RECOMMENDATIONS

I'm not sure if there's been a better written book published yet this year than Ukraine: Zbig's Grand Chessboard and How the West Was Checkmated, but I'm confident there's not been a more important one. With some 17,000 nuclear bombs in the world, the United States and Russia have about 16,000 of them. The United States is aggressively flirting with World War III, the people of the United States have not the foggiest notion of how or why, and authors Natylie Baldwin and Kermit Heartsong explain it all quite clearly.
—**David Swanson,** <u>Ukraine and the Apocalyptic Risk of Propagandized Ignorance</u>

A powerful antidote to mainstream propaganda about the Ukraine Crisis. NATO leaders should read it to avoid sleepwalking into war with the superpowers of the 21st Century.
—**Afshin Rattansi,** *host of RT's Going Underground*

In this must-read book the authors offer an alternative reading of recent American history—a reading shockingly at odds with that of the mainstream press. They inform us that the so-called "Ukraine crisis" and the making of a bogey man of Putin derives from a larger chessgame the West has engaged in from the time we broke our promise to Gorbachev that NATO would not be expanded. They inform us that neocon ideologies are alive and well even in the Obama administration and that the West is in fact playing a losing game to Putin and his emerging ally, China. It is a sad and potentially scary story of ideologies run amok and seems especially ominous in light of the current presidential debates that shed more heat than light on current American history. This book signals a wake-up call even as it blows the whistle on America's kept press for what it has not told us. The authors dare to fill in the gaping holes that constitute our collective ignorance. They have done their homework. They are courageous in their truth-telling. Will Americans listen?
—**Matthew Fox,** *Bestselling Author, Anglican Priest, Educator*

From Zbig's nineties' strategy for US supremacy to the return of Nazism in Ukraine, courtesy of Neo-cons, and how the Russian Bear and the Chinese Dragon are check-mating the US, EU, and NATO across the Eurasian heartland, Ukraine: ZBIG's Grand Chessboard & How the West Was Checkmated is an outstanding example of pragmatic geopolitical analysis and collaborative writing.

—**Deena Stryker**, *international journalist, former State Department speechwriter, Foreign Editor at OpEd News*

For those still taken in by the official Washington/Western narrative regarding events in the Ukraine, Baldwin and Heartsong's book provides a meticulously documented and highly engaging account that all but trashes that narrative. More revealingly, for those still inclined to embrace America's self proclaimed stature as a force for good in an increasingly unstable, chaotic and hostile global environment, the book will give them pause for deeper reflection. The source of most of that instability, chaos and hostility becomes clear for all but the most ideologically myopic and imperially inclined.
—**Greg Maybury** *is a freelance writer who frequently contributes articles to Op Ed News, Consortium News, and Russia Insider*

UKRAINE

ZBIG'S GRAND CHESSBOARD

&

HOW THE WEST WAS

CHECKMATED

UKRAINE
ZBIG'S GRAND CHESSBOARD
&
HOW THE WEST WAS
CHECKMATED

NATYLIE BALDWIN

KERMIT E. HEARTSONG

COPYRIGHT

Copyright © 2015, 2016 by Natylie Baldwin and Kermit Heartsong. All rights reserved.

ISBN-13 (hardcover): 978-0-9906614-6-7
ISBN-13 (softcover): 978-0-9961740-7-7

In accordance with the US Copyright Act of 1976, the scanning, uploading, and electronic sharing of any part of this book without permission of the publisher constitute unlawful piracy and theft of the author's intellectual property. No part of this book may be reproduced or transmitted in any form or by any means, electronic or mechanical, including photocopying, recording, or by any information storage and retrieval system, except for excerpts used for reviews, without permission in writing from the publisher.

Cover Photographs: Courtesy Shutterstock
Cover Design: Wabi Sabi Design Studios (**WSDG**)

The world has achieved brilliance without wisdom, without conscience. Ours is a world of nuclear giants and ethical infants. We know more about war than we know about peace, more about killing than we know about living.

—*General Omar Bradley*

TABLE OF CONTENTS

THE UKRAINE MAP—2015 20
PART I 21
CHAPTER 1 23
THE END OF THE COLD WAR 23
    CONDITIONS IN THE SOVIET UNION 23
    REAGAN AND GORBACHEV 27
    THE FAILURE OF THE PEACE DIVIDEND 29
CHAPTER 2 33
STRANGE BEDFELLOWS 33
    ZBIGNIEW BRZEZIŃSKI'S GRAND CHESSBOARD 33
    THE NEOCONSERVATIVES 52
    THE PHILOSOPHY 52
    MILITARY STRATEGY 58
    THE WOLFOWITZ DOCTRINE 59
    A CLEAN BREAK 61
    ROBERT KAGAN AND VICTORIA NULAND 63
    RESPONSIBILITY TO PROTECT 68
    ORIGINS OF R2P 73
    LIBYA—AN ABUSE OF R2P 74
CHAPTER 3 81
NATO EXPANSION & AMERICAN EMPIRE 81
    NATO: FROM COLD WAR TO GLOBAL WAR 91
    NATO IN THE 1990S 91
    1996 – THE TURNING POINT 98
    NATO IN THE 2000S 103
    THE EU—NATO DANCE 108

UKRAINE..113

CHAPTER 4..117
POST—SOVIET RUSSIA...117

GORBACHEV'S ECONOMIC VISION...............................120
YELTSIN: THE RUSSIAN PINOCHET..............................122
THE ECONOMIC REFORMS...129
FINANCIAL CRISIS OF 2008..134
ECONOMY STILL A WORK IN PROGRESS...................135
CRITICISMS OF PUTIN'S POLICIES................................139

PART II...149

CHAPTER 5..151
UKRAINE I, UKRAINE II..151

COLOR REVOLUTIONS...151
UKRAINE I—THE ORANGE REVOLUTION..................161
GEORGIA, THE DRESS REHEARSAL............................163
UKRAINE II...167
An Offer You Can't Refuse 167
Nazis In The House..186
Crimea..190
Odessa..195
War by any other name: Eastern Ukraine 197
The End Game..208

CHAPTER 6..215
PROPAGANDA & UKRAINE—AMERICAN STYLE ...215

PROPAGANDA IN UKRAINE...222
Peaceful Violence On The Maidan 225
The Maidan Snipers..229
Russian Aggression?...239

- RUSSIA INVADES (AGAIN) 246
- PUTIN IS MAD, CHANNELING HITLER... 253
- WESTERN PROPAGANDA AND THE CRIMEA 259
- MALAYSIAN AIRLINE FLIGHT MH17 265

CHAPTER 7 289
RUSSIA CHECKMATES 289
- CRIMEA 290
- SANCTIONS BACKFIRE 293
- EASTERN PIVOT—BEAR & DRAGON 299
  - MULTI-POLES 304
  - THE SCO 305
  - THE BRICS 305
- NO GAS FOR THE EU 308
- THE DOLLAR FALLS 312

CONCLUSIONS 321
- THE CHURCH OF THE GRAND CHESSBOARD 321
- IMPERIAL WARS & PLANNED CHAOS—TILT! 324
- WORLD WAR III 325

AFTERWORD 331
INDEX 341
APPENDIX I 351
- PHONE TRANSCRIPT NULAND AND PYATT 351

APPENDIX II 355
- PHONE TRANSCRIPT PAET AND ASHTON 355

BIBLIOGRAPHY 363
BIOGRAPHIES 387

INTRODUCTION

At the end of the Cold War, the Russian people had a tremendous amount of goodwill toward Americans. They loved American music and movies and hoped to be accepted into the Western world on equitable terms. A decisive opportunity had presented itself for a more cooperative international framework to emerge through a good faith effort.

On February 9, 1990, George H. W. Bush's Secretary of State James Baker negotiated a gentleman's agreement with Mikhail Gorbachev that, in exchange for allowing a reunified Germany as a NATO member, NATO would not be expanded any farther east. The stage was thus set for global cooperation and the establishment of realpolitik as the operative canon of geostrategic and geopolitical relations. The fruit of such a relationship, many believed, would be a peace dividend.

Tragically, this opportunity was squandered, mostly due to the American political class's triumphalist attitude and a desire to maintain the power and wealth they had established based on an adversarial framework. Thus the march eastward, converting former Soviet satellites to NATO forward operating bases, began a few short years after Baker's promise to Gorbachev.

On September 17, 1997 Zbigniew Brzeziński's book, *The Grand Chessboard: American Primacy and Its Geostrategic Imperatives* was published. It spoke clearly to US financial elites and their political courtesans in regards to maintaining US primacy. Its thesis, as stated by Brzeziński, "It is imperative that no Eurasian challenger should emerge capable of dominating

Eurasia and thus challenging America's global pre-eminence." Since the fall of the Soviet Union the implementation of Zbig's Grand Chessboard strategy has continued unabated and Washington has moved at a feverish pace to bring the endgame, a checkmate, for Russian and ostensibly Chinese power projection in Eurasia.

By 2009, NATO expansion, initiated by Washington, had increased by twelve new nations in central and eastern Europe. To date, NATO stands at the gates of the Russian Federation with provocative actions having taken place in the Ukraine in 2004, Georgia in 2008 and now once again in the Ukraine in 2014. Washington's geostrategic goals—checkmate of Russian and European integration, Russian power projection and suppression of Russian economic viability—collectively represent the final gambit by the West for a checkmate of Russia, so as to render Russia a permanent vassal state.

However, it now appears, a US /NATO checkmate will not be forthcoming as deft economic, political, and tactical countermoves by Russian president Vladimir Putin have turned the tables on the US and NATO. As a result, Russia now stands ready to checkmate the West via its own gambit—the Grand Chessboard strategy.

The potential ramifications are the displacement of the petrodollar, the near-term demise of the US empire, the potential dissolution of NATO, and severe (continuing) Western economic recessions and depressions for decades to come.

Ukraine: ZBIG's Grand Chessboard & How the West Was Checkmated speaks to the historical and geostrategic moves undertaken by the US and NATO, since the fall of the Soviet Union, to control the Eurasian landmass. Further, it details the broken promises of the US and NATO, their geostrategic steps and missteps, and, finally, how the US and NATO, proverbially snatched defeat from the jaws of victory and catalyzed Russia's near-term reemergence as a global power while shifting power eastward.

ACKNOWLEDGEMENTS

We would like to thank Col. Lawrence Wilkerson for taking the time to talk about Ukraine and US foreign policy, as well as Sharon Tennison for her friendship and insight gleaned from over 30 years working in Russia. We'd like to thank Dmitry Orlov for his time and valuable feedback. We would, of course, also like to thank Graham Phillips, George Eliason, and Patrick Lancaster for their courageous and independent reporting from eastern Ukraine. And we'd like to thank Professor Stephen Cohen for his insight, courage, dedication, and truth telling. For whether Orwell is, indeed, the originator or not, the saying—"In a time of universal deceit—telling the truth is a revolutionary act," proves truer today than at any prior time in history.

UKRAINE

ZBIG'S GRAND CHESSBOARD

&

HOW THE WEST WAS
CHECKMATED

THE UKRAINE MAP—2015

PART I
THE OPENING REPERTOIRE & BEYOND

Natylie Baldwin

You don't get to be a serious person in Washington until you are considered pro-intervention.
—*Mike Lofgren, legislative defense analyst*

Baldwin & Heartsong

CHAPTER 1

THE END OF THE COLD WAR
LOST OPPORTUNITIES

CONDITIONS IN THE SOVIET UNION
LEADING TO END OF COLD WAR AND DISSOLUTION OF USSR

By the time Mikhail Gorbachev took over leadership of the Soviet Union in 1985, the Cold War was in the midst of a deep freeze due to a period of poor diplomacy and major distrust on the part of the so-called Superpowers. The economic effects of the Cold War and the arms race it necessitated was having negative consequences for both the Soviet Union and the United States. However, the Soviet Union was more adversely affected and facing diminished economic growth as well as stunted technological development and modernization because of its heavy investment in the defense industry, which had enjoyed priority status within the Soviet economy from the late 1920's (Matlock 2010; Cooper 1991).

The Soviet Union was also in the midst of a guerrilla war in Afghanistan which added to the economic burden and reduced morale. Gorbachev recognized that negotiating an end to the Afghanistan war and the Cold War would enable him to implement reforms by parlaying the money invested in the arms race and militarization into civilian development as well as freeing the nation from the distraction of conflict (Cohen 2011; Matlock 2010).

However, it would be very misleading to assert that the eventual dismantling of the Soviet Union was only due to militarization. In terms of the Reagan administration's increased defense budgets, particularly in hi-tech sectors of defense, it would have been difficult for the Soviets to respond right away due to the their 11th Five-Year Plan (1980–1985) that was already in place and would have required a lengthy undertaking to change. Alternatively, the 12th Five-Year Plan, beginning in 1986, did not reflect any of the changes one would expect in response to these US defense policies. There is no substantive evidence that the USSR did significantly change economic policy in relation to military spending during this period. In fact, changes in defense spending were not seen until 1988 and then it was in the form of reductions (Reynolds 2011; Cooper 1991).

Another element that would be crucial in determining the continued viability of the Soviet economic system was energy. As energy economics expert, Douglas B. Reynolds explains, the Soviet economy up to that time had competed reasonably well with the West, despite its technological lag, lower productivity and the absence of officially sanctioned markets. This is because it was largely cheap fossil fuel energy that had accounted for much of the world's post-war growth. Both the US and the USSR had significant fossil fuel resources until each reached a peak in 1970 and 1988, respectively (Reynolds 2011).

By 1977, the CIA had deduced that the Soviet Union was approaching a peak in their oil production capacity and predicted that the peak would occur by the early 1980's, leading to shortfalls for domestic needs as well as an inability to fulfill supply obligations to its Eastern European satellites and to maintain sales of oil and gas to the West that provided 40 percent of the Soviet Unions' hard currency earnings (CIA Memorandum; Schweizer 1994).

CIA Director William Casey, whom colleagues said viewed the Cold War rivalry with the Soviet Union as a continuation of the good versus evil fight against totalitarianism represented by Hitler's Germany, had presented Reagan in early 1981 with intelligence that reportedly detailed the economic vulnerabilities of the Soviet Union, particularly those relating to oil and gas.

A program was formulated to use intensified covert operations and economic warfare to undermine the Soviet Union. The program included the following parts: 1) increased support for the Solidarity movement in Poland, 2) increased financial and military support to the Afghan Mujahedeen, 3) increased psychological operations, 4) blocking of Soviet access to advance technology, and 5) reduction of Soviet hard currency earnings by driving down the price of oil in collusion with Saudi Arabia while limiting its oil and natural gas exports to Western Europe.

The program was officially given the green light via the signing of several National Security Decision Directives (NSDD) by President Reagan administration throughout 1982.

However, Casey had already begun having meetings in 1981 with officials from Saudi Arabia, which accounted for 40 percent of OPEC's oil production at the time. A deal was gradually worked out with the Saudi royal family, who were strict anti-communists and feared growing Soviet influence in the region, whereby the US would provide defense guarantees to the regime, including the sale of military weapons, in exchange for lower oil prices that would not only weaken the Soviet Union but would have the ancillary benefit of aiding the American economy. Defense Secretary Caspar Weinberger also played a significant role in bringing the deal to fruition (Schweizer 1994).

Indeed, a sharp decrease in oil prices followed, from $66 per barrel in 1980 to $20 per barrel by 1986. It should be noted that, according to a 1983 Treasury Department study, $20 per barrel was viewed as the "optimum" oil price for the American economy. The drop in oil prices was due to a Saudi-induced oil glut which, combined with diplomatic pressure exerted on western European nations, such as France, to curb imports of Soviet oil and natural gas, created a budgetary crisis in the Soviet Union (Sakwa 2012; Schweizer 1994).

As Reynolds (2011) reiterates, American and Saudi policies did not cause the collapse of the Soviet Union but represented a conscious decision to exacerbate an already existing problem of energy depletion within a relatively closed and rigid system.[1] This contributed to the economic and political downward spiral of the Soviet Union by ensuring that it could not procure better technology to alleviate the crisis, consequently creating hard currency and budgetary problems.

By 1987, pursuit of these policies had died off due to political pressures and divisions within the Reagan administration. Nonetheless, the administration was able to participate in the negotiation process with Gorbachev from a position of considerable strength (Schweizer 1994).

---

[1] Post-Soviet oil production was revived due to the introduction of open markets, better technology, and investment in the search for new fields, among other policy changes.

Reagan and Gorbachev
Rise to the Occasion

Although the Reagan administration presided over some abhorrent policies, Jack Matlock—who was the Soviet Affairs expert on Reagan's National Security Council and later ambassador to the Soviet Union—makes a convincing case that Reagan was sincere in his desire to significantly reduce nuclear weapons and to ultimately end the Cold War. However, due to the aforementioned policies during his first term, he understandably hit a brick wall with Soviet Premiers Brezhnev, Andropov, and Chernenko (Matlock 2010).

Suzanne Massie, an author and professor of Russian Studies who specialized in Russian cultural history and served as an advisor to Reagan during his second term, confirms Reagan's sincerity despite the nature of the implemented policies. Her path to advisor status began in the autumn of 1983 when a high-ranking Soviet official warned her during a visit, "You don't know how close war is." Alarmed, she became determined to get President Reagan's ear. She first had to go through National Security Advisor, Robert MacFarlane, who was able to get the White House to agree to send Massie on a "back channel" mission in January of 1984 to explore the Soviet leadership's willingness to negotiate on several key issues, utilizing her established rapport with some officials there.

It was a successful mission and Massie became a regular at the White House from 1984 to 1988. During that time, she observed—and helped to facilitate—Reagan's evolution on how he viewed the Soviet Union and the Russian people. By educating the president on the cultural history of Russia and the nuances of Soviet life, she helped Reagan to gain enough wisdom by the time Gorbachev came to office to treat the new Soviet leader with respect, to keep an open mind while listening to a variety of views on the Soviet issue, and—despite his general loathing of communism and the Soviet system – to recognize Russia's contributions to the world and the fact that the Soviet Union had its own legitimate national interests.

By the time of his 1986 summit with Gorbachev in Iceland, Reagan confessed to Massie that his deepest wish for humanity was "to get rid of those damn nuclear weapons" (Krasnow 2009; Malinkin 2008).

Nevertheless, Reagan and Gorbachev's initial meetings in 1985 did not reflect a terribly auspicious beginning in terms of bridging the chasm between the two nations. But a proposal by Gorbachev calling for complete nuclear disarmament by 1999 got Reagan's attention. Though there was suspicion that this proposal may have been a propaganda ploy on Gorbachev's part, it provided a critical opening between the two leaders. The subsequent Chernobyl catastrophe reinforced the danger of nuclear technology to the Soviet leadership and represented another expensive disaster for which limited funds had to be invested. This provided even more incentive toward a negotiated settlement (Matlock 2010).

According to Matlock (2010), Reagan was very careful during negotiations with Gorbachev to allow him to come to the conclusion that many of the proposed changes were in the Soviet Union's interest due to the economic damage resulting from the military budget necessitated by the Cold War. If Gorbachev would not have been able to negotiate the Cold War's end and the need for allocation of massive resources toward the military, he would not have been able to implement the reforms needed for glasnost and perestroika.

Reagan also was careful never to frame the situation as a victory or defeat. Although George H. W. Bush apparently believed in private that Russia had been defeated, he followed Reagan's approach publicly until his re-election campaign when he declared to the American electorate that, "We won the Cold War" (Matlock 2010; Sarotte 2010).

The Failure of the Peace Dividend

As the end of the Cold War beckoned in the late 1980s and, along with it, the potential for redirection of resources to improve the living standards of communities across America, Seymour Melman—an expert on the military industrial complex (MIC)—noted that 50 percent of the discretionary federal budget at that time went to the Pentagon. Today that percentage is even higher at 55 percent. Meanwhile, 3 percent is allotted to "international affairs," meaning that some portion of that 3 percent goes to diplomacy, which speaks volumes about our leaders' priorities and approach to international relations (Melman 1990; National Priorities Project).

In comparison, Russia's current defense allotment represents 20 percent of its overall budget (Keck 2014). At the same time, the US's spending on defense comprises 39 percent of the world's total military expenditure versus 5.2 percent for Russia (Global Issues 2012). For further perspective, it should be kept in mind that Russia has a history of insecurity on its borders, including World War II, the memory of which, including the loss of 27 million of its people—19 million of them civilians—and the destruction of a significant portion of the country is still strong in the Russian consciousness (Parsons 2014). On the other hand, the US has not had a war on its soil for 150 years and the Civil War did not involve a foreign invasion. Moreover, the US has a vast ocean on either side for protection and relatively stable and friendly neighbors to its north and south.

What all that needless investment into militarism ultimately translates into is investment not made into the infrastructure for American citizens and their day-to-day needs. To illustrate this point, Melman also discussed the state of American domestic infrastructure by 1990 and how it had suffered from the diversion of resources into the MIC:

> *The American ruling class, by 1990, has become a state/corporate managerial entity. Together they control the military-industrial complex....The war economy, in the service of extending the decision power and wealth of America's state and corporate managers, has been consuming the US civilian infrastructure. Roads, bridges, the water supply, waste disposal systems, housing, medical care facilities, schools are in disrepair from coast to coast. (Melman 1990)*

Instead of seizing the opportunity provided by the end of the Cold War and investing in the improvement of Americans' lives, we have continued to feed the same amounts or more into the voracious military economy with our domestic infrastructure in worse shape than ever. The American Society of Civil Engineers Infrastructure Report Card for the US in 2013 was a D+; meanwhile, the *New York Times* recently reported that the federal government will be investing as much as $1 trillion in modernizing our nuclear weapons arsenal over the next 30 years, using the confrontation with Russia over Ukraine as partial justification (Broad and Sanger 2014).

The early stages of another negative trend was observed by Melman (1990) with respect to the deindustrialization of the American economy whereby the nation gradually loses the ability to produce essential goods and to repair the basic infrastructure needed to create and repair those essential goods. For example, in his 1990 and 2001 works, Melman described how the US was becoming dependent upon foreign production of basic machinery and tools that were no longer made in the US (Melman 1990; Melman 2001). This deindustrialization leads to loss of living wage jobs and loss of national independence and self-sufficiency in important areas of the economy. That trend has accelerated in the twenty-four years since and all of the social consequences one would likely expect are visible to most Americans, with the exception of the most wealthy and insulated.

One of the more pernicious consequences of this deindustrialization is that the lack of living wage jobs that used to be available to those with little or no post-secondary education drives more youth into the professional military as they seek a stable income and educational opportunities, reinforcing the militarist feedback loop.

One of the strangest blind spots that American elites seem to have is what their own system has in common with some of the failed aspects of the Soviet Union, with its heavy burden of militarism and empire on its people and economy. They somehow seem to think the US will avoid the same fate.

CHAPTER 2

STRANGE BEDFELLOWS
THE GRAND CHESS BOARD, NEOCONS, AND R2P

Zbigniew Brzeziński's Grand Chessboard

Before getting into a deconstruction of *The Grand Chessboard*, it's important to first take a step back and provide some perspective on who Zbigniew Brzeziński is and why his worldview is particularly relevant to understand in terms of the current events in Ukraine. Brzeziński's view seems to be partly derived from a deep-rooted and irrational antipathy toward Russia—irrational in the sense that it persists despite what Russia actually is or does in objective reality.

Brzeziński was born in Warsaw, Poland in 1928 but his paternal family reportedly originated from Galicia, which was once considered eastern Poland but is now part of western Ukraine. His father was a Polish diplomat who served in Germany from 1931 to 1935 and then served in the Soviet Union from 1936 to 1938 in the midst of Stalin's Great Purge. He was stationed in Canada when both Germany and the Soviet Union invaded Poland in 1939. Poland was later placed in the Soviet sphere of influence at the conclusion of WWII; hence, the Brzeziński family remained in Canada. Brzeziński earned a master's degree from McGill University in Montreal with a focus on the Soviet Union, followed by a PhD at Harvard with a focus on the Russian Revolution and the leadership of Lenin and Stalin. He became an academic at Harvard and then Columbia University where he taught and mentored Madeleine Albright. He served as an advisor to the Kennedy presidential campaign and then was a member of the State Department's Council of Policy Planning from 1966—1968. In 1973, he helped establish the Trilateral Commission with David Rockefeller. Based on ideas Brzeziński spelled out in an article he published in *Foreign Affairs* in 1970, the Trilateral Commission was to be the organizational foundation of a club of developed nations that included those of Europe, Japan and the US to balance world power away from the Soviet Union and China. The club held annual meetings that included the elites of Europe, Japan, and the US, along with notables in world trade, international banking and the establishment media (Lepic 2004).

Throughout the Cold War, Brzeziński supported a policy of engagement with Eastern Europe, including dissidents, believing that divisions within Eastern Europe would destabilize the Soviet Union and hasten its breakup along national lines. He gave little to no support for any rapprochement with the Soviet Union and opposed Charles de Gaulle's vision of a Eurasian project of "Europe from the Atlantic to the Urals."

Brzeziński eventually served as national security advisor in the Carter administration. Touted as the Democratic Party's counterpoint to Henry Kissinger (and implicitly Kissinger's détente approach toward the USSR), his aggressive anti-Russian views often clashed with those of Carter's Secretary of State, Cyrus Vance, who was in the Realist camp and opposed Brzeziński's desire to strengthen ties to China while keeping the Soviet Union at a distance. He and others in the administration argued that such "triangulation" could lead to dangerous and unnecessary perceptions of aggression toward the Soviet Union (Wikipedia, "Zbigniew Brzeziński"; Lepic

2004). Due to Brzeziński's machinations behind Vance's back to convince Carter to undertake the disastrous plan to rescue American hostages in Iran instead of continuing to use diplomatic channels, Vance—who had come to oppose using military intervention to solve international problems—resigned. Upon leaving office, Vance characterized Brzeziński's aggression and Machiavellian tactics as "evil" (Brinkley 2002).

During his tenure, Brzeziński was also the architect of the plan to goad the Soviet Union into its own "Vietnam" quagmire by arming and supporting Islamic mujahedeen against the Soviet-backed government in Afghanistan. The plan, with the assistance of the Pakistan intelligence service, was put into place toward the end of Carter's presidency and in 1979, the Soviet Union, in fact, responded as Brzeziński had hoped, embarking on a decade-long war in the nation that is not called the "graveyard of empires" for nothing.

When the French magazine *Le Nouvel Observateur* interviewed Brzeziński in 1998, he admitted that while he was national security advisor, he played a major role in setting the Afghanistan trap for the Soviet Union to get bogged down in a war. He also reiterated that he had no regrets about the policy, underscoring the fact that he does indeed see the nations and peoples of the world as pieces on a strategic game board, having no regard for the resulting death of a million Afghans and thousands of Soviets, demolition of a country that at the time had minimal religious fanaticism and better conditions for women, or blowback toward his own adopted country (Cohen 2001; Khalidi 1991). A pertinent excerpt of the exchange follows:

> *Le Nouvel Observateur: Former CIA director, Robert Gates, says in his memoirs: the American secret services assisted Afghan*

mujahedeen six months before the Soviet invasion. By that time, you were President Carter's advisor and you played a key role on this. Do you confirm it?

Brzeziński: Yes. *According to the official version of the story, the CIA began to assist mujahedeen in the year 1980, that is, after the invasion of the Soviet army against Afghanistan on December 24, 1979. But the truth that remained secret until today is quite different: it was on July 3, 1979 that President Carter signed his first order on the secret assistance to Kabul's pro-Soviet regime opponents. That day I wrote a memorandum to the President in which I told him that that assistance would cause the Soviet intervention… We did not force the Russian intervention, we just, conscientiously, increased the intervention possibilities.*

NO: *When the Soviets justified their intervention by affirming they were fighting against a secret American interference nobody believed them, though they were telling the truth. Don't you regret it?*

B: *Regret what? That secret operation was an excellent idea. Its objective was to lead the Russians to the Afghan trap, and you want me to regret it? The very same day the Soviets crossed the Afghan border I wrote the following to President Carter: "This is our chance to give Russia its Viet Nam."*

NO: *Aren't you sorry either for favoring Islamic fundamentalism and providing weapons and consultancies to future terrorists?*

B: *What is the most important thing when you look at world history, the Taliban or the fall of the Soviet empire? Some excited Islamists or the liberation of Central Europe and the end of the Cold War? (Lepic 2004)*

In 1989 Brzeziński quit his academic post to work on the "Ukraine project" which worked on behalf of Ukrainian independence.

Brzeziński also became active behind the scenes to use Islamic radicals in Chechnya to destabilize Russia via the American Committee for Peace in Chechnya (ACPC). ACPC was founded by Freedom House—a conservative nonprofit that has historically been used as a front for CIA operations (Chomsky and Herman 1988). ACPC was an organization with a plethora of Neoconservatives on its board and membership roster. It has received up to 80 percent of its funding from the notorious National Endowment for Democracy (NED), an organization funded by the US Congress. NED was established in the early 1980s in response to congressional hearings, namely by the Church Committee, that exposed the CIA's covert efforts to destabilize and overthrow foreign governments that were anathema to the US political elite. Rather than cease these unpopular—and often violent and illegal – covert operations, they were simply transferred to another organization that obscured these nefarious activities under the guise of building civil society and democracy. Government officials who helped draft the legislation creating NED have admitted that NED now does much of what the CIA used to do in this arena (Sourcewatch; Laughland 2004; Blum 2000).

French journalist Arthur Lepic states in his 2004 article on Brzeziński's policies toward the Soviet Union and Russia, "The Outrageous Strategy to Destroy Russia," that Brzeziński was involved in a plan to pave the way for a pipeline deal that would undermine Russia's potential to gain from fossil fuel resources in the Caspian region:

During the '90s he was the special envoy of the American president to promote the most important oil infrastructure project of the world: the Baku-Tbilissi-Ceyhan pipeline which was his best opportunity to prevent the resurgence of Russia. He has also been, since 1999, the president of the American Committee for Peace in Chechnya, whose headquarters are located at the Freedom House facility. This position allows him to intervene in peace negotiations between the Russian government and independence fighters led by Mashkadov. However, the truth behind these good will "democratic" activities [was] to assist independence followers to maintain a war in the area, like the Afghan one, to weaken Russia and to keep it away from the gains of the Caspian Sea. (Lepic 2004)

The Brzeziński calling card of goading Russia into a war or keeping it bogged down in one in order to weaken it has to be kept in mind in analyzing current events.

Flash forward to 2013 when the Ukraine crisis would erupt. With a negotiated end to the Cold War, a dissolved USSR, a Russian Federation that was firmly on the road toward an evolving version of capitalism, expanded economic ties with the EU, and cordial relations with Latin America and a lot of the developing world, Russia and most everyone else had moved on from the idea of Russia as big bad bogeyman. But not an assortment of Russophobes in Washington, like Brzeziński, and those they influence.

Brzeziński influenced both Kerry and Obama, having served as a foreign policy advisor, along with his son, Mark Brzeziński, to the 2004 Kerry presidential campaign and then for the Obama 2008 campaign. Although it is difficult to determine how often Brzeziński directly advises Obama, it is interesting to observe how hawks among both major political parties took their cue from Brzeziński when he compared Putin to Hitler in a March 3, 2014 op-ed for the *Washington Post* (Brzeziński 2014). Within two days, Hillary Clinton, John McCain and Marco Rubio all repeated this absurd claim (Ernesto 2014). It can, therefore, be deduced that Brzeziński still wields considerable influence among the Washington elite. As we will see later, US actions in Ukraine since the fall of 2013 — the culmination of years of US covert operations in that country (Baldwin 2014) — are reminiscent of Brzeziński's previous policies and actions.

Brzeziński continued to offer advice to the president publicly on the crisis via another op-ed, this one published by Politico.com on May 2, 2014, in which he essentially restated his view that America is exceptional and has the right and duty to pull Ukraine away from the Russian sphere of influence into the US-controlled Western sphere based on the premise outlined in his book: namely, that whoever rules Eurasia rules the world. This premise is based upon two assumptions: 1) that one country has the right to rule the world, and 2) that the US is noble or, at least benign, and must be the one to do that ruling lest some other empire crop up and do it. Or, as Terry Malloy said in *On the Waterfront*, "do it to him before he does it to you" (Brzeziński May 2014).

It is clear from the opening pages of *The Grand Chessboard* that Brzeziński is obsessed with imperialism and cannot conceive of a world that is not organized under empire – whether it is the competing regional empires of old or the rise of one global empire as reflected by the US after the Soviet Union's exit from the world stage. He even repeats the common historical fallacy that "hegemony is as old as mankind." If he had even a cursory familiarity with anthropology or pre-recorded history, he would know that throughout the vast majority of humanity's experience, mankind lived in small, relatively egalitarian units of hunter-gatherers. Empire and its attendant effects, such as hegemony, hierarchical social structure, and war, only emerged around 10 –13,000 years ago, roughly coinciding with the widespread adoption of agricultural settlement (Fry 2006).

Brzeziński's Eurasian thesis appears to have been inspired by Nicholas Spykman's Eurasian Rimland concept, which was, in turn, built upon Halford Makinder's Heartland Theory, first formulated in 1904. Spykman's Rimland emphasized the geostrategic importance of the densely populated coastal perimeter surrounding the Heartland of Eurasia. Spykman justified focus on the Rimland instead of the Heartland by arguing that the Rimland contained the majority of the world's people, a large swathe of its resources and an industrial base. Additionally, it served as an entryway to the seas, situated as a buffer zone between the Heartland (source of land power) and sea power. These two theories, like Brzeziński's Grand Chessboard, are widely acknowledged to represent an imperialistic offensive posture dressed up as a defense strategy (Nazemroaya 2012; Wikipedia. "Rimland"; Wikipedia – "Geographical").

In *The Grand Chessboard*, Brzeziński reiterates the factors cited by Spykman and Makinder:

> *About 75 percent of the world's people live in Eurasia, and most of the world's physical wealth is there as well, both in its enterprises and underneath its soil. Eurasia accounts for about 60 percent of the world's GNP and about three-fourths of the world's known energy resources. (Brzeziński 1997)*

He speaks throughout the book with a sense of entitlement on behalf of the US that the American empire should never cede control of these resources to those living near them who may strangely assume a claim to benefit from them.

He emphasizes the following two steps to achieve his imperialist objective of preserving world domination by the US:

> 1) Identify states in Eurasia that have the power to shift the international distribution of power or to be catalysts for doing so; and,
>
> 2) Formulate specific US policies to offset, co-opt and/or control the above as to preserve and promote vital US interests.

Brzeziński goes on to explain the role of Ukraine as a "pivot" state—in other words, a state that, if it remains under Russia's sphere of influence, allows Russia to project power into the rest of Eurasia due to its sea port, major resources, and its role as a geographic defensive buffer—an important psychological factor for a nation that has been invaded from the west numerous times in its history via Ukraine.

Hence, we have a Western-backed coup that toppled a democratically elected leader in Ukraine in order to install a government that would implement the European Association agreement—a stepping stone to NATO membership—and Russia's counter move of reabsorbing Crimea to prevent its naval port from being diverted into potential control by NATO, a move that would have compromised Russia's security and status as an independent nation (An in-depth discussion of the coup itself follows in Part II of this book).

Provocations to get Russia to invade Ukraine—where it would no doubt face a major insurgency in the western part of the country, supported by US/NATO—are a throwback to

Brzeziński's plan to lure the Soviet Union into a quagmire in 1979 which contributed to that country's disintegration. It is an open secret that the Neocons and other Russophobes would consider the destabilization of Russia and a subsequent regime change ousting Putin to be the ultimate prize. Their dubious assumption is not only that this would be possible to do in the first place without risk of a nuclear war, but that any successor to Putin would be weak and compliant—another Yeltsin who will allow them unfettered access to Russia's prodigious natural resources for exploitation—rather than a truly anti-Western hardliner that would be far less accommodating than Putin.

Interestingly, Brzeziński's belief that whoever controls Eurasia controls the world does not necessarily rest on solid ground. As Matlock (2010) points out, history really only shows that whoever controls Eurasia controls Eurasia. Not that such control wouldn't represent tremendous power and influence, especially economic, but there are other factors to consider in terms of world hegemony, such as control of the world's seas, which Russia is not likely to attain any time soon even with firm control of Ukraine and a cemented alliance with China.

With this mindset and background, Brzeziński goes on numerous media outlets, gives speeches and testifies before Congress with his talking points about the Ukraine crisis, asserting who is responsible and how it started, with Russia as the instigator and Putin as the arch-villain described variously as Hitler, Stalin, a thug, and a Mafia gangster.

On June 16, 2014, while participating on a panel at the Wilson Center, Brzeziński continued flogging his theme of Russian imperialism, citing an obscure report by a Russian think tank and pushing the narrative that Russia violated

Ukraine's sovereignty and Western actions in Ukraine are reactive and benign:

> *What we are seeing in Ukraine, in my judgment, is not a pique but a symptom of a more basic problem; namely, the gradual but steady emergence in Russia over the last 6 or 7 years of a quasi-mythical chauvinism…It follows from what I'm saying that the Ukrainian problem is a challenge that the West must address on three levels. We have to effectively deter the temptation facing the Russian leadership regarding the use of force.*
>
> *We have to, secondly, obtain the termination of Russia's deliberate efforts at the destabilization of parts of Ukraine. It's very hard to judge how ambitious these goals are, but it is not an accident that in that one single portion of Ukraine in which the Russians actually predominate, the use of force has been sophisticated. The participants in the effort have been well armed, even with tanks, and certainly with effective anti-aircraft weaponry. All of that is something that even disagreeable, disaffected citizens of a country to which they feel they do not belong would not be storing somewhere in their attic or their basement. These are weapons provided, in effect, for the purpose of shaping formations capable of sustaining serious military engagements. It is a form of interstate aggression. You can't call it anything else. How would we feel if all of a sudden, let's say, the drug-oriented gangs in the United States were armed from abroad, from our southern neighbor, by equipment which would promote violence on that scale on a continuing basis? So this is a serious challenge. So that is the second objective.*
>
> *And the third objective is to promote and then discuss with the Russians a formula for an eventual compromise, assuming that in the first instance the use of force openly and on a large scale is deterred and the effort to destabilize is abandoned.* (Brzeziński June 2014)

Not once does Brzeziński acknowledge the Western role played in the events that led to the ouster of a democratically elected president in February, or the role played by neo-Nazi groups like Svoboda and Right Sector in the violence that took control of the Maidan protests and facilitated the coup. Victoria Nuland and John McCain's egging on the protestors, regardless of their dubious affiliations, is never mentioned. The intercepted phone call between US Undersecretary of Eurasian Affairs Victoria Nuland and American Ambassador Geoffrey Pyatt in which they discuss the US's favored candidate to replace Ukrainian President Viktor Yanukovych —the candidate that *did* subsequently replace him—is never acknowledged (Nuland and Pyatt 2014). Nor is the intercepted conversation between Estonian Foreign Minister Urmas Paet and EU High Representative Catherine Ashton acknowledged wherein it is admitted that, according to eyewitness and forensic medical evidence, it appears that elements from the Maidan-controlled buildings were responsible for fatally shooting protestors and police officers, not Yanukovych's forces (Paet and Ashton 2014). This is all despite the fact that the aforementioned information was readily available to anyone with an internet connection at the time of Brzeziński's speech.

Moreover, whatever military assistance being provided by Russia to the rebels in Eastern Ukraine at that time – which would be in reaction to Western-fomented instability on their border, not due to some unprovoked imperialistic aggression – was a matter of conjecture and had not been proven with any concrete and verified evidence. Much of the military hardware that Brzeziński refers to was available either from Ukrainian military depots that the rebels had access to or gained control of, Ukrainian soldiers who switched sides in the early stages of the conflict, or in later stages, Ukrainian soldiers that deserted and left behind their hardware (Luhn 2014; TASS 2014).

Furthermore, as University of Rhode Island Professor of Politics Nicolai Petro, who just returned from a year spent in Ukraine, pointed out in a September 3, 2014 article in the *National Interest*, there are several credible reports that the numerous pronouncements in the summer of 2014 of Russian troops and heavy weapons crossing into Ukraine were false:

> *This version of official Russian complicity has been challenged by some Western reporters on the scene, most notably, Mark Franchetti who wrote a remarkable piece for the London Sunday Times after spending several weeks embedded with rebel forces. His assessment is backed by the UN High Commissioner for Human Rights and the [Organization for Security and Cooperation in Europe] OSCE observer mission that has been deployed to the border region since the end of July. Both say they have seen no evidence of weapons or military personnel crossing from Russia into Ukraine during this time, even as US and NATO officials say the exact opposite. Moreover, between April and July of 2014, as Russian Ministry of Defense likes to point out, eighteen international inspection teams visited the border region and found "no evidence of undeclared military activity." (Petro 2014)*

Brzeziński's false framing of events, which has been consistently echoed by the White House and the State Department, also suggests that the rebellion in the southeastern parts of Ukraine, which consider themselves to be ethnically, culturally or linguistically Russian, has no indigenous support but is instead contrived through Russian interference. However, Petro cited the results of sociological surveys taken in Ukraine in April, May and June of 2014 that contradict this:

> *Three-quarters of the populations in Ukraine's eastern cities regard the Euromaidan protests as illegal. Specifically, two-thirds of Donbas residents consider the Maidan to have been "an armed overthrow of the government, organized by the opposition, with the assistance of the West." A similar percentage believes that the Right Sector is "a prominent military formation that is politically influential and poses a threat to the citizens and national unity." That may explain why most people in the eastern and southern regions of Ukraine (62 percent) blame the loss of Crimea on Kiev, rather than on Crimean separatists (24 percent), or on Russia (19 percent).*
>
> *Majorities in Donbas (60 percent in Donetsk and 52 percent in Luhansk) disagree with the view that Russia is organizing the rebels and guiding their actions. Moreover, if a referendum were held today (April 2014), only 25 percent would want to join EU, compared to 47 percent wanting to join the Eurasian Customs Union. (Petro 2014)*

During testimony before the Senate Foreign Relations Committee on July 7, Brzeziński continues on with his previous misrepresentation of the events in Ukraine:

> *"[Russia must] accommodate with Ukraine by terminating the assault on Ukrainian sovereignty and economic well-being.... At the same time, it would be made clear that Russia no longer expects Ukraine to become part of the "Eurasian Union", a designation which is a transparent cover for the recreation of something approximating the former Soviet Union or the Tsarist Empire....Putin's second choice is to continue the effort to destabilize Ukraine by sponsoring thinly veiled military intervention designed to disrupt normal life in portions of Ukraine....In brief, the obvious choice for everyone concerned is to find a formula for international accommodation, and that has to*

> *involve the abandonment of the use of force against Ukraine by Russia."* *(Brzeziński 2014)*

In addition to repeating the false narrative already begun in previous articles and interviews, Brzeziński now adds in the implicit accusation of Russia attempting to force Ukraine to become a member of the Eurasian Union, which is mischaracterized as some nefarious imperial project. In reality, the Eurasian Economic Union (aka the Eurasian Union) is a voluntary common market, similar to the EU, currently comprised of Russia, Belarus, Kazakhstan and Armenia (with Kyrgyzstan set to join in 2015). Brzeziński provides no explanation as to why Ukrainians would not have the right to decide for themselves whether to join such an economic union as he makes explicit they have the right to do in connection with the EU. Nor has Brzeziński ever characterized the EU as some Western European neo-imperialist project.

Brzeziński, who is a busy bee, followed this up with an interview with CNN's Fareed Zakaria in which he stated, "I would say that we're not starting the Cold War. He [Putin] has started it." He once again reiterated the false narrative that the Ukraine crisis came about at Russia's instigation and shrieked about Russian imperial ambitions, "What is the alternative? To let war break out in Europe? To let Russia go on to the Baltic states from Ukraine? To let such acts simply be ignored? Is that the choice? Is that the test of leadership?" (Zakaria 2014)

Either Brzeziński is incredibly ill-informed (which is not very plausible) or he is lying on behalf of his own anti-Russia agenda.

Furthermore, his talking points on the Ukraine crisis are almost identical to his talking points to the media about the war between Russia and Georgia in 2008. For example,

Brzeziński said the following during an interview with *Huffington Post*'s Nathan Gardels during the height of hostilities between those two nations:

> *The question the international community now confronts is how to respond to a Russia that engages in the blatant use of force with larger imperial designs in mind: to reintegrate the former Soviet space under the Kremlin's control and to cut Western access to the Caspian Sea and Central Asia by gaining control over the Baku-Ceyhan pipeline that runs through Georgia. (Gardels 2008)*

Brzeziński also made sure to compare Putin to both Hitler and Stalin, comparing the Russian "invasion" of Georgia to Hitler's invasion of the Sudetenland and to Stalin's attack on Finland. Apparently, Brzeziński failed to realize that Dmitry Medvedev was the Russian president and commander-in-chief at that time and there is no dispute that he gave the military orders while Prime Minister Putin was at the Olympics in Beijing.

So, how does Brzeziński's hysteria-laced analysis of the Russian-Georgian conflict hold up to the facts?

According to the EU's "Independent International Fact-Finding Mission on the Conflict in Georgia" issued in September 2009, it was the Georgian armed forces that initiated the conflict, not Russia (EU Report). Georgia's president at the time, Mikheil Saakashvili, was a Western-backed leader who, based on the observations of several world leaders and diplomats, exhibited behavior that indicated he may have been psychologically unbalanced. Saakashvili was apparently operating under the delusion that he could militarily take on Russia and that the US had his back (Roxburgh 2013; European Union; Armstrong 2009).

As for wanting to seize control of the Baku-Ceyhan pipeline, the Russians could have done that easily in the midst of the armed conflict in Georgia, but made no attempt to do so.

So, Brzeziński was either woefully misinformed about that conflict or he was lying on behalf of his anti-Russia agenda then, too. It is troubling that in light of either incompetence or mendacity, he is still being given credibility to comment on the current conflict by mainstream media outlets and the US Congress as well as being invited to the White House for a meeting with the president in early September as a foreign policy "expert" (Landler 2014).

And, with respect to his oft-repeated claim that Putin is an incipient Hitler or Stalin, in the intervening five-and-a-half years between the Georgia conflict and the Ukraine crisis, Russia has not engaged in or threatened any military conflicts with its neighbors. As Russia expert Thomas Graham writes:

> *Russian territorial ambitions beyond its traditional geopolitical zone have been quite limited historically. In this regard, the Soviet period stands out as an anomaly, born of the unique conditions of the mid to late twentieth century: the power vacuum in the center of Europe created by the total collapse of Nazi Germany and the subsequent bitter ideological divide and revolutionary upheaval that produced a global competition between the Soviet Union and the United States. Those conditions no longer prevail, and Russia has reverted to its historical policy of creating a suitable balance of power on the European continent that takes into account the interests of the other great European powers. (Graham 2014)*

Brzeziński never misses an opportunity to accuse Putin of being an imperialist and wanting to revive the Soviet Union — an accusation that is dutifully repeated by other demagogues like John McCain, Hillary Clinton, and Marco Rubio. This accusation is largely based upon a sentence plucked out of a 2005 speech given by Putin and used as Exhibit A of his imperial ambitions. Let's take a look at what Putin actually said:

> *Above all, we should acknowledge that the collapse of the Soviet Union was a major geopolitical disaster of the century. As for the Russian nation, it became a genuine tragedy. Tens of millions of our co-citizens and compatriots found themselves outside Russia's territory. Moreover, the epidemic of disintegration infected Russia itself.*
>
> *Individual savings were devalued, and old ideals destroyed. Many institutions were disbanded or reformed carelessly. Terrorist intervention and the Khasavyurt capitulation that followed damaged the country's integrity. Oligarchic groups—possessing absolute control over mass media—served exclusively their own corporate interests. Mass poverty began to be seen as the norm. And all this was happening against the backdrop of a dramatic economic downturn, unstable finances, and the paralysis of the social sphere.*
>
> *Many thought or seemed to think at the time that our young democracy was not a continuation of Russian statehood, but its ultimate collapse, the prolonged agony of the Soviet system.*
>
> *But they were mistaken.*
>
> *That was precisely the period when the significant developments took place in Russia. Our society was generating not only the energy of self-preservation, but also the will for a new and free life. In those difficult years, the people of Russia had to both uphold their state sovereignty and make an unerring choice in selecting a new vector of development in the thousand years of their history. They had to accomplish the most difficult task: how to safeguard*

their own values, not to squander undeniable achievements, and confirm the viability of Russian democracy. We had to find our own path in order to build a democratic, free, and just society and state.

When speaking of justice, I am not of course referring to the notorious "take away and divide by all" formula, but extensive and equal opportunities for everybody to develop.

Success for everyone. A better life for all.

—Vladimir Putin, Annual Address to the Federal Assembly of the Russian Federation, April 25, 2005

This excerpt of Putin's speech—correctly translated and in context—where he is discussing the conditions of Post-Soviet Russia in the 1990s (which we will explore in detail in Chapter 4) speaks for itself and shows the willingness of Western politicians and pundits to perpetuate misinformation on behalf of an agenda.

It is clear that Brzeziński's psyche is frozen in another era when his fellow Poles were under subjugation from the Soviet Union. This kind of anachronistic and narrow thinking, based on the unresolved emotional wounds of one small segment of the American population who are émigrés or descended from émigrés of former Soviet bloc countries, along with a preoccupation with imperialism, is dangerous if it overtakes US foreign policy, which it appears to have done considering Brzeziński's influence in Washington.

The real issue is whether there will be a multi-polar world or whether the US will insist on continuing its role as the lone hegemon, which will necessitate resorting to more desperate and more brutal measures to maintain. Brzeziński comes out firmly in favor of the latter.

It should be stressed that Brzeziński's reckless Grand Chessboard gambit has little traction with the American people. According to a Pew poll conducted in April of 2014, Americans strongly oppose sending military aid to Ukraine and believe, just as strongly, that what happens in Ukraine has little to do with America's vital interests (Drake 2014).

The Neoconservatives

> *These people are crazy, they're frightening. Believe me, I rubbed up close and personal with them for four years. I can tell you how frightening they are. I sat in the Pentagon and listened to a briefing where Iraq was just the start, then we're going to Syria, then we're going to Iran. You know, these people are nuts....Their long-term plan is American hegemony—now, tomorrow and forever. And when I say hegemony I don't just mean America rules as in Pax Americana. I mean America has its way wherever it goes, whenever it goes and however it wants that way. And this is commercial, financial and economic as much as it is geopolitical.*
>
> —*Col. Lawrence Wilkerson, former Chief of Staff to Secretary of State Colin Powell* (Kall 2014)

The Philosophy

The godfather of Neoconservative philosophy was Leo Strauss. A one-time friend and fellow-traveler in philosophical circles with Carl Schmitt, a German Nazi philosopher and jurist, Strauss developed what would become his ideology in response to a newly dominant post-WWII America that he perceived as crass, materialistic, and devoid of a meaningful sense of community.

According to the well-received 2004 BBC documentary *The Power of Nightmares*, Strauss was an enigmatic figure who never appeared in the media but "devoted his time to creating a loyal band of students." Some of those students went on to hold major positions of power within the George W. Bush (Bush II) administration, though some of them had been influential before then. Paul Wolfowitz, Elliot Abrams, Irving and William Kristol, and Michael Ledeen were all greatly influenced by the teachings of Strauss. Ironically, all were former leftists to varying degrees who had become disillusioned with what they perceived to be the failings of liberalism in the midst of the social tumult of the 1960s and 70s.

The basic idea behind Strauss's teaching was that liberalism and individualism would eventually destroy the fabric of the national community. That community, according to Strauss, seemed only to have a meaningful and coherent identity in relation to an outside "other." This "other," by its very nature, represents a threat that must be fought via a full-scale mobilization of society. Only within this focused and unified fight against an outside "evil" foe can the members of society reinforce their common ties and have a satisfying moral purpose as those on the "good" side of an epic life-and-death struggle.

Underscoring this whole scheme was the need for myths, which Strauss conceded did not need to be based in reality and that the leaders themselves did not have to believe, hearkening back to the concept of the "noble lie" in political philosophy. A successful society would be led by those wise enough to know how to pull the levers behind the curtain to keep society unified and stable (Curtis 2004).

These ideas are reflected in Schmitt's political theology as Strauss himself summed them up in a 1932 letter to Schmitt: "Because man is by nature evil, he therefore needs dominion. But dominion can be established, that is, men can be unified only in a unity against—against other men" (Zuckert 2014).

It is this need for a mythology that paints America as the force for good against an evil foe that has motivated Neoconservatives to opportunistically ally with other elements that at first glance may seem unlikely, such as fundamentalist Christians during Bush II's administration and the Responsibility to Protect (R2P) crowd as we will see later.

Having been largely shunned in the academic community, the Neoconservatives entered think tanks and public service as a way to spread their influence. The first politicians they successfully latched onto were Donald Rumsfeld and Dick Cheney, who served as the Secretary of Defense and Chief of Staff, respectively, under President Gerald Ford. Together they put into place the first attack on Realist Henry Kissinger's détente policy with the Soviet Union by accusing the Soviets of violating the nuclear arms treaties the Nixon administration had negotiated. These allegations were completely baseless, but that didn't stop Rumsfeld from persuading Ford to set up Team B, which would be headed by Paul Wolfowitz, to investigate.

An illustration of the Neocons' tendency to be impervious to arguments or evidence that was contrary to their views comes from Dr. Anne Cahn, who worked with the Arms Control and Disarmament Agency during this time. According to Cahn, the Neocons would sift through data that the intelligence community had already analyzed and come up with conclusions that did not match reality but instead their own pre-conceived fantasies:

> *I would say that all of it was fantasy. I mean, they looked at radars out in Krasnoyarsk and said, "This is a laser beam weapon," when in fact it was nothing of the sort. They even took a Russian military manual, which the correct translation of is "The Art of Winning." And when they translated it and put it into Team B, they called it "The Art of Conquest." Well, there's a difference between "conquest" and "winning." And if you go through most of Team B's specific allegations about weapons systems, and you just examine them one by one, they were all wrong. (Curtis 2004)*

But that didn't stop the Neocons from creating The Committee on the Present Danger, a lobbying group that sought to publicize the bogus "findings" of Team B. One of the politicians who bought into this group's fairy tales was future president Ronald Reagan.

The Neocons gained more influence during the Reagan administration. In fact, many in the Bush II administration would be recycled from the Reagan era. As Matlock (2010) noted in his book, *Superpower Illusions: How Myths and False Ideologies Led America Astray and How to Return to Reality,* although many intelligence professionals and diplomats knew for some time that the USSR was experiencing significant internal challenges, they were drowned out by the neocons' Cold War rhetoric of an evil empire that was voracious in its ambitions to take over the world and threaten America. According to the *Power of Nightmares*:

> *They would set out to recreate the myth of America as a unique nation whose destiny was to battle against an evil in the world. And in this project, the source of evil would be America's Cold*

> *War enemy: the Soviet Union. And by doing this, they believed that they would not only give new meaning and purpose to people's lives, but they would spread the good of democracy around the world. (Curtis 2004)*

Consequently, defense spending was greatly increased with no regard for deficits and military aid was provided to dictators who said the magic words "I'm fighting evil communists." Appeals to religious mythology were incorporated into public debate to obfuscate the real issues (Curtis 2004).

Reagan himself did not fully embrace Neoconservative ideology but some key people around him were greatly influenced by the Neoconservative woo-woo. Reagan's CIA director William Casey, was one such person. He was convinced by the then Special Advisor to the Secretary of State, Michael Ledeen, that "terrorist" groups throughout the world, such as the PLO, the Provisional IRA, and Baader-Meinhof in Germany, were part of a terrorist network overseen by the Soviet Union instead of local groups that emerged to fight various grievances specific to each group. Ledeen was using a book called *The Terror Network* as the basis for this belief. CIA specialists at the time tried to disabuse Casey of this fallacy—namely due to the fact that much of what was in *The Terror Network* was black propaganda that the CIA itself had invented to smear the Soviet Union. Melvin Goodman, who served as Head of Soviet Affairs for the CIA from 1976 to 1987 stated:

> *When we looked through the book, we found very clear episodes where CIA black propaganda—clandestine information that was designed under a covert action plan to be planted in European newspapers—were picked up and put in this book. A lot of it*

was made up. It was made up out of whole cloth. We told him that, point blank. And we even had the operations people to tell Bill Casey this. I thought maybe this might have an impact, but we were all dismissed. Casey had made up his mind. Lies became reality. (Curtis 2004)

Another example of the Neoconservative pattern of not letting facts get in their way. Ledeen's depth of thinking, or lack thereof, was revealed by the following response he gave to the episode:

The CIA denied it. They tried to convince people we were really crazy. I mean, they never believed that the Soviet Union was a driving force in the international terror network. They always wanted to believe that terrorist organizations were just what they said they were: local groups trying to avenge terrible evils done to them, or trying to rectify terrible social conditions, and things like that. And the CIA really did buy into that rhetoric. I don't know what their motive was. I don't know what peoples' motives are, hardly ever. And I don't much worry about motives. (Curtis 2004)

Supposedly, Casey was able to find an academic to produce a document showing that the "terror network" did exist. With this in hand, Casey was finally able to put enough pressure on Reagan to convince him to sign a confidential document to allow funding for covert wars to counter this threat from the Soviet Union (Curtis 2004).

When the Soviet Union's own internal problems came to a head, and Reagan followed his better instincts to engage the new leadership in Moscow to negotiate a peaceful and mutually beneficial path out of the Cold War, the Neocons claimed a victory for their aggressive policies based on more dangerous mythology (Matlock 2010).

When the people controlling foreign policy in America believe that one cannot have a substantive or meaningful identity without something or someone to oppose—in other words, when an enemy disappears, as was the case after the end of the Cold War—an existential crisis ensues. As many analysts observed during the height of the Global War on Terror, if one just substituted the word "terrorist" for "communist" in all the lines of the script, the movie remained pretty much the same.

The profit motive of the MIC, of course, also plays into this interest of keeping conflicts going throughout the world in order to guarantee markets and profits. What were all those powerful arms manufacturers going to do when the Cold War ended? As we will see in Chapter 3, the peace dividend was not going to be allowed to happen.

Military Strategy

Though Leo Strauss gets much of the credit and attention for influencing the group that would become known as the Neoconservatives, a lesser-known inspiration was a RAND Corporation Researcher and Pentagon advisor named Albert Wohlstetter. Wohlstetter found the contemporary nuclear policy of Mutually Assured Destruction (MAD) to be immoral and ineffective due to the fact that it would be so destructive to the civilian population if acted on and therefore no American leader would choose "reciprocal suicide" (apparently, he believed it was plausible that a Soviet leader might). According to authors Alain Frachon and Daniel Vernet in their article, "The Strategist and the Philosopher":

To the contrary, Wohlstetter proposed "staggered deterrence" i.e. accepting limited wars that would eventually use tactical nuclear weapons with high-precision "smart" bombs capable of striking at the enemy's military apparatus.

He criticized the joint nuclear weapons control policy with Moscow. According to him, it amounted to bridling US technological creativity in order to maintain an artificial balance with the USSR. (Frachon and Vernet 2003)

It was purportedly Wohlstetter's influence that led Reagan to pursue his "Star Wars" shield, which was the precursor to the missile defense shield pursued during the Bush II administration and was the reason behind Bush's unilateral withdrawal from the ABM Treaty (Frachon and Vernet 2003).

THE WOLFOWITZ DOCTRINE

Paul Wolfowtiz, a former student of both Strauss and Wohlstetter at the University of Chicago, wrote a draft version of a document called the Defense Planning Guidance for 1994 — 1999 in his capacity as Under Secretary of Defense in the Bush I administration. The draft was leaked to the *New York Times* on March 7, 1992, which led to public outcry about its imperialist overtones, moving official policy from one of "containment" to one of unilateralism and preventing the emergence of any potential rival to the US's hegemony as one of its tenets. The document was subsequently revised by Secretary of Defense Dick Cheney and Chairman of the Joint Chiefs of Staff Colin Powell and was officially released the following month. The original draft became known as the Wolfowitz Doctrine and its precepts re-emerged during the Bush II administration for which Wolfowitz served as Deputy Secretary of Defense (Wikipedia, "Wolfowitz Doctrine"; Wikipedia, "Paul Wolfowitz"). Some of the controversial language of the doctrine that is most germane to the subject of this book includes the following under Section 1.B:

> *Our first objective is to prevent the reemergence of a new rival, either on the territory of the former Soviet Union or elsewhere, that poses a threat on the order of that posed formerly by the Soviet Union. This is a dominant consideration underlying the new regional defense strategy and requires that we endeavor to prevent any hostile power from dominating a region whose resources would, under consolidated control, be sufficient to generate global power. These regions include Western Europe, East Asia, the territory of the former Soviet Union, and Southeast Asia...*
>
> *Finally, we must maintain mechanisms for deterring potential competitors from even aspiring to a larger regional or global role. (Wolfowitz 1992)*

Other disturbing sections of the doctrine that pertain to pushing ideological hegemony and the implicit potential for interfering in the internal relations of other nations include part of Section 1.A:

> *We will seek to promote those positive trends which serve to support and reinforce our national interests, principally, promotion, establishment and expansion of democracy and free market institutions worldwide. (Wolfowitz 1992)*

And Section 7.B:

> *To deterring and, when necessary, defending against threats to our security, and interests; and to exercising the leadership needed, including the decisive use of military forces when necessary, to maintain a world environment where societies with shared values can flourish. (Wolfowitz 1992)*

Basically, this doctrine is giving the United States government permission to decide that potentially any other nation on the planet may be subject to its definition of democracy, free market institutions and an environment where "shared values can flourish." If the US government determines that a nation does not meet these criteria, its rights to sovereignty and to self-determination as enshrined in international law can potentially be overruled, with unilateral military force. In other words, those controlling US government policy ultimately get to decide what form of political government and economic arrangement is best for another nation anywhere in the world, not the people living there and not the recognized leaders of the nation in question.

President Obama, with his frequent citing of America's exceptionalism, has never repudiated this doctrine.

A Clean Break

The concrete policy of regime change has been traced back, according to investigative journalist Robert Parry, to the role of several of the above named Neocon politicians' work on behalf of Israeli hardliner Benjamin Netanyahu's 1996 campaign to become prime minister. As advisors to Netanyahu, they formulated a strategy published under the name "A Clean Break: A New Strategy for Securing the Realm."

The idea behind this strategy was to undermine good faith negotiations, whereby the Palestinians may secure anything resembling a functioning and sovereign state, by destroying the leadership of countries sympathetic to and supportive of Hamas or Hezbollah by way of regime change interventions. The nations included Iraq (then led by Saddam Hussein), Syria under the Assads, and Iran.

While the overt intervention in Iraq and the covert intervention in Syria have resulted in chaos and suffering for the people living there, that chaos has benefitted Israel as Perry points out:

In the end, the regional chaos has helped Prime Minister Netanyahu starve the Palestinians of the financial support they once had, supposedly making them more susceptible to whatever demands the Israelis choose to make. And it has given Netanyahu a freer hand to engage in periodic slaughters of Gazan militants, a process the Israelis call "mowing the grass." (Parry 2014)

The Neocon's unequivocal support for Israel has been observed by others, some even suggesting that there is such a blurred line among Neocons between the Israeli government's interests and the US's interests that the two are often conflated.

Former CIA analysts Kathleen and Bill Christison, in their 2002 *Counterpunch* article, "A Rose by Another Name: The Bush Administration's Dual Loyalties," noted that from the 1990s onward, there was an increasing trend toward not even making any pretense of balance on the Israel-Palestine issue.

In the Clinton administration, the three most serious State Department officials dealing with the Palestinian-Israel peace process were all partisans of Israel to one degree or another… [But] the link between active promoters of Israeli interests and

> *policy-making circles is stronger by several orders of magnitude in the Bush administration, which is peppered with people who have long records of activism on behalf of Israel in the United States, of policy advocacy in Israel, and of promoting an agenda for Israel often at odds with existing US policy. (Christison 2002)*

Douglas Feith, who helped develop the Clean Break strategy for Netanyahu, later contributed to the fabrications that enabled the invasion of Iraq in 2003 by setting up the Office of Special Plans in the Defense Department through which he funneled his own "unverified" intelligence, reminiscent of the fantasies and falsehoods churned out by the Neocons for Team B during the Ford administration (Christison 2002).

ROBERT KAGAN AND VICTORIA NULAND

Robert Kagan, a Neoconservative writer and historian, is not a direct disciple of Strauss, but he buys into the basic Neocon myths about the end of the Cold War; the good versus evil political framework of international politics, and that America always represents the good and, hence, has a duty to intervene on behalf of remaking the world in its own image via regime change.

Kagan is perhaps most infamous for co-founding, along with William Kristol, the think tank Project for a New American Century (PNAC) in 1998. One of PNAC's main projects was to encourage a policy of regime change in Iraq via publication of policy papers and political lobbying. It wasn't until Bush II occupied the White House that they would find a receptive audience.

Kagan's views developed while serving as a policy staffer in the State Department during the Reagan administration where he later became a speechwriter for Secretary of State George Schultz. His thinking and experience culminated in an article published by *Foreign Affairs* magazine in 1996 in which he lamented "America's reduced role in a post-Cold War world." Instead he suggested America should serve as a "benevolent global hegemon."

Despite the fact that, by any reasonable standard — such as the reality that most of his predictions about regime change and war in Iraq have been proven to be completely wrong — his basic ideas have not fundamentally changed, nor have they ceased to be taken seriously in Washington.

Kagan still believes the US has a legitimate duty to expand its power and dominion throughout the world in pursuit of "common universal values," which is still code for our definition of democracy and free market institutions (Beaumont 2008).

With new opportunities for the spreading of chaos and destabilization via regime change having exhausted themselves temporarily in the Middle East by 2008, Kagan began transposing his theme of bringing good old American "democracy" by force to a different geographic area: Eurasia.

As he told Peter Beaumont of *The Observer* that year, "Democracies need to be working together to promote their fundamental values in the new confrontation with the globe's newly confident autocracies" (Beaumont 2008).

Those "newly confident autocracies" he was referring to were Russia and China.

Around this same time, Kagan served as a foreign policy advisor to John McCain, who has consistently expressed public hostility toward Russia.

More recently, Kagan has been busy spewing his interventionist ideology in media outlets such as *The New Republic* and the *Washington Post*. The latter published a column in July of 2014 in which Kagan made the following comment:

> In my view the willingness of the United States to use force and to threaten to use force to defend its interests and the liberal world order has been an essential and unavoidable part of sustaining that world order since the end of WWII. (Kagan 2014)

Apparently, Kagan missed the history lesson on US interventions since WWII that have removed democratically elected leaders and replaced them with brutal dictators (e.g., Iran in 1953 and Chile in 1973) and the American provision of support for paramilitaries who slaughtered anyone suspected of opposing their agenda (e.g. Central America in the 1980s) (Blum 2000). As a reputed historian, he also seems to have missed the fact that there is no historical evidence that a functioning democracy can be imposed by an outside force. Furthermore, the theory of democratic peace that he implicitly believes in has been shown to be erroneous. Two nations both having some form of democratic government is no guarantee that they will not go to war (Wikipedia, "List of Wars Between Democracies").

In response to Kagan's essay in the May 2014 issue of *The New Republic*, "Superpowers Don't Get to Retire," Obama said he wanted to have lunch with Kagan to compare world views.

Kagan is now starting to distance himself from the label "Neoconservative" and has publicly stated that he prefers to be called a "liberal interventionist." Moreover, he has maintained bipartisan connections by serving on a civilian advisory board for Hillary Clinton during her tenure as Secretary of State. He has even intimated that he may support her if she runs for president in 2016:

> *I feel comfortable with her on foreign policy. If she pursues a policy which we think she will pursue, it's something that might have been called neocon, but clearly her supporters are not going to call it that; they are going to call it something else. (Horowitz 2014)*

In regards to the Ukraine crisis, he has pushed the standard line of misinformation and distortion and used it as a pretext to justify a more muscular and interventionist policy in Eurasia:

> *When Vladimir Putin failed to achieve his goals in Ukraine through political and economic means, he turned to force, because he believed that he could. What might China do were it not hemmed in by a ring of powerful nations backed by the United States? (Kagan 2014)*

In this case, Kagan's distortions are particularly egregious and willful because he knows full well the role his wife, Victoria Nuland, played in fomenting the current chaos in Ukraine.

Nuland, a former chief foreign policy advisor to Dick Cheney in the Bush II administration and later ambassador to NATO, served as a spokesperson for the Obama State Department prior to her current gig as Assistant Secretary for European and Eurasian Affairs. She is one of the Neocons that Obama inexplicably kept around—part of the new tactic that many Neocons had embarked on by 2008, which was to embed themselves within the broader Washington establishment, according to former Neocon Jacob Heilbrunn, now an editor at the Realist publication *The National Interest*:

> *Whether it's the Foundation for the Defense of Democracies or the National Endowment for Democracy, the Weekly Standard or the New York Sun, the neoconservatives are battle-hardened fighters who have created a permanent base for themselves. They will not disappear. (Lobe 2008)*

Heilbrunn provides unique insight into the Neocon mindset by describing what amounts to an internalized case of post-traumatic stress disorder in connection with the Jewish holocaust that makes for an eternal vigilance about the failures of German and European liberal democrats to standing up to Hitler and the Nazis as well as to Communism. "Neoconservatives see Munichs everywhere and anywhere. [They] have shaped a romantic narrative for themselves in which they are the new Churchills staring down the forces of evil" (Lobe 2008).

This is the kind of mindset that can find within a leader like Russian President Vladimir Putin, who is a pragmatic mixed bag of political and economic policies and cannot be bent to the US's will, a new Hitler.

After having the wheels greased via funding of numerous political and media organizations in Ukraine by the National Endowment for Democracy (NED) led by its Neocon president Carl Gershman, Nuland actively encouraged the protests at Maidan Square along with Neocon Senator John McCain who was photographed with leaders of Svoboda in front of their neo-Nazi banner (Taylor 2013).

Responsibility to Protect
(aka R2P or Liberal Intervention)

> *War is essentially an evil thing. Its consequences are not confined to the belligerent states alone, but affect the whole world. To initiate a war of aggression, therefore, is not only an international crime, it is the supreme international crime differing only from other war crimes in that it contains within itself the accumulated evil of the whole.*
>
> —*Judgment of the Nuremberg Tribunal, 1945—1946*

John Horgan in his book, *The End of War* scientifically analyzes war throughout human history via anthropological, historical, psychological, and sociological studies of warfare and atrocities. One of his conclusions is that the old cliché about justice being a prerequisite for peace is wrong. Actually, the opposite is true—peace is a prerequisite for justice and for the pursuit of other noble goals. By the very nature of war and the conditions it produces, justice, democracy and physical well-being cannot flourish (Horgan 2012; Jacobson 2012).

Those who believe that war can be the means for bringing peace, democracy, and human rights to an area in conflict or breakdown are required to delude themselves with notions of "short, clean, surgical" wars, which have no basis in reality. To believe such is to be actually or willfully ignorant of what modern war is, which includes soldiers who have typically undergone training that has been refined over the past 70 years to produce higher kill rates through operant conditioning, the use of weapons and munitions that are guaranteed to be non-discriminatory due to their awesome power of destruction or continuing danger after the cessation of hostilities, and theaters of operation that do not have clearly delineated lines separating the battlefield from the non-battlefield (Grossman 1997; Zinn 2002).

"Humanitarian interventions" based on the theoretical promotion of human rights and democracy is a modern variation of the crusader mindset. It is a mindset that has been used to justify colonialism in the past, such as Christian missionary work, "civilizing" the pagans and savages, and the "white man's burden." It has also proved a very successful way to get traditionally anti-war and anti-imperialist segments of the left to support such wars even though there is little reason to believe that "great powers" like the US are suddenly pursuing something different than they have in the past when they choose to intervene militarily or otherwise embed themselves by force in another country: economic gain and geopolitical advantage (Bricmont 2006).

As alluded to earlier, one need only look at the US's documented record of military interventions and covert operations in other countries since the end of WWII to realize that a country's human rights record or functional democratic institutions are not the criteria by which the US determines what leaders or governments it will support, install, prop up or ally with. A more consistently recognizable pattern involves receptivity to US corporations and geostrategic advantage against perceived competitors on the world stage (Blum 2000).

Diana Johnstone, author of *Fool's Crusade: Yugoslavia, NATO and Western Delusions* and a critic of R2P, points out that genocide and ethnic cleansing actually tend to occur within the context of or as the result of wars. The Jewish Holocaust and the Khmer Rouge genocide are obvious examples. The Rwandan genocide happened during a civil war that took place from 1990-1994 (Johnstone 2013).

Another example, although less clear to the American public due to the dominant portrayal offered by the US government and establishment media, is the Serbian genocide of the Milosevic government against Kosovar Albanians immediately following the initiation of the US/NATO military intervention—a humanitarian catastrophe that NATO expected as a result of its actions, according to international law expert Francis Boyle, who represented the Republic of Bosnia and Herzegovina in proceedings at the International Court of Justice (Boyle 2013). Indeed, a July 2014 report by the chief prosecutor of the Special Investigative Task Force set up by the EU to conduct a criminal investigation into allegations of war crimes by the US/NATO-installed Kosovo Liberation Army (KLA) found that a criminal indictment is justified against senior officials of the KLA. This finding was based on sanctioned actions that constitute ethnic cleansing and crimes against humanity against large portions of the Serb and Roma populations, as well as violent persecution of political opponents within the community of Kosovo Albanians (Williamson 2014).

The United Nations (UN) was established to protect the concept of national sovereignty with the understanding that in order to save future generations from war, it was necessary to highlight the sanctity of national borders from violation by more powerful and belligerent nations. Johnstone argues that advocates of the R2P doctrine seek to undermine this legal concept of national sovereignty:

> *In fact, Hitler initiated World War II precisely in violation of the national sovereignty of Czechoslovakia and Poland partly in order, he claimed, to stop human rights violations that those governments allegedly perpetrated against ethnic Germans who lived there. It was to invalidate this pretext, and "save succeeding*

> *generations from the scourge of war", that the United Nations was founded on the basis of respect for national sovereignty.*
>
> *In practice this [R2P] can give the dominant powers carte blanche to intervene militarily in weaker countries in order to support whatever armed rebellions they favor. Once this doctrine seems to be accepted, it can even serve as an incitement to opposition groups to provoke government repression in order to call for "protection." (Johnstone 2013)*

Furthermore, R2P campaigns are often undertaken in order to address problems that were created by imperialist or colonialist powers to begin with. This dynamic is being played out at the time of this writing as President Barak Obama has ordered military airstrikes and an increase in forces to protect the northern city of Erbil from advances by Islamic State of Iraq and Syria (ISIS) fighters and to help the thousands of people belonging to the Yazidi religious sect that are reportedly stranded on a mountain in the middle of hostilities (Queally 2014). It should be noted, however, that the Kurdish territory in which Erbil is situated is home to 25 percent of Iraq's oil reserves (Democracy Now 2014). For those who argue that this is a cynical statement about the US's true motives, one can rest assured that the US will "incidentally" ensure some kind of direct or indirect control of those nearby oil resources.

By invoking the Responsibility to Protect doctrine Obama is ostensibly addressing a problem that is a result of the US government's invasion and occupation of Iraq, which created the conditions of a civil war in the first place, in addition to providing support to an armed rebellion in Syria next door in the hopes of overthrowing the Assad regime. A segment of those same rebels eventually became the radicals who joined Islamic State of Iraq (ISI)—a splinter group of Al

Qaeda in Iraq—to become Islamic State of Iraq and Syria (Parry 2014).

Acting without congressional authority, Obama has placed no time limit on airstrikes and has authorized the use of military force to defend diplomatic personnel in Erbil instead of evacuating them. At the time of this writing, there are reportedly more than 1,000 US military personnel in Iraq (Democracy Now 2014). These kinds of actions have historically been precursors to deeper and longer military involvement (Queally 2014; McCauley 2014).

Considering the fact that Israel just finished a military campaign that resulted in the deaths of over 2,000 Gazans—the vast majority of which were civilians—as well as the demolition of what little civil infrastructure was left in the area, all without any substantive concern expressed by the US government, much less invoking R2P, it is apparent that the US is picking and choosing which violations of humanitarian laws deserve action. This is all the more pronounced when the invocation of R2P in the case of Israel's actions in Gaza would not require direct military intervention and the costs associated with it, but only the withholding of the annual $3 billion in aid the US provides Israel each year on the condition that Israel stop violating international law. Additionally, the US could decide not to continue using its veto power at the UN to shield an increasingly defiant Israel from the consequences of its actions. Neither of these approaches would cost the US blood or treasure.

Origins of R2P

The Responsibility to Protect doctrine was inspired, in large part, by the failure of the international community to stop the genocide in Rwanda in 1994 and controversy over NATO's "humanitarian" actions in the Balkans in that same decade. Subsequently, then Secretary General of the UN Kofi Annan sought guidance and clarification on when the international community should intervene for humanitarian purposes.

R2P later emerged from the report of the International Commission on Intervention and State Sovereignty (ICISS) in December of 2001. The commission had a thorny issue to deal with as it involved the principle of state sovereignty and when it may presumably be breached for humanitarian reasons, namely genocide. It is recognized that the Iraq War of 2003 dealt a setback to R2P, as a partial justification proffered for that war was humanitarian intervention. Subsequent humanitarian disasters in Darfur, however, kept interest in R2P alive and attempts were made to revise and clarify the doctrine.

What emerged by 2005 at the World Summit was an agreement by the heads of states and governments to three general ideas. Those three ideas evolved into the Three Pillars of the Responsibility to Protect doctrine unveiled by the Secretary General of the UN Ban Ki-Moon in his 2009 report, "Implementing the Responsibility to Protect":

> Pillar One: States have the primary responsibility to protect their populations from genocide, war crimes, ethnic cleansing and crimes against humanity;
>
> Pillar Two: addresses the commitment of the international community to provide assistance to States

in building capacity to protect their populations from genocide, war crimes, ethnic cleansing and crimes against humanity and to assisting those which are under stress before crises and conflicts break out; and,

<u>Pillar Three</u>: focuses on the responsibility of the international community to timely and decisive action to prevent and halt genocide, ethnic cleansing, war crimes and crimes against humanity when a state is manifestly failing to protect its populations. (Greppi 2009)

A resolution of the UN General Assembly was introduced in September of 2009 and it was agreed by that body to continue consideration of R2P. Informal interactive dialogues on the issue have taken place every year since 2010.

Libya—An Abuse of R2P

Despite the noble intentions of most of those behind this doctrine, which is still in the process of becoming a customary norm and is not enshrined in any legally binding treaty, it is not without serious problems and criticisms.

International law expert Marjorie Cohn has expressed concern with the possibilities for abuse of the doctrine by powerful actors, citing its invocation in Libya:

> *Security Council Resolution 1973 begins with the call for "the immediate establishment of a ceasefire." It reiterates "the responsibility of the Libyan authorities to protect the Libyan population" and reaffirms that "parties to armed conflicts bear the primary responsibility to take all feasible steps to ensure the*

> *protection of civilians. The resolution authorizes UN Member States "to take all necessary measures…to protect civilians and civilian populated areas."*
>
> *But instead of pursuing an immediate ceasefire, immediate military action was taken instead. The military force exceeds all bounds of the "all necessary measures" authorization. "All necessary measures" should first have been peaceful measures to settle the conflict. Yet peaceful means were not exhausted before the military invasion began….After passage of the resolution, Libya immediately offered to accept international monitors and Qaddafi offered to step down and leave Libya. These offers were immediately rejected by the opposition. (Cohn 2011)*

Moreover, Obama, along with then French President Nicolas Sarkozy and British PM David Cameron, admitted in an *International Herald Tribune* op-ed that NATO would continue its military campaign in Libya until Qaddafi was gone – in other words, the R2P invocation in the UN Resolution was used as a cover for regime change:

> *However, so long as Qaddafi is in power, NATO must maintain its operations so that civilians remain protected and the pressure on the regime builds. Then a genuine transition from dictatorship to an inclusive constitutional process can really begin, led by a new generation of leaders. In order for that transition to succeed, Qaddafi must go and go for good. (Obama, et al. 2011)*

Eventually, Qaddafi was captured by rebel forces, tortured, and murdered. Then-Secretary of State Hillary Clinton was caught on camera gloating at the news of this blatant violation of international law, exclaiming, "We came, we saw, he died" (Parry 2014; Clinton 2011). Since then, Libya has degenerated into tribal conflict.

Robert Parry describes the Libyan intervention, instigated by White House R2P advocates Samantha Power and Susan Rice, as a war that "the Neocons and the R2Pers teamed up for" (Parry 2014). Indeed it seems to have been the beginning of a strange partnership in which the Neocons do their part to destabilize and bust up a state—to paraphrase Wolfowitz—by taking a minority opposition and arming it in the target country so that it attracts increasingly nuttier elements, thereby setting up the nation for an intervention with an R2P pretext as the leadership of the target country predictably reacts to the armed rebels with force.

A September 2013 report by the Belfer Center for Science and International Affairs of the Harvard Kennedy School found that the US government's narrative about the events in Libya that supposedly required a "humanitarian intervention"—repeated by the mainstream media—was wrong. In fact, the uprising in Libya was armed and violent from the beginning and Qaddafi's military response did not target civilians or use indiscriminate force. These findings were supported by the UN, Amnesty International, and Human Rights Watch (Kuperman 2013).

A similar process was attempted in Syria but was thwarted by a combination of Russian diplomacy and elements of Obama's military leadership being weary of a full-fledged military engagement on the erroneous assertion of Assad's responsibility for a sarin gas attack (Hersh 2014; Lloyd 2013).

Parry (2014) cites a Washington insider as confessing that these two ideologies "now represent the dominant foreign policy establishment in Official Washington." The source went on to observe that "the Neocons are motivated by two things, love of Israel and hatred of Russia. Meanwhile, the R2Pers are easily enamored of idealistic young people in street protests" (Parry, April 2014).

Putin, educated in international law, publicly expressed grave concern at the pattern of intervention being established by both Bush and Obama. At the outset of intervention in Libya, Putin said the following to international journalists:

> *About the UN resolution, which gives grounds for the present military intervention—this resolution is defective. If we look at what is written there, it becomes obvious that it allows anyone to take any action against a sovereign state. It reminds me of the medieval call for a crusade. When countries call on each other to go out and liberate something.*
>
> *But, you know, I don't worry more about this military intervention—there are a lot of military conflicts going on and, unfortunately, will unfold in the future. I'm more worried about the ease with which decisions are being made to use force in international affairs nowadays. For example, it has become a steady trend in US policy. During Clinton's era, they bombed Yugoslavia and Belgrade. Bush invaded Afghanistan. Iraq was invaded under far-fetched false pretenses, liquidating an entire administration, including Saddam's children. And now it's Libya's turn. It opens with a pretext to defend civilians, but it's the civilians who die under the bombs during airstrikes. Where is the logic and conscience here? Both are absent. There are already victims among the civilians. (Putin 2011)*

The R2P doctrine still has traction among mainstream western commentators, however, as Jean Bricmont observes in his book *Humanitarian Imperialism: Using Human Rights to Sell War*, those who exercise power typically utilize an ideology that is meant to convince those on the receiving end that the power being exercised over them is for their own good. Such language was found among Hitler's supporters in Germany and renowned American commentators during the Vietnam War.

He goes on to explain that ideology is the most important in "open" and "democratic" societies where it constitutes the main form of social control by marginalizing debate outside of a narrow set of parameters. These methods are arguably much more effective than the control by fear that autocratic societies utilize:

> *Today's secular priesthood is made up of opinion makers, media stars of all kinds, and a considerable number of academics and journalists. They largely monopolize public debate, channeling it in certain directions and setting the limits on what can be said, while giving the impression of a free exchange of ideas. One of the most common ideological reinforcement mechanisms is to focus debate on the means employed to achieve the supposedly altruistic ends claimed by those in power, instead of asking whether the proclaimed aims are the real ones, or whether those pursuing them have the right to do so. (Bricmont 2006)*

Hence, respectable debate in our so-called open and "liberal" media in the US is focused on the effectiveness of means and tactics of the policy and not the legitimacy of the aims or the policy itself. In contrast to an autocratic society, the purveyors of propaganda among the secular priesthood in open societies typically believe the distortions and obfuscations they peddle.

Based on what transpired in the Balkans and in Libya after US/NATO intervention, as well as what turned out to be faulty evidence or outright mendacity regarding the reasons for the interventions in both areas in the first place, along with the near intervention in Syria following the same pattern, the argument that US/NATO military interventions is the way to stop or prevent genocide, ethnic cleansing and other crimes against humanity is refuted.

On September 1, 2014, when French and Russian diplomats and parliamentarians convened a dialogue on the Ukraine crisis, the participants stated that these abuses had degraded the efficacy of international law:

> *The Ukrainian crisis is in fact a product of the destruction of the framework of international law that we have experienced since the middle of the 1990s and which manifested itself around the subjects of Kosovo (1998-99), of Iraq (2003)—the magnitude of whose consequences are today being measured—and, more recently, of Libya. Today we are tasting the bitter fruits of this destruction of the rules of international law; a destruction for which the United States and NATO bear the responsibility. It is not possible to find a framework for resolving this crisis without rules that are acknowledged by all. International law is still based on two rules, which are profoundly contradictory: respect for the sovereignty of states and the right of peoples to determine for themselves. Mediation between these two principles has been dramatically and permanently weakened by the actions of NATO states and the United States since the end of the 1990s. It is these mediations that we must rebuild. (Slavyangrad 2014)*

No further movement seems to be imminent to get the R2P doctrine incorporated into an international treaty, and its evolution into an eventual customary norm has hit some snags among countries in the global south. In fact, during the UN General Assembly's "High Level Meeting on the Rule of Law at the National and International Levels" in September of 2012, the resulting Declaration expressed no further support or even mention of the R2P doctrine (Boyle 2013).

Cohn points out that during General Assembly discussions on the issue back in 2009, the Cuban delegation raised some prescient and thought-provoking issues that are worth quoting here:

> *Who is to decide if there is an urgent need for an intervention in a given State, according to what criteria, in what framework, and on the basis of what conditions? Who decides it is evident the authorities of a State do not protect their people, and how is it decided? Who determines peaceful means are not adequate in a certain situation, and on what criteria? Do small states have also the right and the actual prospect of interfering in the affairs of larger States? Would any developed country allow, either in principle or in practice, humanitarian intervention in its own territory? How and where do we draw the line between an intervention under the Responsibility to Protect and an intervention for political or strategic purposes, and when do political considerations prevail over humanitarian concerns? (Cohn 2011)*

CHAPTER 3

NATO EXPANSION & AMERICAN EMPIRE

> *Expanding NATO would be the most fateful error of American policy in the entire post-cold-war era. Such a decision may be expected to inflame the nationalistic, anti-Western and militaristic tendencies in Russian opinion; to have an adverse effect on the development of Russian democracy; to restore the atmosphere of the cold war to East-West relations, and to impel Russian foreign policy in directions decidedly not to our liking.*
>
> *Russians are little impressed with American assurances that it reflects no hostile intentions. They would see their prestige (always uppermost in the Russian mind) and their security interests as adversely affected.*
>
> —George F. Kennan, author of US "containment" policy for the Soviet Union (Kennan 1997)

> *They probably rubbed their hands rejoicing at having played a trick on the Russians.*
>
> —Mikhail Gorbachev in a 2009 interview with Germany's Bild newspaper on the West's broken promise not to extend NATO east in return for German reunification (RIA Novosti 2009)

In December of 1989, a few weeks after the fall of the Berlin Wall, President George H.W. Bush (Bush I) participated in a summit with Mikhail Gorbachev in Malta. During that summit, Washington promised that it would not "take advantage" of the political upheaval taking place in Eastern

Europe in light of Gorbachev's decision not to use force to maintain control in the region (McGovern 2015).

Subsequently, on February 9, 1990, Bush's Secretary of State James Baker negotiated a gentleman's agreement with Gorbachev that, in exchange for allowing a reunified Germany as a NATO member, NATO would not be expanded any farther east. The following day, West German Chancellor Helmut Kohl reiterated this same offer, which is when Gorbachev actually accepted it. Due to the Soviet Union's history of having been invaded twice by Germany during the 20th century, Gorbachev was understandably hesitant to allow reunification. However, Baker had explained that it would be better to have a unified Germany in NATO, where it was implied that any contemplated military actions would be kept in check, than to have an independent Germany. Gorbachev ultimately agreed with this reasoning but made a grave error in not demanding that the agreement be put in writing, which has provided US leaders with plausible deniability when it suited them (Sarotte 2010).

According to ex-CIA analyst and Soviet specialist Ray McGovern, when he first asked Viktor Borisovich Kuvaldin, one of Gorbachev's advisers at the time, why there was no written record of Baker's promises insisted upon, McGovern described Kuvaldin's response as follows:

> *He tilted his head, looked me straight in the eye, and said, "We trusted you." (McGovern 2015)*

NATO Secretary General Manfred Woerner reflected Gorbachev's understanding of the agreement in a speech three months later in Brussels where he stated, "the fact that we are ready not to place a NATO army outside of German territory gives the Soviet Union a firm security guarantee" (Pushkov 2007).

That "firm security guarantee" has translated into a total of twelve new members, all from Central and Eastern Europe, that have joined NATO since the end of the Cold War, with overtures having also been made toward Kazakhstan and Azerbaijan (Nazemroaya 2012).

The agreement was first broken by President Bill Clinton who encouraged the entry of Hungary, Poland, and the Czech Republic into the alliance. This followed both an intensive lobbying effort by the arms industry, which needed a mission to justify its continued share of public largesse after the Cold War, and a political battle between Clinton and Bob Dole for the Polish-American vote during that year's presidential campaign (Hartung 1998; Chicago Tribune 1996). Later, Bush II actively lobbied for the entry of seven more Eastern European nations into the alliance, including the three Baltic states of Estonia, Latvia and Lithuania on Russia's border (Matlock 2010).

Jack Matlock, who served as US ambassador to the Soviet Union in the Bush I administration, explains that when Clinton was advised by Russian representatives and Soviet/Russia experts, even some of whom had participated in the negotiated end of the Cold War, that he was about to make a serious geopolitical blunder in encouraging NATO expansion, he did it anyway.

> *"[One of two decisions] turned Russian public opinion during the years of the Clinton administration from strongly pro-American to vigorous opposition to American policies abroad. The first was the decision to extend the NATO military structure into countries that had previously been members of the Warsaw Pact. There was no need to expand NATO to ensure the security of the newly*

> *independent countries of Eastern Europe. There were other ways those countries could have been reassured and protected without seeming to re-divide Europe to Russia's disadvantage...Combined with rhetoric claiming "victory" in the Cold War, expanding NATO suggested to the Russian public that throwing off communism and breaking up the Soviet Union had probably been a bad idea. Instead of getting credit for voluntarily joining the West, they were being treated as if they had been defeated and were not worthy to be allies."* (Matlock 2010)

The obvious question to ask is why we needed to keep NATO if the reason for its existence had disappeared and the Warsaw Pact, its Soviet-era counterpart, had been disbanded? Alexey Pushkov, Russian legislator and Professor at the Moscow State Institute of International Relations, recalls that this question was indeed put to the West over the years: "The standard response to the arguments against NATO's eastward expansion was that Russia's neighbors felt unsafe. [But] neither Warsaw nor Prague could point to any signs that Russia had aggressive designs towards Eastern Europe" (Pushkov 2007).

Pushkov states that proposals were offered to guarantee security for the countries of Eastern Europe that did not require the expansion of NATO, as Matlock suggests above, but such offers were rejected in Washington and Brussels. He goes on to describe his experiences over the years in trying to explain Russia's concerns about NATO expansion to the West:

> *Throughout the 1990s, I often made the point that by expanding NATO eastward, Russia would be pushed out of the Euro-Atlantic community. From the geopolitical point of view it is as if the West were saying to Russia, "From now on, your security is of no interest to us. You are on your own." The answers I was repeatedly getting were amazing and extremely short-sighted:*

"What can you do to oppose the expansion? Move your troops to your Western borders? What practical measures can you take?" As for the guarantees given in 1989 and 1990, I was told that none of them had been codified in any formal treaty or agreement and that, even if Western leaders such as Helmut Kohl or John Major reiterated what Baker or Woerner had said, they were now of no consequence." (Pushkov 2007)

Despite warm personal relations between Bush II and Putin at the start of the new millennium, Russia's security concerns ultimately did not fare any better with the new administration.

After the September 11th attacks, Putin was the first world leader to call Bush, seeing it as an opening for cooperation (Matlock 2010). After supporting the US War on Terrorism, including logistical and intelligence assistance, as well as providing access for what were to be temporary military bases to conduct the war in Afghanistan—a decision Putin had to persuade nay-sayers among his defense and security chiefs to agree to—Putin undoubtedly thought there would be some meaningful reciprocity. However, he eventually realized that little would be forthcoming (Roxburgh 2013).

In October of 2001, Putin met NATO Secretary General George Robertson in Brussels and boldly inquired as to when Russia would be invited to join NATO. Robertson told him that he'd have to apply for membership, go through a vetting process, and then an invitation would be issued (Roxburgh 2013). Putin shrugged this off with a dismissive comment to the effect that Russia would not wait in line with smaller, less important countries (Roxburgh 2013).

As a way to placate Russia, British Prime Minister Tony Blair came up with a plan in 2002 to create the NATO—Russia Council, a measure "stopping well short of membership but at least giving them a sense of belonging to the club." Russia would have a permanent ambassador to NATO and would participate in NATO discussions. But problems soon arose, including complaints from Russia that they were often excluded from informal discussions prior to official meetings and would consequently face a coordinated bloc. These effects, combined with Blair's underlying attitude in creating the plan —as stated by one of his aides (Roxburgh 2013), that "even if they [Russia] weren't really a superpower anymore, you had to pretend they were," created the impression that the West was merely being condescending. This is particularly striking when one reads Putin's words at the signing ceremony about his desire for Russia's needs to be heard and to be respected:

> *The problem for our country was that for a very long time, it was Russia on one side, and on the other practically the whole rest of the world. And we gained nothing good from this confrontation with the rest of the world. The overwhelming majority of our citizens understand this all too well. Russia is returning to the family of civilized nations. And she needs nothing more than for her voice to be heard and for her national interests to be taken into account. (Roxburgh 2013)*

Bush II's senior director for Russia on the National Security Council, Thomas Graham, admitted to Reuters in an April, 2014 interview that an alternative that was not pursued by the US was to dissolve NATO and create a new pact that reflected new global realities and eventually included Russia (Rohde and Mohammed 2014).

The unwillingness to allow Russia into NATO or to come up with an alternative alliance that could be in everyone's interest represented another lost opportunity that would prove to have fateful consequences. Putin's cooperation and stated yearning to be accepted into the western world not only didn't get him a meaningful chance at NATO membership, but it didn't stop Bush's insistence on unilaterally pulling out of the ABM Treaty to pursue a missile defense shield—a move that basically tells Russia that the US reserves the right to a nuclear first strike without retaliation.

According to Soviet/Russia expert, Patrick Armstrong (2009), the West's mentality toward post-Soviet Russia has been one of either condescension or hostility or a strange combination of both. The condescension justifies having economic advisors go in and induce "shock therapy" on the nation in the 1990s, as well as lambasting it when convenient for not being a full-fledged liberal democracy after only 20-some years of attempts following one thousand years of authoritarian rule, including the czars and the Soviets.

The aforementioned NATO membership charade was preceded by Bill Clinton, his amiable relations with his Russian counterpart notwithstanding, when he delivered these patronizing words to a departing Boris Yeltsin, over whose objections he began NATO expansion, representing one of the few times Yeltsin briefly lashed out at the US after being rather subservient on the matter:

> *Boris, you've got democracy in your heart, you've got the trust of the people in your bones, you've got the fire in your belly of a real democrat and reformer. I'm not sure Putin has that. You'll have to keep an eye on him and use your influence to make sure that he stays on the right path. Putin needs you, Boris. Russia needs you...You changed Russia. Russia was lucky to have you. The world was lucky you were where you were. I was lucky to have you. We did a lot of stuff together, you and I...We did some good things. They'll last. It took guts on your part. A lot of that stuff*

was harder for you than it was for me. I know that. (Roxburgh 2013)

As will be discussed in Chapter 4, rather than being the flaming democrat that American politicians and mainstream media hailed at the time, Yeltsin was corrupt, utterly compliant to the US's desires, and more authoritarian in many respects than Putin. He was also deeply unpopular among his own people by the time he left office (Roxburgh 2013; Klein 2007).

In a candid conversation with his deputy secretary of state, Strobe Talbot, in 2006, Bill Clinton made an admission that reflected the American political elite's attitude toward post-Soviet Russia, saying "We keep telling Ol' Boris, 'Okay, now here's what you've got to do next—here's some more shit for your face'" (Bhadrakumar 2006).

The hostility is exemplified by NATO expansion, missile defense shields and accusations that Russia has imperial ambitions if it asserts its political and economic independence or insists that it also has legitimate interests in its own backyard.

This evaluation, however, really only tells the story of the mindset of the politicians and advisors around the presidents who have had the most influence from Clinton to the present. Another attitude does exist among some leaders and advisors, but it has been overruled by the assortment of Russophobes and Neo-Imperialists operating under the banner of neoconservatives, humanitarian interventionists, or Brzeziński advocates of the Grand Chessboard previously discussed.

As a case in point, in the Bush II administration, there was a split about the proper approach to Russia. There was, according to former BBC Moscow correspondent Angus Roxburgh, the "Russophiles" led by Secretary of State Colin

Powell, who believed in trying to understand Russia's concerns and their legitimate right to consideration of their interests. This perspective was more in line with some of Western Europe, particularly France and Germany. In addition to trade and economic ties, there was the view there that Russia was like a prodigal son that should be welcomed home due to a sense of shared history and culture. It was also believed that this approach was the best way to strengthen democracy in Russia (Roxburgh 2013). Indeed, as some independent analysts have pointed out, had the West made a good faith attempt to integrate post-Soviet Russia into the European community, there would have been no "civilizational" clash for countries like Ukraine to be caught in the middle of (Petro 2014).

The other camp was led by the Neoconservatives who adhered to the belief that the United States "won" the Cold War and that Russia should accept its position as a vanquished nation that would have little say over anything the US did, even in its own border regions, no matter how myopic or reckless it turned out to be. Jack Matlock has publicly denounced this dangerous re-writing of history:

> *"Reagan normally rejected [the Neoconservatives] advice if it involved refusing to talk to adversaries. But when his policies actually worked, instead of conceding that Reagan was right and they were wrong, they have sought explanations for the end of the Cold War that bolster the myths that have plagued us. Thus the idea is perpetuated that it was US force and threats, rather than negotiation, that ended the Cold War, and also that Reagan's rhetoric "conquered" communism, and that the collapse of the Soviet Union was the equivalent of a military victory. These claims are all distortions, all incorrect, all misleading, and all*

dangerous to the safety and future prosperity of the American people." (Matlock 2010)

By 2002, seven more nations of Eastern Europe were invited to join NATO (they were admitted in 2004), creating another strain in the American relationship with Russia. By March of 2003, further problems emerged as Russia, correctly recognizing that Saddam Hussein had nothing to do with Al-Qaeda or terrorism, made a last minute, behind-the-scenes diplomatic push to avert the war. When that failed, they partnered with France and Germany to oppose the invasion at the UN (Roxburgh 2013).

Two months later, Bush made a stop in Poland—a country whose political class has historically had Russophobic tendencies and had supported the US invasion of Iraq, like all of the new post-Cold War members of NATO—before heading to St. Petersburg for its 300th anniversary celebrations. This insult was the nail in the coffin for Putin's attempts to establish a mutually respectful and beneficial relationship with the US. He was later overheard telling French Prime Minister Chirac at the event: "My priorities were the following: first a relationship with America, second with China, third with Europe. Now it's the other way around—first Europe, then China, then America" (Roxburgh 2013; Nazemroaya 2012; Rozoff 2010).

As we shall see later, it was the successful results of that revised program of prioritizing a relationship with Europe and China that the US later viewed as a threat.

NATO: From Cold War to Global War

The refusal in Washington to give up the Cold War mentality was foreshadowed as early as 1989, as Russia scholar Stephen Cohen relates in describing his debate, at the invitation of the White House, with Cold-War professor Richard Pipes over the possibility of a US-Soviet strategic partnership: "Declarations alone could not terminate decades of warfare mentality... Many of the top level officials present clearly shared my opponent's views, though the President did not" (Cohen 2011).

This residual Cold War mentality, along with the profit motive of the military-industrial complex and the ideological mix of Neoconservatives, humanitarian interventionists, and Grand Chessboard advocates who wielded influence, doomed the possibility of a true rapprochement between the US and Russia as well as a more cooperative international framework. Indeed Brzeziński himself had stated publicly in the 1990s that the fate of NATO was either to expand or become obsolete. In 1997, he went further by claiming that NATO preservation was "vital" to keeping the US relationship with Europe to the US's advantage on the Eurasian "chessboard" (Brzeziński 1997).

NATO IN THE 1990s
LAYING THE GROUNDWORK FOR EXPANSION

> *If we treat Russia as irredeemably hostile, then we will initiate a self-fulfilling prophecy ...we must engage Russia instead with a clear determination to foster security cooperation. As we approach the 21st century, the main task of Europe is to find a place for Russia. This was done for Germany in the post-Second World War period. If they can't for Russia, Central Europe will return*

> to being what it was during the interwar period, the chessboard of European powers.
>
> —NATO Secretary General Willy Claes, Munich Security Conference, 1995 (Federation of American Scientists)

In 1991, President George H.W. Bush was determined to "kick the Vietnam Syndrome." In other words, he wanted the American public to get over its apprehension toward military intervention overseas that had resulted from the long, brutal and increasingly dubious war in Vietnam. On behalf of that goal, Bush rejected proposals for Iraq's withdrawal from Kuwait, including one brokered by Gorbachev and supported by US military leaders, after a destructive Coalition bombing campaign. Bush saw a ground war as an opportunity for a cheap and easy victory against weakened Iraqi forces (Parry 2014).

NATO had quietly participated in the military operations that comprised the Iraq War (or Gulf War I). This motivated military leaders in both the Pentagon and NATO to consider expanding its use in other geographic and operations areas outside of its stated jurisdiction.

Meanwhile, certain political insiders were already angling for NATO expansion. For example, an ethnic lobbying group called the Polish American Congress (PAC) called for Poland's entry into NATO at their National Directors Meeting in June of 1991, six months before the dissolution of the Soviet Union. In September, they also called for the entry of Hungary and Czechoslovakia – also known as the Visegrad Group of nations (Poland, Hungary, Czechoslovakia, or later Czech Republic and Slovakia). One of PAC's most prominent members and a major advocate of NATO expansion was Jan

Nowak who had worked for years for Radio Free Europe until it was exposed in the 1970s as a CIA propaganda outlet. After leaving Radio Free Europe he went on to serve as an advisor to the Carter administration, including to his friend Zbigniew Brzeziński (Polish American Congress; Gati 2013; Lukasiewicz 2014).

In the autumn of 1993, PAC stepped up its advocacy for NATO enlargement by adopting a resolution to push the US government to facilitate Poland's entry into the alliance as soon as possible. A strongly worded letter enclosing a copy of the resolution was sent to President Clinton on October 28th (Polish American Congress).

The following month, an article appeared in the *Washington Post* about the contents of another article by a history doctoral candidate named William Larsh. Larsh's obscure piece, published in an academic journal, was critical of WWII-era diplomat Averell Harriman, asserting that Harriman was naïve about Stalin and facilitated a deal to replace the previously recognized government of Poland with Stalin's puppet leaders in the days when the war was winding down. This was followed up by another article in the *Washington Post* ten days later, "Ghost of Yalta," in which the authors reiterate the theme of the sell-out of Poland by the Roosevelt administration during the resolution of Allied boundaries at the close of the war in Europe (Polish American Congress).

In reality, it was British Prime Minister Winston Churchill who paved the way for Soviet control of Eastern Europe, including Poland, when he sent his foreign minister, Anthony Eden, to Moscow to propose a deal with Stalin. In exchange for control of Eastern Europe, Britain would have control of Greece, an important geostrategic buffer for Churchill. Stalin was receptive and Churchill flew to Moscow in October of 1944 to seal the deal—six months before Yalta (Polk 2014).

Nevertheless, these articles helped to gain traction for the "not another Yalta" meme that would follow, which had its genesis among members of the political class that emerged from post-Soviet Central and Eastern European nations, such as Vaclav Havel, who was a Czech dissident playwright. While Poland and Czechoslovakia both had a long history of being carved up and subjugated among various empires, unlike the aftermath of WWI or WWII when the victors drew up borders based purely on their own interests, the USSR/Russia peacefully withdrew all its troops from East Germany and the other satellite countries of Central/Eastern Europe under voluntary agreement at the end of the Cold War. Therefore, to compare the release of the Central/Eastern European nations from Soviet control to the Yalta conference of WWII is problematic—even more so as time goes on, when every Russian leader since Gorbachev has stated that they wanted to be part of the West—albeit as a partner, not a vassal.

Furthermore, Havel's views did not represent a monolithic view about how to best secure the futures of Poland, Czechoslovakia, and Hungary among Soviet era dissidents in these countries. For example, some wanted to strengthen the Organization for Security and Cooperation in Europe (OSCE) in the hopes of eventually creating a pan-European arrangement that included Russia (the USSR was already a member as would be its successor state the Russian Federation), replacing both NATO and the Warsaw Pact. But the approach advocated by Havel to enlarge NATO to include these three nations, which would conveniently maintain the US's dominant role in European security, quickly won the day among the new leadership of these countries.

The Clinton administration, taking the helm at the beginning of 1993, did not jump at this proposal to enlarge NATO; in fact, only National Security Advisor Anthony Lake really supported the idea in the beginning. Elements in both the State Department and the Pentagon were initially leery of taking on the added burden of providing security for the Central/Eastern European states. Also, it was recognized that NATO enlargement would complicate Clinton's foreign policy priority of assisting post-Soviet Russia in its transition to market democracy. Eventually, Havel of the Czech Republic, Lech Wałęsa of Poland, and Arpad Goncz of Hungary played on Clinton's neo-Wilsonian philosophy of the need to facilitate the spread of "democracy" and sold the president on the convoluted belief that inclusion of their respective nations in NATO would prove their credentials as Western market democracies and would encourage Russia on its own path toward democracy. Clinton subsequently expressed openness toward eventually allowing these nations into the alliance. The narrative of NATO's purpose also began to change from that of a Cold War defensive alliance to that of "an inclusive alliance protecting the democratic states and open societies of the continent" (Asmus 2002).

When the Clinton administration would actually put this enlargement idea into practice, however, was another matter. The Partnership for Peace program—a voluntary and somewhat vague program connected to NATO in which the various parties tended to project what they wanted to on to it—was established and soon became a vehicle for the possibility of NATO membership for those nations that eventually joined. The Clinton administration saw it as a means to eventually enlarge NATO, but at a gradual pace to placate Russia for the time being and to address the reservations of other NATO members in Europe.

After a summer that saw a controversial conference and public communique between Wałęsa and Russian president Boris Yeltsin in which it appeared that Yeltsin had allowed Wałęsa to talk him into allowing Polish entry into NATO – a meeting that observers noted was later beset with yelling matches among Yeltsin and his advisors who demanded that he withdraw such language from the communique—Russian Foreign Minister Andrei Kozyrev clarified to US Ambassador Tom Pickering Russia's position that it did not oppose NATO enlargement as long as it could be the first post-Cold War nation to join. Yeltsin subsequently moderated his view in a letter stating that NATO enlargement was interpreted as only a theoretical possibility at the time and suggested that both NATO and Russia could provide reciprocal security guarantees to the Central/Eastern nations in question. In November, the head of the FSB (successor to the KGB) presented its own report on the possibility of NATO enlargement and concluded that it was a threat to Russia's security and would require a reset of the nation's defense policy (Asmus 2002).

In December, Brzeziński made a personal appeal to National Security Advisor Anthony Lake for the entry of Poland, Hungary and the Czech Republic into NATO. Lake was, of course, sympathetic, but the administration was still holding back (Asmus 2002).

The results of the mid-term elections in November 1994 provided a shot in the arm to NATO expansion as the Republicans used the administration's slow pace and cautious public wording to argue that the Democrats were pussyfooting around on an enlargement commitment and were too quick to appease Russia. NATO enlargement became one of the few foreign policy provisions of the Contract with America by calling on the US to reaffirm its commitment to enlargement and to include the democracies of Central/Eastern Europe. It also contained a goal for the entry of Poland, Hungary, and the Czech Republic into NATO by January of 1999 (Asmus 2002).

By this time, Poland had already been subjected to "shock therapy" to prepare it as a proper market democracy and, hence, entry into NATO. When the heroes of the Solidarity movement were able to take power in Poland in 1988, they faced an economic mess due to years of Communist Party mismanagement and the movement's leaders were looking toward the kind of system that Gorbachev initially had in mind for Russia: a gradual move toward a mixed economy with a strong public sector modeled on the Scandinavian countries. But before they could implement the reforms necessary to do this, they needed debt relief and initial aid money.

With Western economic elites licking their chops at the possibility of opening up state controlled assets in Central/Eastern Europe to privatized foreign investment, the International Monetary Fund (IMF) allowed Poland's debt and inflation levels to deepen in order to increase desperation and the subsequent acceptance of austerity and privatization conditions for receipt of loans. Harvard economics wunderkind Jeffrey Sachs (who will make another appearance in Chapter 4), along with international speculator George Soros, went to Poland in 1989. Without wasting any time, Sachs introduced a program that included the sudden elimination of price controls and subsidies as well as the sell-off of public resources to private entities. Sachs convinced the reluctant leadership of Solidarity—a movement that had arisen in response to price increases imposed by the Communist government in Moscow and had advocated direct worker ownership—to make these painful sacrifices that would hurt their rank and file on the promise that it would be for the best in the long run (Klein 2007).

1996 – THE TURNING POINT

> *Far from promoting democracy in Eastern Europe, Washington is promoting a system of political and military control not unlike the one practiced by the Soviet Union. Unlike that empire, which collapsed because the center was weaker than the periphery, the new NATO is both a mechanism for extracting Danegeld [tribute levied to support Danish invaders in medieval England] from new member states for the benefit of the US arms industry and an instrument for getting others to protect US interests around the world, including the supply of primary resources such as oil.*
>
> —John Laughland, trustee of British Helsinki Human Rights Group (Laughland 2002)

The turning point for the entry of Poland, Hungary, and the Czech Republic into NATO occurred as Clinton was pressured by presidential election rival Bob Dole's campaign to acknowledge that Poland should join the alliance in order to court the Polish-American vote. Moreover, this is around the time that intense lobbying by the military-industrial complex to enlarge NATO as a new market for arms-related sales started yielding results.

The US Committee to Expand NATO was a lobbying group founded in 1996 by Bruce P. Jackson, director of global development for Lockheed Martin, and Ronald Asmus, a former RAND analyst who worked with the future leadership of the Visegrad states as soon as the Cold War ended. Asmus became known as the intellectual architect behind the idea of NATO enlargement and how to frame the idea in an acceptable way. The committee's membership during its active years reads like a Neocon all-star list: Robert Kagan, Richard Perle, Paul Wolfowitz, Stephen Hadley, Condoleezza Rice, and John McCain. But Democratic hawks were also deeply involved in the group and its mission, including Brzeziński disciple Madeline Albright, a Czech-American (Gerth and Weiner 1997).

The Committee regularly wined and dined US Senators as well as politicians from Poland, Hungary, and the Czech Republic in addition to conducting free "defense planning seminars." Maps used during these presentations to the Poles reportedly showed arrows pointing from Russia as the origin of a hypothetical attack. The message was not subtle.

They also coordinated their lobbying efforts with the Hungarian American Foundation and Polish American Congress (PAC). In fact, the legislative director for PAC at the time admitted that PAC was working with the Committee in their effort to win NATO membership for Poland. Arms manufacturers also provided funding for various relevant ethnic lobbying groups like American Friends of the Czech Republic and the Romanian-American community (Hartung 1998).

It would be unfair, however, to suggest that the Committee and the arms dealers and political influencers it represented had to carry the entire burden of lobbying for NATO expansion and the arms sales it would portend. They got significant help during the Clinton administration from many sectors of the federal government, such as the State

Department. As darkly comical as it may sound, our department of diplomacy at Foggy Bottom promoted the sale of American-made instruments of warfare via the Office of Defense Trade Controls, which advised the merchants of death on how to "cut red tape" and facilitate faster and easier approval of arms sales. According to defense spending expert William Hartung's March 1998 report, "The Hidden Costs of NATO Expansion," "State Department personnel posted overseas are graded for promotion based in part on how helpful they are to US defense firms in marketing military equipment in the host country."

US ambassadors to Poland, Hungary, Romania, and the Czech Republic were encouraged to push strenuously for the sale of American attack helicopters, fighter planes, and missiles to ostensibly prepare their militaries for NATO membership readiness.

The Commerce Department also made it a priority to pitch for arms export sales during the Secretaries' overseas trade missions, including air shows and weapons exhibitions. And, of course, the Pentagon promotes arms sales through the Defense Security Assistance Agency, which administers the Foreign Military Sales Program.

This lobbying blitz from 1996 to 1998 saw two-thirds of countries receiving the Pentagon's largest direct subsidy program for weapons exports, the Foreign Military Financing Fund, from the Central/Eastern European area or former Soviet Republics. Each of these nations, including Poland, Hungary, and the Czech Republic as well as Bulgaria, Romania, and the three Baltic states (all part of the second wave of new NATO entries in 2004) received at least $155 million per year during this period to facilitate preparation for NATO membership and "acquisition of NATO compatible equipment." Tax-payer-subsidized loans worth $647.5 million from the Pentagon's Central European Defense Loan Fund were provided to "assist in the gradual enlargement of NATO by providing loans to creditworthy Central European and Baltic States for acquisition of NATO-compatible equipment" (Hartung 1998). Another Pentagon loan program, known as Defense Export Loan Guarantee (DELG), provided up to $15 billion in loans for the export of US arms and military paraphernalia to thirty-nine nations—a quarter of which targeted Central/Eastern European nations (Hartung 1998). A spokesperson for the DELG program admitted that a "disproportionate interest" in the $2.4 billion worth of requests they had received came from the Central/Eastern European nations. These subsidized loan programs have a history of simply writing off billions of dollars owed, which increases the burden on US taxpayers.

Another racket of the Pentagon that benefits nations receiving arms exports is the regular practice of giving away what they label "surplus" quantities of military equipment and then ordering brand new equipment to replace it. Not only are American taxpayers getting ripped off by giving away equipment that has been paid for, they are then hit up for the cost of more expensive replacements. The Excess Defense Articles grant program authorized twelve Central/Eastern European nations to receive free US weaponry in fiscal year 1998—eleven of which gained entry into NATO by 2009.

Finally, there were the Export Import Bank loans, which were allowed to fund military exports again in the 1990s after a period of prohibition following abuses during the Vietnam War. The largest loan by this bank for military equipment during this period was for $90 million to Romania to finance the purchase of five Lockheed Martin radar systems.

In all, $1.2 billion was estimated to have been spent on grants and loans to begin NATO enlargement between 1996 and 1998 (Hartung 1998).

By 1998, the US Senate had voted in favor of accession of Poland, Hungary, and the Czech Republic into NATO. Senators William Roth and Barbara Mikulski held a press conference in Warsaw on November 16, on American support of NATO expansion. Senator Roth stated in his remarks that "NATO is a threat to no one. It is a defensive alliance, and all we seek is peace, security and stability for all of Europe." This echoes Brzeziński's comments at a Senate Foreign Relations Committee hearing the year before wherein he advocated NATO enlargement and responded to criticisms of the project by denying that the project was anti-Russia or a moral crusade of retribution for historical wrongs against Eastern Europeans. However, neither Roth nor Brzeziński state who or what is the actual threat to Europe that is so grave that it requires not only that NATO continue on, despite the fact that no opposing military alliance exists anymore, but must be enlarged. Both admitted that Russia was not a threat at the time. Indeed Polish Defense Minister Janusz Onyszewicz had stated by the middle of the decade that the motivation to join NATO was "not to defend against a Russian attack. We see that attack as a virtual impossibility." This is buttressed by the fact that the Central/Eastern European nations, including Poland and the Czech Republic, had all decreased their defense budgets, shortened terms of military conscription, and disbanded many of their army divisions by 1995. Not exactly the actions of nations terrified of the bear next door (Brzeziński, October 1997; Federation of American Scientists).

It appears at this point that the US political class had no intention of using the historic opportunity provided by the end of the Cold War to incorporate Russia into the West as an equal and respected partner, but instead to subdue it through political cooptation and economic exploitation (as we'll see in Chapter 4) and—if that didn't work—to view it as a future enemy. Either way, money would be made and power maintained by those sitting at the top of the American food chain.

NATO IN THE 2000S

When three of the four Visegrad states were formally inducted into NATO at its Washington summit in 1999, no new nations were extended official invitations, but the Membership Action Plan (MAP) was soon introduced, which provided a procedural framework for the vetting process and objective criteria for the future membership of any nation – at least, in theory. The MAP procedure was different from the first wave of post-Cold War enlargement that occurred on the unilateral initiative of the US. Nine countries were named for the initial MAP process: Albania, Bulgaria, Estonia, Latvia, Lithuania, Macedonia, Romania, Slovakia, and Slovenia.

In May of 2000, a conference was held in Vilnius, Lithuania attended by the foreign ministers of nine of the MAP countries. The representatives agreed to work cooperatively toward NATO admission for all. They became known as the Vilnius Group and would add Croatia as a member the following year, making it the Vilnius 10.

Four successive summits of the Vilnius Group were held at breakneck speed over the next two-and-a-half years: at Bratislava, Sofia, Bucharest, and Riga.

Their cause was bolstered by a letter signed by seventeen US senators to President Bush, in April of 2001, urging further NATO enlargement. Two months later, Bush gave a speech in Warsaw in which he announced strong support for all the democracies of Europe to be included as full members of the alliance (Tarifa 2007).

The public focus on this latest round of NATO enlargement was on the commitment and capability of the candidates. The Vilnius 10 nations implemented economic, military, and judicial reforms to prepare for accession.

The terrorist attacks of September 11, 2001 created an additional rationale for more rapid expansion of NATO both in terms of membership and geographic reach.

In 2002, NATO invited Romania, Bulgaria, Slovenia, Slovakia and the three Baltic states of Latvia, Lithuania, and Estonia to join the alliance at its summit in Prague. Bruce Jackson—the Lockheed Martin executive, co-founder of the US Committee to Expand NATO, PNAC board member, and a chum of neocon vice president Dick Cheney—called the plan to get the Vilnius 10 into NATO the "Big Bang." During his testimony before Congress in April of 2003 advocating for NATO enlargement to include seven of the Vilnius 10, he used the now-established rationale that NATO enlargement represented the inclusion of these nations into an innocuous club of peaceful democracies. He cited the words of both Brzeziński and Neoconservative politicians to underscore this dubious claim (Engdhal 2006; Jackson 2003).

Seven of the Vilnius 10 would be admitted in 2004 and two more in 2009. Membership for the tenth candidate, Macedonia, was vetoed by Greece.

Meanwhile, Article 5 of the NATO Treaty was invoked to use NATO in the Global War on Terror and specifically in

Afghanistan where it eventually took over military operations via control of the International Security Assistance Force (ISAF) in 2003. NATO was also involved in air operations during the invasion of Iraq that same year and participated in the occupation of the country from 2004 to 2011 under the "NATO Training Mission—Iraq" (Nazemroaya 2012).

All of the new NATO members and future members would eventually participate in the Iraq War in some capacity, prompting Donald Rumsfeld's quip about "Old Europe" as opposed to a newly developing focus on the eastern nations (BBC 2003).

According to Mahdi Darius Nazemroaya, author of *The Globalization of NATO*, the Global War on Terrorism, viewed as an example of Samuel Huntington's "Clash of Civilizations" theory, enabled EU and NATO power projection into Eurasia's surrounding areas from two different fronts: from the western front in Europe and from the eastern/southern front via Japan, South Korea, the Arabian Peninsula, and Afghanistan—which are now littered with US military bases as well as ties to NATO and three branches of the global missile shield system.

By 2009, not only had NATO expansion greatly increased in terms of membership by twelve new nations in Central and Eastern Europe, its mandate had also expanded to include peacekeeping, international policing, and counter-terrorism activities—a far cry from its start as a defensive alliance to protect Western Europe from invasion by the long dead Soviet Union (Nazemroaya 2012).

Around this time, former UN Assistant Secretary General and UN Humanitarian Coordinator for Iraq Hans von Sponeck wrote an article published in a Swiss journal, in which he expressed deep concern for the direction NATO had been taking since the 1990s. He believed that the United Nations was at a crossroads, reflected in its relationship with NATO:

> *The world of the 192 UN member states has come to a fork in the road. One way leads to a world focused on the well-being of society, conflict resolution, and peace, i.e. to a life of dignity and human security with social and economic progress for all, wherever they may be – as stated in the United Nations Charter. Down the other road is where the nineteenth century "Great Game" for power will be further played out, a course which, in the twenty-first century, will become more extensive and dangerously more aggressive than ever. This road supposedly leads to democracy, but in truth it is all about power, control, and exploitation. (von Sponeck 2009)*

In those two preceding decades, he argued, NATO had been attempting to usurp the UN's authority on the "monopoly of the use of force" by greatly expanding its objectives as well as its geographic reach by first trying to cast itself in the role of military arm of the UN, including invocation of what would evolve into the Responsibility to Protect doctrine in the Balkans. Then it went further, serving as an occupation force in Iraq (von Sponeck 2009).

In 1999, NATO acknowledged that it was moving beyond the mandate of a defensive alliance to include, "The protection of the vital resources' needs of its members. Besides the defense member states' borders, it set itself new purposes such as assured access to energy resources and the right to intervene in 'movements of large numbers of persons' and in conflicts far from the borders of NATO countries" (von Sponeck 2009).

In his article, von Sponeck asked how NATO's now broadened mission could be reconciled with international law, particularly with the UN charter. In this vein, he was particularly worried by an accord signed between the UN and NATO in September of 2008, which did not consult the Security Council. He believed that an accord between the two institutions undermined the UN's neutrality when three members of the Security Council are members of NATO which have a hostile posture toward the other two Security Council members and aims to assert power interests by use of force. Additionally, NATO is a "military alliance with nuclear weapons" and Article 2 of the UN Charter "requires that conflicts be resolved by peaceful means" (von Sponeck 2009).

In 2011, the troubling trends of NATO continued when the alliance blatantly breached the UN mandate to implement a no-fly zone in Libya (Nazemroaya 2012).

More recently, NATO, which now outspends the Russian military by eleven to one and has four times as many soldiers (Lekic 2014), has continued the insidious extension of its tentacles into still more areas of the world. In May of 2013, NATO entered into an agreement increasing military assistance to the African Union, including the Africa Standby Force. As a result of this agreement, NATO has a significant voice in determining where and how to use these forces.

According to geopolitical scientist Manlio Dinucci, NATO signed another security agreement in 2013 with Colombia, a likely precursor to membership. Dinucci (2014) describes the Pacific Rimpac 2014, which took place this past July, as "the world's largest maritime exercise, directed against China and Russia." It involved 25,000 soldiers from 22 nations utilizing 55 ships and 200 warplanes, all under US command (Dinucci 2014).

The EU—NATO Dance

To understand the mechanisms that facilitate NATO expansion, the purpose behind it, and the underlying rivalries that could one day possibly undermine it, one must understand the role of the European Union, the dynamics within it, and its relationship to the United States.

Within the European Union (EU) there are two recognized axes of power and influence, which are also recognized axes within NATO. The first axis is the Anglo-American (also known as Atlanticist) partnership, which arose from the relationship between Britain and the United States after Britain's post-WWII decline which coincided with the US's ascent. This axis has more power in NATO with its military might supported by 48 percent of the world's total military expenditures. And although the US is not an actual member of the EU, Britain is largely recognized as its proxy across the pond. Moreover, the US invests significantly in the European Central Bank (ECB) as well as throughout the EU in general.

The second axis is the Franco-German axis, which was cemented between France and West Germany after WWII, partly to put a check on the first axis. But a rivalry between the continental powers and Britain had much longer historical roots as Britain had periodically shifted its alliance to whichever continental power seemed weaker to counterbalance the stronger one (Nazemroaya 2012). The unification of Germany after the Cold War strengthened the Franco-German axis, which has also historically tended to lean toward a Pan-Europeanism or even a Eurasian partnership. With

Germany as the strongest economy in the EU, this axis has more influence and power within that entity (Nazemroaya 2012).

Since Title 10 of the Washington Treaty, which created NATO, requires a potential member to be European, it should be pointed out that Europe is not truly a continent unto itself but part of the Eurasian landmass that includes an area with a diversity of culture and politics, including the UK, France, Germany, Scandinavia, Greece, Italy, Russia, and arguably, Turkey. This is important when considering the definition of "European" as it relates to both the European Union's assumption that it solely represents some "European" interest and NATO's pushing the boundaries of that definition when it is advantageous to its expansion (Nazemroaya 2012).

Since the main post-Cold War thrust of expansion of both the EU and NATO has been aimed at the former Soviet satellite countries in Central and Eastern Europe, the goal has also been to prevent economic alliance with Russia. Indeed, Brzeziński stated in *The Grand Chessboard* that the "essential point regarding NATO expansion is that it is a process integrally connected with Europe's own expansion." He simultaneously makes it clear that Russia will not be considered for inclusion except perhaps at some point far into the future after they've been encircled and pass America's definition of democracy and free market institutions—in other words, after they've accepted a subservient role (Brzeziński 1997).

Although many countries become NATO members first and then make their way into the EU, plans to reverse that sequence have been formulated with NATO membership not being far behind once EU membership has been established. There are various instruments that the EU utilizes under its

European Neighborhood Policy (ENP) to expand EU membership. One is the European Neighborhood and Partnership Instrument (ENPI) that facilitates the conversion of economies to a privatized Neoliberal capitalist system. After the privatization of state and public assets takes place in the target country, a Stabilization and Association Process (SAP) is implemented in which these assets are scooped up by French, British, German, Italian, Canadian, and American corporations, thereby preventing economic independence (Nazemroaya 2012).

Recent recipients of the ENPI brand of political and economic manipulation are Ukraine, Georgia, and Moldova via the new-fangled Eastern Partnership (EaP) instrument—a kind of preliminary SAP that opens up borders and mandates economic restructuring towards the privatized Neocolonial process stated above, but makes no promises of EU membership or any of its reputed privileges. These same three countries have also been wooed by the Eurasian Union (Nazemroaya 2012).

Analysts have recognized a disturbing pattern with countries that resist the ENPI program—they are usually targeted for military operations and attempts at regime change. Until the Ukraine crisis, this had been most apparent in the Southern (MED) arm of the ENPI project, which has included Libya and Syria—an example of the fluid and opportunistic definition of European (Nazemroaya 2012).

In 2006, the EU's Security Strategy was absorbed into NATO during its annual summit. The emphasis of that summit was on securing energy resources with the goal of "co-managing the resources of the EU's periphery from North Africa to the Caucasus" (Nazemroaya 2012). Also implied was the goal of redefining the EU's security borders in synch with both Franco-German and Anglo-American economic and geopolitical interests, indicating a rapprochement of the rift that temporarily cropped up between the axes as a result of the Iraq War. Around this time, the idea of ultimately creating a common economic union of Europe and North America was floated, along with one day totally integrating the EU with NATO (Nazemroaya 2012).

In February 2007, then-Secretary of Defense Robert Gates admitted to Congress that Russia and China were officially viewed as threats. Several days later, the chief of the Russian Armed Forces, General Yuri Baluyevsky, told the Russian public that they faced a threat from the US and NATO greater than during the Cold War and urged commensurate preparations. Shortly thereafter, Putin complained during the Munich Conference on Security Policy that NATO was targeting Russia (Nazemroaya 2012).

> *I am convinced that the only mechanism that can make decisions about using military force as a last resort is the Charter of the United Nations. And in connection with this, either I did not understand what our colleague, the Italian Defense Minister, just said or what he said was inexact. In any case, I understood that the use of force can only be legitimate when the decision is taken by NATO, the EU, or the UN. If he really does think so, then we have different points of view. Or I didn't hear correctly. The use of force can only be considered legitimate if the decision is sanctioned by the UN. And we do not need to substitute NATO or the EU for the UN. When the UN will truly unite the forces of the international community and can really react to events in various countries, when we will leave behind this disdain for international law, then the situation will be able to change. Otherwise the situation will simply result in a dead end, and the number of serious mistakes will be multiplied. Along with this, it is necessary*

> to make sure that international law has a universal character both in the conception and application of its norms...
>
> I think it is obvious that NATO expansion does not have any relation with the modernization of the Alliance itself or with ensuring security in Europe. On the contrary, it represents a serious provocation that reduces the level of mutual trust. And we have the right to ask: against whom is this expansion intended? And what happened to the assurances our Western partners made after the dissolution of the Warsaw Pact? Where are those declarations today? No one even remembers them. But I will allow myself to remind this audience what was said. I would like to quote the speech of NATO General Secretary Mr. Woerner in Brussels on 17 May 1990. He said at the time that: "the fact that we are ready not to place a NATO army outside of German territory gives the Soviet Union a firm security guarantee." Where are these guarantees? (Putin 2007)

The configuration of NATO currently reflects a Pan-European entity ensconced in an Anglo-American security apparatus, but given the aforementioned dynamics and rivalries, it doesn't have to remain that way. Recent events playing out in Eurasia reflect the strong engagement of Russia with the European Union over the past decade, much to the consternation of the Anglo-American axis as Nazemroaya states:

> The alliance is increasingly being viewed as a geopolitical extension of America, an arm of the Pentagon, and a synonym for an evolving American Empire... Ultimately NATO is slated to become an institutionalized military force...Nevertheless for every action there is a reaction and NATO's actions have given rise to opposing trends. The Atlantic Alliance is increasingly coming into contact with a zone of Eurasia that is in the process of emerging

with its own ideas and alliance. What this will lead to next is the question of the century. (Nazemroaya 2012)

UKRAINE

In Jack Matlock's 2010 book, *Superpower Illusions*, he provided a description of modern Ukraine's complex political history and demographics that proved prophetic with respect to the post-coup problems we are currently witnessing: "Well over half of Ukrainian citizens oppose the country's entry into NATO. To understand why, one must bear in mind that Ukraine's biggest security problem is not Russian "imperialism" but political, social, economic, and linguistic divisions inside the country." Prior to WWI, the western area of modern-day Ukraine was part of the Austro-Hungarian Empire and the southeastern areas part of the Russian Czarist Empire.

Matlock concluded that any attempts to bring Ukraine into NATO would have dire consequences. Putin made this very argument to then-National Security Advisor Condoleezza Rice during an October 2006 meeting that became heated when the subject of Ukraine's potential future entry into NATO came up. According to Russian Foreign Minister, Sergei Lavrov, who was present, Putin tried to impress it upon Rice that efforts to bring Ukraine into NATO would be disastrous all the way around: "Putin explained what Ukraine was—at least a third of the population are ethnic Russians—and the negative consequences that could arise, not only for us but for all of Europe if Ukraine and Georgia were dragged into NATO" (Roxburgh 2013).

American Ambassador Bill Burns who was with Rice at the meeting stated that Rice responded by declaring that each sovereign nation had the right to decide for itself which institutions or alliances it wanted to join. Putin reportedly replied in what would turn out to be prescient terms: "You do not understand what you are doing. You are playing with fire" (Roxburgh 2013).

To demonstrate the disingenuousness of Rice's argument, try to imagine the following: Russia convinces Mexico to join a military alliance hostile to the US. In response, US leaders proclaim that Mexico has the right to join any alliance it chooses and they have no concerns.

Of course, no one in their right mind believes this is what would transpire.

In February of 2008, Ambassador Burns sent a classified cable back to Washington summing up a meeting with Foreign Minister Lavrov about Ukraine's intent to seek a NATO Membership Action Plan as "Nyet Means Nyet: Russia's NATO Enlargement Redlines." The Russians had reiterated again that Ukraine in NATO was unacceptable, citing among other concerns, that the issue could precipitate division in the country, perhaps leading to civil war, which would put Russia in the difficult position of having to choose whether to intervene or not – a decision it was stressed that Russia did not want to be faced with (Burns 2008).

Furthermore, Ukrainians themselves demonstrated their antipathy toward NATO membership from January to March when the Ukrainian parliament (the Verkhovna Rada) was blocked from functioning by an opposition coalition that resulted from the "Orange Revolution" leaders Viktor Yushchenko and Yulia Tymoshenko trying to push the country into the alliance (Rozoff 2014).

The geopolitical reality is that Ukraine needed to be a buffer and a bridge between the West and Russia with the opportunity to have beneficial economic relations with both, since Russia has been Ukraine's largest trading partner and the country from which it received various subsidies, such as discounted gas. To ensure that buffer role, however, it was imperative for all parties that NATO membership was off the table.

Despite denials in some quarters, the economic agreement with Europe that deposed Ukrainian President Viktor Yanukovych refused to sign included language that would lay the groundwork for NATO membership (Stea 2013). This presented another serious problem in addition to the economic exclusivity and austerity program, it would have required of an already poor country that relies heavily on trade with Russia. While Yanukovych may have been playing both ends against the middle with Russia and the EU, it was certainly not irrational for him to have rejected the terms of this agreement.

As Stephen Cohen stated in a June 2014 interview with Thom Hartmann, no country anywhere in the world, regardless of their leader, would allow an adversarial military alliance to park itself on their borders. It would be considered an act of aggression (Hartmann 2014).

During the Franco-Russian roundtable dialogue on the Ukraine crisis, the participants acknowledged the contribution of NATO and its dynamics to the current problems:

> *The position of the European Union is held hostage by certain countries, especially Poland, who are doing nothing for the resolution of this crisis....[They described] what was now happening as a "cycle of stupidity", in which some, particularly in the EU and NATO, bear a heavy and historical responsibility." (Slavyangrad 2014)*

CHAPTER 4

POST—SOVIET RUSSIA
FROM "SHOCK THERAPY" TO AN EMERGING POWER

> *The result [of Boris Yeltsin's "shock therapy" program] was the worst economic and social catastrophe ever suffered by a major nation in peacetime. Russia sank into a corrosive economic depression greater than that of the American 1930s. Investment plunged by 80 percent, GDP by almost 50 percent; some two-thirds of Russians were impoverished; the life expectancy of men fell below 59 years; and the population began to decline annually by almost a million people. In 1998, with nothing left to sustain it, despite several large Western loans, the Russian financial system collapsed. State and private banks defaulted on their domestic and foreign obligations, causing still more poverty and widespread misery.*
>
> —Stephen F. Cohen, *Soviet Fates and Lost Alternatives (Cohen 2011)*

Ambassador Matlock described conditions in the aftermath of the Soviet dissolution as follows: "In Russia, the Soviet collapse was followed by runaway inflation that destroyed all savings, even worse shortages of essential goods than existed under communism, a sudden rise in crime, and a government that, for several years was unable to pay even [its] miserable pensions on time. Conditions resembled anarchy much more than life in a modern democracy" (Matlock 2010).

When the communist command economy was dismantled, Neoliberal economic advisors often insisted that Russians not rely on the state for any economic assistance during the transition under the guise of leaving communism behind. One illustrative story relayed by Matlock involved a member of the Moscow city council who wanted to encourage small private businesses in his district. He had developed a plan to "offer long-term low-interest loans from the city budget to entrepreneurs...When he explained his idea the Hoover (Institution) economists objected, saying that he must not involve the government...If the government provided loans or subsidies, that would be perpetuating socialism" (Matlock 2010).

The city council member was taken aback and asked where entrepreneurs would get their seed capital. After being told that it would have to come from private sources, he inquired, "You mean from our criminals? If they provide the capital, they control the business. That's not what we want to happen" (Matlock 2010).

Unfortunately, that is what happened.

Exploitive conditions were foisted on Russia when economic advisors from the Harvard Institute for International Development and other advocates of the "Chicago School" of economics colluded with Russian predators like Anatoly Chubais, Mikhail Khodorkovsky and others who would emerge as Russia's pack of oligarchs (Wedel 1997).

In the meantime, Russians were excited at the new possibilities of the democratic transformation they were undertaking. However, the dissolution of the Soviet Union, which had held together numerous republics that consisted of various ethnic groups and had provided a modest but stable livelihood for most, also resulted in destabilization and trauma. Russians tried to learn how to form and navigate democratic institutions and move toward a privatized economy, yet had no meaningful experience with either in their long history of authoritarian rule, the last 70 years of which constituted a closed totalitarian state.

Sharon Tennison, an American author, citizen diplomat and founder of the Center for Citizen Initiatives who has worked all throughout Russia (and its predecessor the Soviet Union) since 1983, captured the hopes, fears and confusion of Russians during this harrowing time when she relayed a conversation she had with a Russian scientist named Tatiana in 1991:

> *We are not like Americans. We don't have the natural instincts your people have cultivated for generations. We have another set of instincts, another mentality. It will take us a very long time....and it will be a very painful process for us to learn a new mentality. First, we will be flat on our stomachs for probably seven years, then we will have to hobble on our knees for probably seven more years, then maybe we will get on our feet in the next seven years. We don't know — we can't see what is ahead at the end of this black tunnel. It is a totally unknown future we are walking into. (Tennison 2012)*

The Russians are a very smart, resilient, and resourceful people. But they also have a different ethic about the role of social and economic rights, a different geographic reality they are sensitive to—having been invaded numerous times in their history and possessing a strong memory of profound destruction and suffering from The Great Patriotic War (WWII)—and a more conservative cultural view due to the closed nature of the Soviet Union that even today is barely 23 years into the past. Therefore, as Russians embarked on their journey toward democracy and a new economic order—a journey that is still in progress—they could not be expected to become a carbon copy of the United States, or even of other European nations. They would need to find their own path consistent with their culture, geography, and history. This is part of the right of self-determination, a right that is often not respected by international players in powerful positions who must continuously feed an insatiable need for more profits, more markets, and more geopolitical power. The unfolding of events in post-Soviet Russia is a case in point.

Gorbachev's Economic Vision

As Naomi Klein chronicles in her book, *The Shock Doctrine: The Rise of Disaster Capitalism*, after overseeing a remarkable period of democratization that included the emergence of a free press, a parliament, an independent constitutional court, and the establishment of local councils and elections, Gorbachev's desire—to be implemented over a period of ten to fifteen years—was to create a mixed economy, similar to the Scandinavian social democracies, consisting of free markets balanced with robust social programs, including public control of certain essential industries.

But Gorbachev, recognized by the West to be in a weak position and in need of economic aid and guidance, received a very unsettling message from the leaders of the G7 nations when he attended their annual summit in 1991. They wanted Gorbachev to apply a "shock therapy" economic program like Poland had just undergone, only in an even more extreme form: on a shorter time frame and without any debt relief (Klein 2007).

To reinforce the message and ratchet up the pressure to accept such a proposal, the IMF—at the behest of the US Treasury Department—demanded harsh austerity measures in exchange for loans, followed by the World Bank making similar demands (Klein 2007; Engdahl 2014).

Gorbachev knew that such a program would never be accepted by the Russian people. As post-Soviet polls indicated, 67 percent of Russians favored worker co-ops as the best way to facilitate privatization and 79 percent believed the government should play an active role in promoting full employment (Klein 2007). Consequently, Gorbachev faced a choice between the political democracy he had fought so hard to achieve and economic dictatorship. Mainstream media in the West at the time, such as *The Economist* and the *Washington Post*, openly encouraged Gorbachev to adopt an authoritarian stance to implement what they deemed the necessary policies for creating their definition of a liberal market economy. In fact, they suggested that Russia exercise the "Pinochet Option"—a reference to the brutal Western-backed dictator who had overthrown the democratically elected Socialist president of Chile, Salvador Allende, in 1973—if Gorbachev proved to be too squeamish to go along with the program (Klein 2007).

The Chicago School economic advisors in the US, who followed Milton Friedman's scorched earth philosophy of Neoliberal economics that worshipped a mythical market that was unmoored from the needs of humanity, found their Russian Pinochet personified by Boris Yeltsin. Yeltsin, president of the republic of Russia, had gained popular support later in 1991 by climbing in protest atop one of the tanks driven threateningly up to the steps of the Parliament building by a contingent of disaffected Communist officials. He rode that wave of popularity all the way to a power grab when he formed an alliance with the leaders of two other Soviet republics and forced the dissolution of the Soviet Union, thereby rendering Gorbachev—who was trying to keep the Soviet Union together—powerless (Klein 2007; Cohen 2011).

Yeltsin: The Russian Pinochet

Yeltsin wasted no time in appointing the Chicago School advisors from the US, including Jeffrey Sachs, to comprise his economic team (Klein 2007). Yeltsin, with the help of these advisors, was looking for a quick infusion of cash like that promised by the G7, IMF, and World Bank. Of course, the strings attached were well understood at that point. In order to pull this off without facing a backlash from the Russian populace, Yeltsin went to the Parliament with an outrageous proposal: to be granted permission to circumvent Parliament and rule by decree for one year on the pretext of solving the nation's economic mess. In recognition of the fact that they were desperate for aid, Parliament agreed.

In the year that followed, Parliament would come to regret their decision. After placing an authoritarian named Yury Skokov in charge of the military and security departments to control potential dissent, Yeltsin embarked at break-neck speed on a plan of lifting price controls on food, cuts to various subsidies and other policies that resulted in an inflation rate of 2,500 percent at its height. With the ruble having lost its value, the life savings of millions disappeared and workers went months with no pay. Many people were forced to sell their belongings on the sidewalk, farms were abandoned as farmers were forced to seek recompense elsewhere, food distribution networks collapsed, store shelves were empty, and the search for food often became the top priority as people spent hours in lines to obtain food imported from the outside (Klein 2007; Wedel 1997; Tennison 2012).

During the first few years of this "shock therapy" program, Russia faced its greatest mortality crisis since WWII as many middle-aged men drank themselves to death or met an early demise from other health problems related to neglect as well as suicide and homicide. All the sacrifices endured to emerge victorious in The Great Patriotic War, combined with re-building the Soviet Union, had suddenly come to nothing. The sense of being needed, particularly strong in Russian and Soviet culture, had evaporated for many of the men in this demographic whose identity and sense of being needed was rooted in their role as economic providers as well as guardians and beneficiaries of a steadily improving "radiant future" under the Soviet state. Between 1993 and 1994 alone, around one million Russians died prematurely (Parsons 2014).

A Mafia-style criminal element also emerged from the ruins made up of disenfranchised police officers, KGB officials, and black market operatives who soon formed protection rackets targeting the small to mid-sized businesses that had started. The protection money that had to be paid, which increased any time production went up, stunted the new entrepreneurial class (Tennison 2012).

By November of 1992, Anatoly Chubais had been appointed as Yeltsin's economic czar. He began working with the Harvard Institute for International Development (HIID), which was funded by USAID and now headed by Jeffrey Sachs. One of HIIDS's cheerleaders in the Clinton administration was Lawrence Summers at Treasury. The HIID team and its enablers included former World Bank consultant Jonathan Hay who had previously served as a senior legal advisor to the Russian state's privatization committee (GKI) and would now be serving as HIID's general director in Moscow (Wedel 1997).

In late 1991 and early 1992, the Chubais economic team concentrated the accumulation of property into a few well-connected hands in contravention of a privatization program previously passed in the country to prevent corruption. One of their projects was a voucher privatization program paid for with $325 million in US taxpayer money. It is reported that hundreds of investment funds simply resold the vouchers to domestic criminals, Western investment banks, and global money launderers. These schemes were the impetus for Yeltsin's rule-by-decree. Many of the decrees were written by Hay and his cronies (Wedel 1997; Williamson 1999).

When the year was up in March 1993, with popular support, Parliament attempted to rein in Yeltsin's abuses by repealing the decree powers they had granted him. In response, Yeltsin declared a state of emergency; however, the constitutional court ruled that Yeltsin's abuse of power violated the constitution on eight counts. A short time later, Parliament passed a budget that would put the brakes on the austerity measures demanded by the IMF. Yeltsin, with the support of Washington—particularly, Lawrence Summers at the Treasury Department, who put additional pressure on the IMF to rescind a major loan to Russia at a strategic moment—issued a decree dissolving Parliament and abolishing the constitution. Parliamentarians then called a special session and voted to impeach Yeltsin (Klein 2007).

With President Clinton continuing to support him, the US congress voting to provide $2.5 billion to his government, and the American mainstream media cheering him on while painting the Parliamentarians in Orwellian terms as Communist hangers-on and backwater anti-democrats, Yeltsin sent troops in to surround the Parliament building and ordered all utilities cut. Klein reported that Boris Kagarlitsky, director of the Institute of Globalization Studies in Moscow, and present at these events, told her that supporters of Russian democracy

> *... were coming in by the thousands trying to break the blockade. There were two weeks of peaceful demonstrations confronting the troops and police forces, which led to partial unblocking of the parliament building, with people able to bring food and water inside. Peaceful resistance was growing more popular and gaining broader support every day. (Klein 2007)*

Word came out at this time that Polish citizens had just voted out the party that had forced "shock therapy" on them. Consequently, Yeltsin's advisors saw early elections to break the standoff as too risky. Shortly thereafter, Yeltsin's troops fired machine guns into a crowd of mostly unarmed demonstrators who had marched to a major television station to demand announcement of their heightened opposition to Yeltsin's rule. This was followed by Yeltsin's orders to storm the Parliament building and destroy it. As Klein sums up the episode that killed around 500 people, wounded 1,000, and forever changed the direction of Russia:

> *Communism may have collapsed without the firing of a single shot, but Chicago-style capitalism, it turned out, required a great deal of gunfire to defend itself: Yeltsin called in five thousand soldiers, dozens of tanks and armored personnel carriers, helicopters and elite shock troops armed with automatic machine guns – all to defend Russia's new capitalist economy from the grave threat of democracy. (Klein 2007)*

A sample of headlines from US media outlets reporting on this turn of events included, "Victory Seen for Democracy" by the *Washington Post* and "Russia Escapes a Return to the Dungeon of its Past" in the *Boston Globe*. Clinton even sent Secretary of State Warren Christopher to Moscow to congratulate Yeltsin on keeping Russia safe for predatory capitalism (Klein 2007).

By contrast, Putin has some authoritarian tendencies, which the West never tires of bemoaning, with casual epithets of "thug," "gangster," and "Stalin" tossed about; however, he has never rolled tanks into the streets, ordered Russian troops to fire on their own people, or destroyed government buildings.

Yeltsin continued to steamroll over any last shreds of democracy by dissolving elected bodies, suspending the constitution and the court, ordering military patrol of the streets, and imposing censorship. Meanwhile, with no Parliament to place a check on them, the Chicago School devotees—led by the HIID team—ran amok, implementing deep budget cuts, removing more price controls, and privatizing faster and more broadly.

The HIID team facilitated Chubais and other Russian predators' ability to create and fund private organizations whereby they could circumvent the Russian Parliament and other regulatory agencies, or be considered Russian or American depending on what was advantageous in terms of attaining wealth and resources or avoiding penalties and taxes (Wedel 1997).

In 1995, Chubais also ran the notorious loans-for-shares program that auctioned off state-owned companies worth billions for token amounts to a select group of Russians; however, the Harvard Management Company (HMC), which manages the university's endowment, and George Soros were two non-Russians allowed to partake in the pillaging. Both HMC and Soros ended up with significant shares in one of Russia's largest steel mills as well as in Sidanko Oil. Soros was involved in other speculative ventures in Russia and is reportedly eyeing similar vulture opportunities in Ukraine (Wedel 1997; Hudson 2014).

Western bankers enabled these kleptocrats in keeping the proceeds in offshore accounts, thereby evading taxes. Klein described the turn of events as follows:

> *A clique of nouveaux billionaires, many of whom were to become part of the group universally known as the "oligarchs" for their imperial levels of wealth and power, teamed up with Yeltsin's Chicago Boys and stripped the country of nearly everything of value, moving the enormous profits offshore at a rate of $2 billion a month. Before shock therapy, Russia had no millionaires; by 2003, the number of Russian billionaires had risen to seventeen, according to Forbes list. (Klein 2007)*

The oligarchs' wealth and power facilitated Yeltsin's re-election in 1996. In fact, two associates of Chubais were caught red-handed leaving a government building with $500,000 cash for Yeltsin's campaign. Tape recordings later emerged in which Chubais and his accomplices are heard discussing how to hide evidence of their illicit activities and how to use PR tactics to deflect accusations of wrongdoing in the political sphere (Klein 2007; Hudson 2014; Wedel 1997).

Between 1992 and 1996, HIID alone received $57.7 million from US taxpayers via USAID for their "economic development" of Russia. The vast majority of that money was granted absent any competitive bidding, all with the blessing of five different agencies of the US government, including the Treasury Department and the National Security Council (Wedel 1997).

By now, the reader can probably deduce why Yeltsin – the hero of the West – was voted the least popular leader of the last 100 years by the Russian people. At the time of his departure from office, 90 percent of Russians polled did not trust him and 53 percent thought he should be put on trial (Wahlberg 2012; Cohen 2011).

There were, no doubt, other options that would have been more fair and acceptable among the Russian people. As mentioned previously, a full two-thirds of Russians polled during the transition period preferred co-ops as a more equitable means of privatization. An even higher percentage advocated for a government role in support of economic justice. Similarly, there were programs in development by Russians that would have facilitated a more distributist approach to privatization. For example, there was the idea for modest government-subsidized loans for the start of small businesses in various localities that was put forth by the Moscow city council member and shot down by Western advisors. Another program was designed by a Russian free market economist named Larisa Piasheva. Her program would have distributed property among average Russian citizens and would not have been dependent upon Western loans.

As Anne Williamson, a long-time American journalist who specialized in covering the Soviet Union and Russia, stated in her testimony before Congress on this topic in September of 1999:

> *When the administration says it had no choice but to rely upon the bad actors it did select for American largesse, Congress should recall Larisa Piasheva. How different today's Russia might have been had only the Bush administration and the many Western advisors from the IMF, the World Bank, the International Finance Corporation, the European Bank for Reconstruction and Development, and the Harvard Institute for International Development then on the ground in Moscow chosen to champion Ms. Piasheva's vision of a rapid disbursement of property to the*

people rather than to the "golden children" of the Soviet nomenklatura [elite bureaucrats].

...Clearly, an equitable and transparent privatization that would have delivered property widely to Russia's many eager hands should have preceded the freeing of prices. And during privatization, native producers should have enjoyed some protectionism at least, as did developing American industry and manufacture in the 19th century.

...Today the Clinton administration's chief defense for their hand in Russia's ruin is that somebody had to keep the communists at bay. But there were no communists in Russia by late 1991, only nascent investment bankers looking to nail down a stake any which way. (Williamson 1999)

THE ECONOMIC REFORMS
OF THE PUTIN AND MEDVEDEV ERA

The conditions described in the previous section constituted the mess that Vladimir Putin faced when he took over as President of the Russian Federation in 2000. It should be noted that Putin started his presidency having to navigate these crises amidst ruthless political clans within the Kremlin that were inherited from the Yeltsin era, without the support of a political party, and the very real threat of being assassinated or overthrown if he trusted the wrong person or stepped too heavily on the wrong toes.

Some observers who were on the ground in Russia during this time believe that this is the reason Putin brought in trusted, dependable, and often life-long friends and colleagues from St. Petersburg to comprise his political team. Western media, out of ignorance or malice, began referring to these new Putin appointees as the St. Petersburg "Chekists"—a pejorative for Soviet era secret police (Tennison 2012).

Putin's team gradually implemented policies that stabilized the country, improved infrastructure and standards of living for many Russians, and led to a decrease in crime and chaos.

Sharon Tennison has visited different parts of Russia regularly over her three decades-long career there. She describes the changes over the past fourteen years as follows:

> *During this time, I've traveled throughout Russia several times every year, and have watched the country slowly change under Putin's watch. Taxes were lowered, inflation lessened, and laws slowly put in place. Schools and hospitals began improving. Small businesses were growing, agriculture was showing improvement, and stores were becoming stocked with food.*
>
> *Highways were being laid across the country, new rails and modern trains appeared even in far out places, and the banking industry was becoming dependable. Russia was beginning to look like a decent country—certainly not where Russians hoped it to be long term, but improving incrementally for the first time in their memories. (Tennison 2014)*

Tennison observed the same improvements starting to appear in areas farther away from the major cities:

> *In September [2013] I traveled out to the Ural Mountains, spent time in Ekaterinburg, Chelyabinsk and Perm. We traveled between cities via autos and rail—the fields and forests look healthy, small towns sport new paint and construction. Old concrete Khrushchev block houses are giving way to new multi-story private residential complexes which are lovely. High-rise business centers,*

fine hotels and great restaurants are now commonplace—and ordinary Russians frequent these places. Two and three story private homes rim these Russian cities far from Moscow.

We visited new museums, municipal buildings and huge supermarkets. Streets are in good repair, highways are new and well marked now, service stations look like those dotting American highways. In January [2014] I went to Novosibirsk out in Siberia where similar new architecture was noted. Streets were kept navigable with constant snowplowing, modern lighting kept the city bright all night, lots of new traffic lights have appeared. It is astounding to me how much progress Russia has made in the past 14 years since an unknown man with no experience walked into Russia's presidency and took over a country that was flat on its belly. (Tennison 2014)

Moreover, those who didn't have an agenda of Russia-bashing acknowledged the impressive infrastructure at the Sochi Olympics, including "state-of-the-art bridges, roads, and tunnels." The majority of this infrastructure is permanent for the city (Kovacevic 2014).

When Putin, at the outset of his first term as president, met with his circle of economic advisors to come up with a plan to restore stability and improvement, it is reported that, due to the fact that he was a novice, he spent a lot of the time at these meetings listening and asking questions. The one question he consistently asked when a policy was being considered was what its effect on social welfare would be (Roxburgh 2013).

According to Angus Roxburgh, the concept of the "collective" interest was not merely a communist contrivance – it has deep roots in Russian culture. Many Russians have expressed nostalgia for the Soviet era because during that time they felt a relative sense of belonging and common identity as well as stability (Roxburgh 2013; Cohen 2011).

The economic team Putin had put together included, among others, lawyer-businessman German Gref, Deputy Finance Minister Alexei Kudrin, and liberal economist Andrei Illarionov. One of the major problems to be addressed was solving Russia's revenue crisis due to much of Russia's wealth leaving the country, along with poor people refusing to pay high tax rates on meager incomes.

Subsequently, they came up with a plan to reduce the tax rate in the hopes that it would be paid. Personal income tax rates were decreased from as high as 30 percent to a flat rate of 13 percent. Corporate rates were dropped from 35 percent to 24 percent. It should be noted that the IMF did not like the plan. When the Russian government stated that it would stick with the plan regardless, the IMF left the country (Roxburgh 2013).

It was a gamble that paid off as Russians started to pay their taxes and eventually the government had surpluses. Additionally, Putin had ordered the oligarchs to pay taxes and stay out of politics if they wanted to keep the loot they'd acquired from the Yeltsin years, which also added to the revenue stream.

A revolutionary land code was established allowing for buying and selling of residential property. A new legal code that sought to fight money laundering and to break up certain monopolies was implemented – though some monopolies remained, namely Gazprom in the gas industry (Roxburgh 2013).

The Partnership and Cooperation Agreement (PCA) that went into effect in 1997 paved the way for increased trade relations between Russia and the EU. Trade consisting mainly of mineral fuel products (77.3 percent) along with some manufactured goods, chemicals and raw materials, were worth 115 billion euros ($150.6 billion). EU exports to Russia were worth 65.6 billion euros ($86 billion). By 2012, overall trade between Russia and the EU totaled 325 billion euros ($426 billion), with EU as Russia's largest trading partner at 41 percent. Trade between Russia and Germany alone in 2013 amounted to 76 billion euros ($100 billion) (Euronews 2014).

From 1999 to 2008, Russia's GDP had increased by an average of 7 percent per year. A Stabilization or rainy day fund was established that included a $140 billion Reserve fund and a $30 billion National Welfare fund to ensure that pensions could be paid. The rate of Russians living in poverty decreased from 30 percent in 2000 to 14 percent in 2008, with average wages having quintupled, though this was skewed due to the existence of a small ultra-wealthy group. Moreover, Russia had decreased its inflation rate from 20 percent to 9 percent (Roxburgh 2013; Mellow 2013; RIA Novosti 2008).

By 2006, Russia had paid off most of its external debt, including all money owed to the IMF. When the Russian Ministry of Finance approached the Paris Club, a group of billionaire bankers, and offered to repay all Russia's external debts early, they were rebuffed as the international bankers preferred to have the debt outstanding as long as possible in order to maintain control, which is what these international financial arrangements are really about. But, as of 2012, Russia was still paying the debt ahead of schedule (Johnson 2012).

Financial Crisis of 2008

Russia has refused to play the debt and austerity game and has been seeing positive results. In response to the 2008 financial meltdown, Russia implemented a large stimulus package facilitated by the rainy day funds mentioned above. Public debt, as of 2013, is 7.7 percent of GDP compared to 72.5 percent for the US. The Russian government will not borrow more than 1 percent of GDP and keeps reserve funds at a 7 percent minimum, according to Russia's Finance Minister, Anton Siluanov, and has been running virtually no budget deficit (Roxburgh 2013; Mellow 2013).

From the post-crisis period of 2009 to the present, all 10 of Russia's top exports (mineral oils (58 percent), iron and steel, pearls, gems and precious metals, fertilizers, machinery, wood, and aluminum) posted double-digit increases. These gains ranged from 24 percent for aluminum to 257 percent for non-industrial diamonds (World's Top Exports 2013).

Furthermore, Russia's unemployment rate was 5.8 percent in 2013—lower than the US (7.4 percent) and the EU (12 percent) (World's Top Exports 2013; BLS 2014; Eurostat 2014).

In early September of 2014, the Global Competitiveness Report showed that Russia had gained 11 points and was among 3 nations that recorded increased values in all areas since 2010, representing Russia's biggest jump in that report's findings.

According to the report, "Russia is better than 40th in four categories—market size (7th), macroeconomic environment (31st), higher education and training (39th), and infrastructure (39th)" (RT 2014).

Economy Still a Work in Progress

Despite the phenomenal success enjoyed by Russia since 2000 — largely achieved by not following the Neoliberal prescriptions of the West — Medvedev and Putin have both admitted that Russia's economy is still too dependent upon fossil fuels and raw materials exports.

Putin himself also conceded in a 2013 conference sponsored by a state-owned bank in Russia that productivity is lagging compared to other developed nations (Mellow 2013).

And, of course, there is the continuing issue of corruption in government bureaucracy and in the business community, which erodes confidence and increases costs of those wanting to do business in Russia, whether they're Russians or foreigners. The Global Competitiveness Report cited above noted that a "major overhaul" was still needed to eradicate corruption and favoritism. In his December 2013 Annual Address to the Federal Assembly — the equivalent of the State of the Union — Putin pushed for the Duma (Russian legislative body) to draft a law streamlining an arbitration court system for resolution of economic conflicts. This law would also develop a federal portal that would provide transparent information on all inspections of businesses and publish a national rating of the investment climate in the nation's various regions. The portal has since been implemented (RT 2014).

To grasp the possible significance of the portal, one must understand the background and nature of corruption in Russia. It is mostly a problem among local officials (90 percent of all corruption is estimated to be at the local level) throughout the country. Along with the powerful class of oligarchs that came to control the Kremlin in the 1990s were the 89 regional governors throughout the Russian Federation who ruled their respective fiefdoms, enriching themselves through massive bribery. Lower on the food chain were local officials who earned paltry salaries and bilked new entrepreneurs for bribes in exchange for signing off on official documents as well as contriving inspections on charges of flimsy or non-existent violations, requiring the payment of additional bribes for clearance.

Part of the reason this kind of corruption persists is due to the strong historical roots of getting essential things done via "connections" and its associated prestige rather than the rule of law as a foundation. This was the case in Czarist Russia as tributes were typically paid in the form of goods or money to officials as part of the feudalism-like system, which was gradually dismantled in the rest of Europe but continued in Russia. Due to Russia's sprawling geographic size and its lack of a developed transportation system, interaction with the outside world and the attendant exposure to new ideas was hindered until the 19th century. Russians' relationship with governmental authority was modeled on the administrative state system inherited from the Mongols. Consequently, their social contract had never been that of a citizen with rights or sovereignty but as subjects that were granted varying amounts of social protection, and later some limited decision-making within autonomous peasant communities, in exchange for submission to state authority. Submission was enforced by a harsh bureaucracy.

This arrangement of deference to authority and reliance on "connections" to obtain necessities continued under the Soviet system, with deference to authority demanded in exchange for security, stability and a degree of social protections. There was also the Communist Party bureaucracy with party managers who lorded over their respective regions (Tennison 2012; Szamuely 1974).

A further step to address corruption is a draft bill being drawn up as of October 2014 to stop tax evasion and "gray capital outflows" through offshoring. Another key reason for this legislation involves keeping money in Russia to provide internal financing to bring productive capacity online for import substitution and increased general industrial and technical buildup, which requires internal credit sources (Business New Europe 2014).

Despite the almost $9 billion worth of exports in machinery and almost $5 billion in electronic equipment in 2013, Russia's manufacturing base is not where it could be. However, as Fred Weir wrote in the *Christian Science Monitor* in July of 2014, sanctions could have the serendipitous effect of prompting progress on this front. Some analysts he spoke to argued that "the Russian government can use its nearly half-trillion dollars in foreign currency reserves to bolster the ruble and back investments in domestic industries. That could make up for the coming loss of virtually all Ukrainian imports and redirect Russia's economy from raw materials exports to modern manufacturing and services" (Weir 2013). Stopping the bleeding of offshoring is a step in that direction.

Another approach discussed in Weir's article was kicking Russia's growing economic ties with the world outside of the Atlanticist bloc—as exemplified by BRICS—into high gear (Weir 2013).

A common response in the Anglo-American media to Russia's recent retaliatory measure of banning most agricultural imports from the US and EU was that Russians would go hungry and were, therefore, shooting themselves in the foot. Within a matter of days of the announcement, however, numerous Latin American countries, namely Argentina and Brazil, got in line to fill the gap. In addition, China started selling produce directly to Russia and plans to set up a cross-border wholesale market and warehouse complex on its northeastern border (Brown 2014; RT 2014).

More importantly, according to the Food and Agricultural Organization, Russia ranks in the top three producers in the world for a range of agricultural products, from various fruits and vegetables to non-wheat grains, potatoes and poultry. It is not among the top 10 food importers and has had plans in place since 2013 to significantly boost its already respectable production of organic produce from small farms and gardens (Brown 2014).

Natural Society reported in May of 2013 that 35 million Russian families are growing an impressive percentage of Russia's fruits and vegetables on 20 million acres:

> *According to some statistics, they grow 92% of the entire countries' potatoes, 77% of its vegetables, 87% of its fruit, and feed 71% of the entire population from privately owned organic farms or house gardens all across the country. These aren't huge Agro-farms run by pharmaceutical companies; these are small family farms and less-than-an-acre gardens. (Sarich 2013)*

Additionally, the UK *Telegraph* reported in April of 2013 that the Russian government will be adding support and certification to organic farmers that will become effective in 2015. They also reported that 60 percent of consumers in St. Petersburg and Moscow had no problem paying higher prices for homegrown organic produce. That percentage is likely to remain fairly high with the patriotic element added in as a result of Russia's sanctions on imports (Sarich 2013; Ukolova 2013).

The agricultural sanctions will create some problems, mainly short-term shortages of some meat products and price increases due to the need to work out infrastructure issues to accommodate imports from countries at a greater distance; however, it is reasonable to conclude that Russians will not be going hungry any time soon.

Sharon Tennison, during her trip to Moscow and St. Petersburg this past September, reported that the general reaction to Western sanctions was as follows:

> *The general outlook of Russians I spoke with is one of quiet confidence, saying that sanctions will turn out good for Russia in the long run—that Russia must become self-sufficient—remarking that Russia became infatuated with foreign products in the 1990s. At that time they felt Russia didn't need to manufacture high-end products; that they could purchase them from other countries. However, the situation has changed. Today production has become the "in" discussion wherever one goes. The sanctions have helped bring this about. Several Russians remarked that they hoped the sanctions lasted for three years or more, since that would give Russians sufficient time to learn to manufacture formerly imported items themselves. The Russian government is offering financial support to entrepreneurs who are ready to move into consumer production. (Tennison 2014)*

Criticisms of Putin's Policies

In an article for *Foreign Affairs* in November 2013, "The Seduction of George W. Bush," author Peter Baker posited that Bush was naïve to consider trusting Putin as an international partner and that any problems leading to a rift in their relations were all due to a combination of Putin's endless character flaws and ill-informed Stone Age policies. If the accounts in Baker's article are to be believed—and many of the events and conversations are presented with little or no historical or political context that may shed light on what shapes Russia's perspective and, hence, Putin's comments and actions—Putin told Bush that he believed centralization provided stability for Russia (Baker 2013).

While somehow ignoring his own administration's centralizing of power with its unitary executive philosophy, Bush's reaction to Putin's comment—and the implicit attitude underlying it—was that it was the wrong path for Russia, regardless of whether post-Soviet Russia's conditions may indicate that this course made some degree of sense in terms of bringing stability to a politically and economically chaotic nation that was on the brink of being a failed state. There is also no attempt to objectively analyze whether this course of action has benefitted Russia and its people in any significant way and, therefore, may be valid for Russia, at least for a period of time.

One institution that attempted to objectively assess this policy in economic terms was the Institute for Economies in Transition, a project of Bank of Finland. In a 2008 Discussion Paper, the results of a comprehensive statistical analysis of corporate governance between the period of 2001 and 2004 in Russia revealed a positive correlation between state involvement and improved corporate governance with the trend more marked in companies where the state owned a minority share as opposed to full ownership. Furthermore, Transparency International's most recent report states that the Russian company Gazprom scored higher than Apple, Amazon and Google, which are notorious for having poor scores, while Rosneft actually scored higher than Exxon Mobil. Since the idea of any state involvement in business having positive effects is antithetical ideologically to the US-led West, these reports got little to no press coverage in the Western establishment media (Yakovlev 2008; Lossan 2014).

But Bush, with little working knowledge of Russian history, culture or nuances of policy, presumed that he knew what was best for Russia more so than the Russian president — another instance of the patronizing American attitude.

President Obama, for all the early suppositions that he was more enlightened and less arrogant than his shoot-from-the-hip predecessor, has shown a similar lack of knowledge or understanding of Russia as illustrated in his August 2014 remarks to *The Economist* that Russia didn't make anything and that immigrants didn't flock there. In actuality, Russia, after the United States, is the second most popular destination in the world for immigrants (Adomanis 2014). And, as discussed, Russia does indeed make a few things. One of the items it manufactures is the RD-180 rocket engine that gets US satellites off the ground. The RD-180 is the most advanced rocket engine in the world and it is estimated it would take as long as five to eight years to bring an American alternative online (Howell 2014).

Putin has clearly spelled out his reasons for centralizing control in Russia in the first decade of the 21st century stating in speeches that this policy was a necessary move to deal with a Russia that was in political and economic chaos.

Matthew Johnson, an academic specialist in Russian history and philosophy, wrote in the *Eurasian Review*, that the United States has itself engaged in some of the same policies in times of crisis that it has criticized Putin for:

> *During WWII, the federal government took over the economy for war production. This is not considered authoritarianism, but a response to an emergency....As the Russian economy collapsed by 1995, Russians demanded action. The state was required to take action against organized crime, begin collecting taxes again and reform the armed services. Only a fairly strong state could accomplish this. (Johnson 2014)*

Though Putin has made it clear in both words and actions that he believes in markets and global trade, he has also shown discernment in rejecting elements of Neoliberal globalization and fundamentalist market theory that is anathema to long-term economic stability, independence, or social justice.

During a 2012 presidential campaign speech, Putin discussed how government support may still be needed in a focused manner, for example, to improve industrial policy in Russia:

> *It is often argued that Russia does not need an industrial policy and that, when choosing priorities and creating preferences, the government often makes mistakes by supporting ineffective players and getting in the way of competition. It's hard to argue with such assertions, but they are valid only if all other conditions remain the same. We went through de-industrialization and the economic structure is severely deformed. Large private capital does not willingly flow into new sectors – in order to avoid higher risks. We will certainly use tax and customs incentives to encourage investors to allocate funds to innovative industries. But this could show its effects several years from now – or not if more attractive investment options emerge in the world. Capital, after all, does not have borders. Are we ready to put Russia's future at such great risk for the sake of purity of an economic theory? (Putin 2012)*

It is that "purity of an economic theory" as propagated by the disciples of Milton Friedman that is non-negotiable to American elites; world leaders who seriously question it all too often end up in those American elites' crosshairs.

Johnson, in his insightful article "Globalization and Decline of the West: Eurasianism, the State and Rebirth of Ethnic-Socialism," analyzes the West's preoccupation with "democracy" and "openness," especially in relation to criticisms of Russia. He deconstructs what the West, led by the US, actually seems to mean by these terms with respect to their practical application.

> *The ideas of "democracy" and "openness" are mere buzzwords that are explicitly connected to the economic interests of those who created the globalization project....The main focus of Western capital is that "openness" becomes universally conflated with cultural and ideological standardization. "Democracy" can then become universally conflated with securing the maximum return on investment. (Johnson 2014)*

What Johnson is touching on here is the fact that there is nothing that Western elites fear and disdain more than authentic and substantive democracy—not the perversion of the term that they have created in which it is conveniently equated with liberalized markets whereby they can exploit everyone's resources for their own benefit, combined with dog and pony show elections where most of the candidates are pre-approved by the elites in order to provide a pretense of political democracy.

This is reflected in the US's characterization of Yeltsin as a "democrat" on one hand, and shrieks about or distortions of every little thing Putin does that they don't approve of—and the stated reasons for disapproval are often not the actual ones

—on the other hand. It is also tragically reflected in a review of post-WWII US foreign policy, in which democracy is reduced to a mere annoyance, as when Iranians freely elected Mohammad Mossadegh but the US/UK saw fit to overthrow him in 1953 for the crime of wanting to nationalize the fossil fuel industry so its proceeds could benefit the Iranian people rather than foreign corporations. As a replacement, they installed the brutal Shah as dictator. A similar scenario played out the following year when the democratically elected leader of Guatemala, Jacobo Arbenz Guzman, was overthrown in a CIA-backed coup after nationalizing agricultural land, including that owned by the American corporation, United Fruit Company (Risen 2000; Kornbluh and Doyle).

Johnson also points out that neoliberal capitalists implicitly believe that a country should have no "national interest" separate from those of Western capital, such as national independence, stability, or social justice.

By 2006, Putin had made it clear that foreign investment in Russia would have limitations and conditions placed upon it – namely, that such investment must be beneficial to the Russian people rather than exploitive and that it must not undermine the security or independence of Russia. This was exemplified in moves that year by the Russian government to regain control of oil and gas deposits that had been virtually given away by Yeltsin under Production Sharing Agreements to Exxon Mobil and Royal Dutch Shell (Engdahl 2006).

Putin had shown this inclination three years earlier when he had Mikhail Khodorkovsky arrested and jailed for tax evasion. However, tax evasion was merely the tip of the iceberg in terms of what this recalcitrant oligarch, who ran Yukos Oil, was in the midst of trying to pull off.

At the time of Khodorkovsky's arrest at Novosibirsk airport in October of 2003, he had succeeded in buying a huge number of votes in the Duma four weeks prior to elections. Having control of Russia's legislature would have allowed him to alter laws whereby he could effectively seize control of Russian oil and gas deposits and pipelines. Furthermore, he could have legislation passed that would position him for the Russian presidency.

Additionally, Khodorkovsky was colluding with Dick Cheney and other powerful players in the US to sell a stake ranging from 25 to 40 percent in Yukos to Exxon Mobil and Chevron, giving the US major influence over decisions relating to Russian fossil fuel resources, the engine of the country's economic growth and recovery. The final details of the sale were set to be ironed out when Putin intervened.

Of course, Khodorkovsky's cadre of friends in the West, like NATO enlargement cheerleader/war profiteer Bruce Jackson, George Soros, and Stuart Eizenstat—who had worked in the Treasury Department during the Clinton administration, representing the halcyon years for the oligarchs pillaging Russia's assets—immediately set up a PR campaign characterizing the Putin government as the bad guys bullying an innocent "dissident" oligarch who only yearned for Western style democracy. A major lobbying effort to get Khodorkovsky freed was undertaken, but the Russians were not in a forgiving mood (Engdahl 2006; Clark 2003).

It appears that the concept of a Eurasian (Economic) Union represents Putin's attempt to integrate the benefits of global markets without compromising other important interests like maintenance of sovereignty and regulation of economic relations to prevent or counter major imbalances that can lead to destabilization and dangerous levels of social inequality. The common market space it encompasses, at least initially, was comprised of two nations on Russia's borders, Belarus and Kazakhstan, which have long-standing historical, geographic and ethno-cultural ties. It is gradually expanding to include other nearby nations, such as its newest member Armenia, and Kyrgyzstan, which will be following suit in 2015. This trend will only increase if it demonstrates a successful and appealing model. Russia had been in discussions regarding potential membership with Ukraine during Yanukovych's leadership – a move that Yanukovych was open to as long as it didn't preclude Ukraine's being integrated also with the EU (Bespalova 2013).

The fact that Ukraine might have joined the Eurasian Union and that a successful Eurasian Union might one day link up to the EU was an especially upsetting thought in the minds of US elites.

Putin has consistently made the connection between stability and security with social justice and equitable development. For example, during his speech before the Munich Conference on Security Policy in 2007:

> *And there is still one more important theme that directly affects global security. Today many talk about the struggle against poverty. What is actually happening in this sphere? On the one hand, financial resources are allocated for programmes to help the world's poorest countries - and at times substantial financial resources. But to be honest—and many here also know this—linked with the development of that same donor country's companies. And on the other hand, developed countries simultaneously keep their agricultural subsidies and limit some countries' access to high-tech products.*

And let's say things as they are—one hand distributes charitable help and the other hand not only preserves economic backwardness but also reaps the profits thereof. The increasing social tension in depressed regions inevitably results in the growth of radicalism, extremism, feeds terrorism and local conflicts. And if all this happens in, shall we say, a region such as the Middle East where there is increasingly the sense that the world at large is unfair, then there is the risk of global destabilization. (Putin 2007)

In discussing various aspects of the financial crisis that had recently affected the world at the Davos Economic Forum in 2009, Putin again addressed these interconnections by discussing the untenable levels of inequality the crisis had laid bare:

The benefits that were generated were distributed very disproportionately. In fact, such disproportions could be seen between layers of the population in individual countries and even in highly developed countries, as well as between different countries and regions of the world.

For a significant part of mankind, comfortable housing, education and qualit[y] medical care are still inaccessible. And the world upsurge of recent years has not radically changed this. (Putin 2009)

Putin has continued to encourage policies in Russia that acknowledge social responsibility. In his 2013 Address to the Federal Assembly, he outlined plans to raise salaries for teachers, professors, and doctors and for investment in affordable housing construction with the requisite social infrastructure for middle-income families (Putin 2013).

A conspicuous consumption tax was enacted on luxury cars in May of 2013 to increase revenues—fulfillment of a campaign promise made by Putin in 2012. And while it was conceded that the revenues produced would be modest, at least at the outset, Putin supported it because in his words, "It is the right thing to do; there should be such a tax. And the question of social equity, the gap in incomes is a sharp and very important question." A similar tax on luxury real estate is also being considered (Putin 2013; Putin 2012).

As international political journalist Deena Stryker (2014) states, "Russia is no longer a socialist country, but it hasn't thrown out the baby with the bathwater and hence should be labeled as an aspiring social-democracy that has yet to develop an advanced parliamentary system such as exist in Northern and Western Europe."

For any intellectually honest and independent analyst who has studied Putin's words and actions over the course of years, it is apparent that he is attempting to gradually and methodically raise the standard of living for the Russian people. It is also apparent that he views stability, both within Russia and in the outside world that Russia must co-exist with, as crucial, and that the most reliable way to achieve and maintain stability is through a multi-polar world, international law with a strengthened UN as the arbiter, and more equitable development.

It should become clearer to most readers as they continue through this book why the Western elites hate Putin. And it has nothing to do with whether he is democratic or authoritarian.

PART II
THE WEST CHECKMATED

Kermit E. Heartsong

"The Russians have already won beyond their wildest dreams. It's very late in the game."
—Henry Kissinger

CHAPTER 5

UKRAINE I, UKRAINE II

It is important prior to discussing the recent events in Ukraine, beginning in February 2014, and those that took place in Ukraine in 2004, to speak to the mechanisms responsible for them. Mechanisms, which time and time again, Western governments have utilized to destabilize countries, to covertly remove their governments (undesired regimes in favor of pliable or easily controlled regimes), while simultaneously undermining the regime's sanity, credibility, and morality via a psychological-warfare campaign, designed to make the various charges adhere.

The events that have been unfolding in the Ukraine over the course of the past year thus follow a well-established precedent for what may be described as a new type of warfare that has been and is being employed in numerous countries around the world.

COLOR REVOLUTIONS

The types of wars range from hot and cold to guerrilla and asymmetrical to economic (unilateral economic sanctions) and political to what might be called "swarm-warfare."

Swarm warfare targets the social, political, and economic organs of a given government/nation and infects it, much like a virus. As the contagion spreads, swarm-warfare causes the host state to lose any and all viability (governance, control, policing capability), whereby it quickly dies and is transformed into something entirely different (a zombie nation—see Libya). The Madison Avenue brand name for this tactic of swarm warfare is a "color revolution."

Color revolutions generally have no front lines, are primarily waged in urban areas, utilize social media as viral replicators and thereby a means to more properly direct the infection to a nation-state's vital organs. The overriding strategy is to manipulate and control the state in an attempt to cause paralysis and ultimately its political death. Simultaneously, outside states responsible for the infection create a self-serving diagnosis, which is promulgated to the media in order to preempt the infected state's own diagnosis and further drive the infection via public opinion. Fear, propaganda, psychological warfare, agent provocateurs, and false flag terrorist actions form the basis of the outside state's diagnostic narrative (brutal dictatorship) and treatment (regime change).

The goal of color revolutions as stated by Vladimir Zarudnitsky, the Russian Chief of the General Staff's Main Operations Department, is that they are:

> *Geared toward destroying a state from within by dividing its population. Commonly accepted rules of warfare are ignored, since official state-run armed forces are not used. Instead, criminal and terrorist forces and private military companies are allowed to act with impunity. (Zarudnitsky 2014)*

While an early form of color revolutions was first developed and implemented in the mid-twentieth century in Mohammed Mosaddeq's Iran (1953), a more advanced strain of color revolutions was developed in the final quarter of the 20th century.

A social scientist, Gene Sharp, was commissioned by NATO to conduct a study on how to make Europe unconquerable. His study, "Making Europe Unconquerable: A Civilian-Based Deterrence and Defense System," with a foreword by George Kennan, diplomat, political scientist, and "the father of containment" strategy, was published in 1983. Sharp's study became the operating manual for successive US Governments and their intelligence agencies with regard to viral Warfare (of the non-biological variety) or what would come to be known as "color revolutions."

The test case or the first practical application of Sharp's study as implemented by the CIA, was undertaken in China in 1989. The event would later become known as the *Tiananmen Square Massacre*. The leader of Communist China, Deng Xiaoping, was the target of the first color revolution, as sponsored by the US. As French journalist and author, Thierry Meyssan (2012) describes in his article, "Perfecting the Method of Color Revolutions":

> *The United States wanted to topple Deng Xiaoping in favor of Zhao Ziyang. The intention was to stage a coup with a veneer of legitimacy by organizing street protests, in much the same way as the CIA had given a popular facade to the overthrow of Mohammed Mossadegh by hiring Tehran demonstrators (Operation Ajax 1953). The difference here is that Gene Sharp had to rely on a mix of pro-Zhao and pro-US youth to make the coup look like a revolution. (Meyssan 2012)*

Tiananmen Square thus bore all the hallmarks of a color revolution—mass student protests blocking government buildings, a steady supply of goods to the protestors (Coleman stoves, training, instruction, and logistics manuals—at the time, unusual for students to have been able to afford), and Molotov cocktails, the seeming weapon of choice for most color revolutions. Additionally, a sub-segment of the *rioters* trained as agent provocateurs would escalate the violence at the predesignated time. In the case of Tiananmen Square, it would be this third group of *protestors*, who would use the Molotov cocktails to attack police and soldiers, who were initially unarmed (burning a number of them alive).

However, despite the claims of Western governments and media about the tragedy of the Tiananmen Square Massacre, there was, actually, no massacre at all. Cables of the communications among diplomatic personnel, and in particular from a Chilean diplomat to his US counterpart released in a Wikileaks cable, confirms that:

> *He [Chilean diplomat] watched the military enter the square and did not observe any mass firing of weapons into the crowds, although sporadic gunfire was heard. He said that most of the troops which entered the square were actually armed only with anti-riot gear—truncheons and wooden clubs; they were backed up by armed soldiers," a cable from July 1989 said. (Wikileaks 2011)*

It was also later discovered, after much disinformation and propaganda had been spread, that the Chinese government's version of the truth regarding Tiananmen Square was, indeed, accurate and that no massacre had ever taken place.

This color revolution, however, proved unsuccessful, as Deng quickly arrested Sharp and expelled him from China.

Despite the failure, Sharp was able to learn important lessons regarding the mobilization of young activists and how to successfully manipulate them toward a desired end. The method as summed up by Meyssan:

> *Exacerbate all underlying frustrations, blame the political apparatus for all the problems, manipulate the youth according to the Freudian "patricidal" scenario, organize a coup, and then propagandize that the government was brought down by the "street." (Meyssan 2012)*

Sharp would take the lessons learned from this first experiment and, with the assistance of Colonel Reuven Gal, then chief psychologist of the Israeli Army, set up "training programs for young activists, with the objective of organizing coups" (Meyssan 2012). Sharp and Gal's strategy would be coupled with a concept, developed by the RAND Corporation in the late 1990s, called "swarming." Swarming, as alluded to earlier, is the concept of utilizing the communication patterns and movements of insects to direct spontaneous protests against targeted leaders via GPS satellite images, chat rooms, instant messaging, cell phone text messaging, and blog sites (Engdahl 2009).

The test case for the full implementation of this advanced form of a color revolution, as coupled with the swarming technique, came in Belgrade, Yugoslavia in the year 2000. The target for regime change via this improved version of color revolution was President Slobodan Milosevic.

The Clinton Administration began its color revolution against President Milosevic with a $41 million budget that was run from the American Consulate via the office of Ambassador Richard Miles (Engdahl 2009). The campaign involved coordinating popularity polls and the training of thousands of opposition activists in organizing strikes, communicating with symbols (in order to obscure their messages), overcoming fear, and undermining the authority of the Milosevic regime. Of tantamount importance was the organization of a parallel vote count to sow doubt should the initial vote not go as desired (Engdahl 2009). As Engdahl states:

> *Thousands of spray paint cans were used "by student activists to scrawl anti-Milosevic graffiti on walls across Serbia," and throughout the country around 2.5 million stickers featured the slogan "Gotov Je," meaning "He's Finished." Milosevic was deposed by a successful high-tech coup that became "the hallmark of the US Defense policies under (Rumsfeld) at the Pentagon." It became the civilian counterpart to his "Revolution in Military Affairs" doctrine using "highly mobile, weaponized small groups directed by 'real time' intelligence and communications. (Engdahl 2009)*

The campaign waged against Milosovec would now serve as the basis for all future color revolutions to be directed at leaders who embraced a different concept of what was good for their state and their people.

Subsequent color revolutions would follow in the Rose Revolution (Georgia 2003), the Orange Revolution (Ukraine 2004), Tulip Revolution (Kyrgyzstan 2005), Cedar Revolution (Lebanon 2005), Blue Revolution (Kuwait 2005), Saffron Revolution (Myanmar 2007) and the Green Revolution (Iran 2009), to name but a few.

The results of the various successful color revolutions, despite their lofty promises and without exception, have brought social, political, and economic suffering for the targeted nation's masses via the Western plundering of resources, privatization, and extortion as implemented by the World Bank and the IMF's austerity programs. Or succinctly put, the end goals of color revolutions are chaos, instability, and asset pillage. As stated by Sergey Kuzhugetovich Shoygu, Russian Minister of Defense:

> *The Arab Spring, for example, has destabilized the Middle East and North Africa. Now, a whole range of African states are near collapse because of the effects of events in Libya. Afghanistan is also increasingly unstable. (Shoygu 2014)*

In the end, color revolutions are indeed a form of swarming social warfare, carefully staged by intelligence operatives often embedded in non-governmental organizations (NGOs) that seek to manipulate rebellion, class divide, and social discord to orchestrate political change, regime change, and asset stripping in a given country. Key end goals of the various color revolutions—as they are sold to the masses, however, are *hope and change, freedom, democracy, EU candidacy* (when appropriate) and other objectives that the demonstrators can "believe in," despite their ultimate hollowness.

HOW THEY WORK—THE DETAILS

Color revolutions as developed by Gene Sharp and refined by Colonel Reuven Gal, provided the US with an operating manual. The RAND Corporation provided the tools, soft weapons, and the concept of swarming as subsequently allied to the development of social media.

The forward operating bases, intelligence agents, and command staffs for color revolutions are often found in organizations such as the Albert Einstein Institute (AEI), National Endowment for Democracy (NED), International Republican Institute (IRI), National Democratic Institute

(NDI), Freedom House and the International Center for Non-Violent Conflict (ICNC).

The funding apparatus for the above organizations is the US Agency for International Development (USAID), which is the de facto financial branch of the State Department. As Eva Golinger (2010) states in her article, "Color Revolutions: A New Form of Regime Change, Made in USA:"

> *Today, USAID has become a critical part of the security, intelligence and defense axis in Washington. In 2009, the Interagency Counterinsurgency Initiative became official doctrine in the US. Now, USAID is the principal entity that promotes the economic and strategic interests of the US across the globe as part of counterinsurgency operations. Its departments dedicated to transition initiatives, reconstruction, conflict management, economic development, governance and democracy are the main venues through which millions of dollars are filtered from Washington to political parties, NGOs, student organizations and movements that promote US agenda worldwide. Wherever a coup d'etat, a colored revolution or a regime change favorable to US interests occurs, USAID and its flow of dollars is there. (Golinger 2010)*

The operating instructions for color revolutions, which interestingly enough, are run like a marketing campaign, are as follows (Golinger 2010):

- Find a country with significant natural resources—like oil or gas—that is geostrategically positioned to advance Western interests or that conducts a foreign policy independent of or at odds with the West in general, or Washington, in particular. And if the country, as determined by any one of the above criteria, is unstable, socially stratified, financially weak, or militarily impotent, all the better.

- Identify and enlist student and various youth movements and organizations to spearhead the campaign. They will serve as the "Fresh face (the 'Fodder Units')," attracting others to join in as though it were the fashion, the 'in' thing to do."

- Next, pick a color (rose, orange, green), a symbol (fist, open hand, Nazi Wolfsangel, etc.), and a brand to unite and rally the masses to a common, identifiable cause—freedom, democracy, acceptance by the West.

- Plan protest and/or destabilization campaigns in conjunction with an upcoming electoral campaign and make sure to organize a very visible parallel vote count, which will be necessary in the end to highlight voter tension, raise questions of rampant fraud, and to discredit the elections and exit polls, should the color revolution's desired candidate fail to win.

- Target the security forces and police with the intention to win them over, engage them with the message of commonality, that they too will benefit from a change in the current regime and the freedoms that will be won once the current regime is gone (Golinger 2010).

And *voila*, color revolution, though the disclaimer should probably read: "Results may vary, but know that the *hope and change, the freedom and democracy* envisioned was little more than a cynical, prefabricated pipe dream." In reality, the color revolution regime change endgame, as imposed by its interlocutor, the IMF, will inevitably take the form of a structural adjustment program that will—

- Dramatically cut social services and funds for education
- Limit and or reduce wages and pensions
- Impose layoffs in the public sector
- Call for investment guarantees for foreign private corporations
- Open the door for large-scale privatization of state assets
- Necessitate devaluing the currency
- Transform residents of said country to (low) wage slaves, the disenfranchised, or something far worse

The financial *"pound of flesh"* for such a color revolution will invariably lead to a significant reduction of the country's GDP, the plundering of its various national assets—precious metals (think gold reserves), minerals, gas, oil, land (to Western oligarchs and multinationals), and adherence to the West's geopolitical script. Said adherence will require the proper voting (or abstention) record in international forums, compelled "Coalition of the Willing" duty, and the necessary Central Bank and free market reforms.

Perhaps it is true that memories are short, as Ukraine's initial experience with the IMF's structural adjustment program came in 1992, lasted until 1995, and led to the reduction of Ukraine's GDP by 60 percent.

Ukraine I—The Orange Revolution

The Ukraine's Orange Revolution of 2004 would be a textbook example of the various color revolutions that preceded it and those yet to come.

In November 2004 presidential candidate Victor Yanukovych won the run-off election against Viktor Yushchenko, a former governor of Ukraine's Central Bank. However, following Yanukovych's victory, numerous unsubstantiated claims of fraud arose from the Yushchenko camp and his supporters.

While Yanukovych, like Yushchenko, favored increased ties with the West, Yanukovych was not an enthusiastic supporter of Ukraine joining NATO, as his primary constituency was the pro-Russian Eastern Ukraine. This became an issue for the West. Yuschenko, on the other hand, had Central Bank credentials and hard-wired affiliations with the West. His wife was a former official in the Reagan and George H.W. Bush Administrations and Yuschenko favored NATO and EU membership. Yuschenko was thus the color revolution's darling (see Yatsenyuk).

Ukraine's first Orange Revolution began immediately after the run-off, with its call of tainted elections and its target, the pre-emptive regime change of Yanukovych. The media fell into lockstep with the "Orangists" and became a willing accomplice and a staunch detractor of Yanukovych.

Mass street protest, civil disobedience, sit-ins and general strikes, as per the color revolution manual, were immediately and systematically rolled out.

Within weeks, Ukraine's Orange Revolution had precipitated the Ukrainian Supreme Court's annulment of the November run-off results and ordering of a new election for

December 26, 2004. Yushchenko won the election and was inaugurated on January 23, 2005.

However, despite winning the color revolution/Regime Change battle, the Western soft-war in Ukraine would inevitably be lost. As detailed in the article, "The Orange Revolution Peeled" (Raimondo 2010):

> *[Yushchenko's] Regime turned out to be just as incompetent and rife with cronyism as his corrupt and venal predecessors, if not more so. A great deal of Western "aid" money disappeared down several rabbit holes. Worse, the economy was paralyzed by the imposition of price controls, and corrupted by brazen influence-peddling. Under Yushchenko's power-sharing agreement with the volatile Yulia Tymoshenko, the "gas princess" and Amazonian oligarch, the country disintegrated, not only economically but socially as centrifugal forces of culture, language, and the weight of history were brought to bear on the unity of the country, and things began to come apart. (Raimondo 2010)*

Embezzlement, infighting, systemic corruption, and betrayal between the new regime's leaders, Prime Minister Yulia Tymoshenko and President Yuschenko, derailed the goals of the West. Yanukovych was then elected in 2010 and began to ameliorate relations with Russia, while actively courting the West as well. And while corruption was also part and parcel of Yanukovych's term, geopolitical pragmatism and realpolitik would win in the short term.

However, refusing to be thwarted, Washington would, over the course of the next decade, "invest" $5 billion in Ukraine to finally have its way. The invested monies would be spent to train subversive groups (Svoboda, Right Sektor, Fatherland Party) and to prepare and educate select sectors of the country in order to launch a redux of the first Orange

Revolution. The tactics would remain the same: foment agitation for EU membership; purge from Ukrainian's Rada (parliament) highly "questionable" political groups (Communist Party, Party of Regions); implement draconian financial measures via the IMF and the World Bank; and plunder, privatize and strip mine a range of Ukrainian assets (gold, oil, gas, industry, etc.).

With the actors trained and the stage set, it would now be time for a dress rehearsal to iron out the kinks, so to speak, for Orange Revolution II.

Georgia, The Dress Rehearsal

Georgia's color revolution was color-coded as rose and had taken place in 2003, but the West had unfinished business in that former Soviet state. It had "regime changed" Georgian President and former Soviet Foreign Minister, Eduard Shevardnadze, and ushered in Mikheil Saakashvili as president.

Saakashvili, American-educated and staunchly pro-West, immediately sought to have Georgia join both the European Union and NATO (Shakarian 2014).

Over the course of the next several years, Saakashvili continually engaged in provocative, anti-Russian rhetoric, which led to a steadily deteriorating relationship between Russia and Georgia.

During this period, the Pentagon, NATO, and allied militaries concentrated their efforts and actions on attempting to mold the Georgian military into a capable fighting force and thus another belligerent pawn at Russia's front line. As reported in the *Financial Times*, in the months before the

Georgian attack, the Pentagon had provided combat training to Georgian special-forces commandos (Chomsky 2008).

On August 7, 2008, during the Olympic Games in Beijing, China, President Saakashvili authorized the Georgian military to attack the city of Tskhinvali in the breakaway region of South Ossetia. The Georgian military fired an artillery bombardment upon Russian peacekeepers and civilians, in the disputed South Ossetia territory. As reported by Mikhail Barabanov (2008) in his article, "Three military Analyses of the 4 Day War Between Russia and Georgia":

> *The attack on South Ossetia was not spontaneous. Over the course of several days in early August, the Georgians appear to have secretly concentrated a significant number of troops and equipment in the Georgian enclaves in the South Ossetian conflict zone, under cover of providing support for the exchange of fire with Ossetian formations. On August 7, at about 22:00, the Georgians began a massive artillery bombardment of Tskhinvali, the capital of South Ossetia, and by dawn the next day began an attack aimed at capturing Tskhinvali and the rest of the territory of South Ossetia. By 08:00 on August 8, Georgian infantry and tanks had entered Tskhinvali and engaged in a fierce battle with Ossetian forces and the Russian peacekeeping battalion stationed in the city. (Barabanov 2008)*

Moscow's retaliation was lightening fast and led to a four day war in which Russia expelled the Georgian military from South Ossetia and the Kodori Gorge, Georgia's only remaining foothold in Abkhazia. Further, the war destroyed Georgia's war-making apparatus (as supplied by the West). South Ossetia and Abkhazia were both recognized as independent states by Russia. Saakashvili, in response, would sever all ties with Moscow.

The Western press, in lockstep from CNN to the New York Times to the BBC, was quick to formulate their "diagnosis," and they assigned blame to Russia for *aggressively invading* Georgia. The Western media immediately categorized the Russian *invasion* as a bid to, "reestablish the territories of the former Soviet Union." The West and its attendant media then leveled charges continually against Russia, despite a glaring lack of supporting evidence and investigative feet on the ground. It was necessary for Western governments and their attendant media to collectively form a repulsion to anything that resembled actual truth. The Western narrative regarding Russia's "invasion" of Georgia continues to this day in the face of investigative reports that have clearly stated otherwise.

One such report, conducted by an independent EU fact-finding mission and headed by Swiss diplomat and Caucasus expert, Heidi Tagliavini, that took the better part of a year to complete and numbered a thousand pages, disputed President Saakashvili's statements and press releases (Bidder 2009). Whereas President Saakashvili had claimed that Georgia's artillery bombardment of the South Ossetian capital of Tskhinvali was a preemptive strike directed against advancing Russian armored columns that were already in South Ossetia (Bidder 2009), the report's findings came to the following conclusion:

> *Georgian claims of a large-scale presence of Russian armed forces in South Ossetia prior to the Georgian offensive on 7/8 [2008] August could not be substantiated by the mission. It was Georgia which triggered off the war when it attacked (South Ossetian capital) Tskhinvali. (Bidder 2009)*

The findings of this report, however, have not, as of the release of this book, found their way to Western mainstream media outlets and, as a result, Western mainstream media continue to labor under the erroneous conclusion that Russia started the 2008 Georgian conflict.

The toll of the Georgian conflict left 133 civilians and 59 Russian peacekeepers dead. The Russian invasion and aerial bombardment of Georgia, according to the *Financial Times*, left 146 Georgian soldiers and 69 civilians dead (Chomsky 2008).

In the end, Saakashvili, like so many before him, was abandoned by the West, who lacked the will or the power to protect him. There would be no Western or NATO boots on Georgian ground. The Georgian debacle of 2008, however, would serve as a potent foreshadowing of things to come.

Saakashvili's regime gradually collapsed, and in October of 2012 his party, the United National Movement, lost to the Georgian Dream coalition headed by billionaire Bidzina Ivanishvili.

Ivanishvili's term in office would see a more pragmatic approach than his predecessor with regard to relations with Russia.

Ukraine II

> *The US mainstream news media is reaching a new professional low point as it covers the Ukraine crisis by brazenly touting Official Washington's propaganda themes, blatantly ignoring contrary facts and leading the American public into another geopolitical blind alley.*
>
> —Robert Parry, Investigative Reporter, formerly with AP and Newsweek

ZBig's Grand Chessboard strategy has long held to the stratagem that control of Ukraine was the key to unbroken US world domination, the suppression of Western European independence, the checkmate of Russian power projection across the Eurasian bridge (Ukraine), and the sabotage of Russian and Western European integration.

In light of the Grand Chessboard strategy, the events that have unfolded and that continue to unfold in Ukraine should be seen and understood clearly for what they are—a fundamentalist geopolitical ideology.

It is important that one be as accurate as the available data and evidence allow. Of further importance is the timeline or the order in which events have taken place in the Orange Revolution II—those known publicly at the time and those later discovered, that were covertly running in parallel.

AN OFFER YOU CAN'T REFUSE

> *With astonishing unanimity, NATO leaders feign surprise at events they planned months in advance. Events that they deliberately triggered are being misrepresented as sudden, astonishing, unjustified "Russian aggression." The United States*

> *and the European Union undertook an aggressive provocation in Ukraine that they knew would force Russia to react defensively, one way or another.*
>
> —Diana Johnstone, *"Tightening the US Grip on Western Europe: Washington's Iron Curtain in Ukraine"*

From **May 31-June 3, 2012,** world leaders met in Chantilly, Virginia, for the Bilderberg Meeting, as some would argue, to analyze the economic "fundamentals" of their elite agenda, to determine how those fundamentals would be efficiently marshaled in their best interest, and how to remove any and all obstacles to the successful implementation of those fundamentals.

Attendees at the Chantilly meeting included Royal Dutch Shell CEO Peter Voser; Royal Dutch Shell Chairman Jorma Ollila; BP CEO Robert Dudley; Massachusetts Senator John Kerry, now US secretary of state; Keith B. Alexander, director of the National Security Agency; Thomas E Donilon, then White House national security advisor; Michael J. Evans, then vice chairman of Goldman Sachs & Co; Donald E. Graham, then chairman and CEO of The Washington Post Company; Reid Hoffman, co-founder of LinkedIn; Henry Kissinger; John Micklethwait, editor-in-chief of *The Economist*; Charlie Rose, interviewer/reporter; Martin H. Wolf, chief economics commentator for The Financial Times; Robert B. Zoellick, president of the World Bank, along with a host of other "VIPs" (Bilderberg.com 2012). The full list of the Bilderberg meeting can be found by Googling "Bilderberg Meeting May 31st - June 3, 2012."

One of the foremost experts on the annual Bilderberg meetings is reporter Daniel Estulin, who provides via articles and books a general summation (presumably via inside sources), as to what exactly the fundamentals are for each of the Bilderberg meetings and how they will be attained.

A couple of the key economic fundamentals for the May 2012 Bilderberg meeting were: 1) hydrocarbons (oil, tar sands) and 2) export routes (Keystone XL, South Stream, Energy East). Certainly, while there were many whose economic interests were tied to these particular "fundamentals," perhaps, Royal Dutch Shell, Suncor, and Cenovus Energy should be considered primary beneficiaries.

The attainment of the organizations' hydrocarbon fundamentals would be achieved by discouraging, sabotaging, and bringing alternative sources to bear via new pipeline routes, with the intent of circumventing the EU's Fuel Quality Directive (FQD). The FQD restricts imports of heavy crude such as tar sands oil, which US and Canadian companies have been intent on developing and exporting to the EU (Nelson 2014).

The primary obstacle to the implementation of the economic fundamentals, as determined at the meeting, was Russian President Vladimir Putin, due to his unwillingness to see Russia encircled by US and NATO military bases and his clear insistence on Russian sovereignty—the marshaling of Russia's hydrocarbon resources and plans for a second natural gas pipeline to Europe. This second pipeline would circumvent entirely Ukraine and provide the EU with a more stable supply of gas. This would, of course, de-privilege the aforementioned Western hydrocarbon fundamentals, while potentially establishing a rapprochement between Western Europe and an independent Russia (Nelson 2014). The conclusion was that Putin would have to first be demonized, Russia brought to its knees economically, and then Putin removed via regime-change.

In September of 2013, a gathering of Western elites met in Yalta, Crimea to strategize on the future of Ukraine's relationship to the European Union. Paid for by Ukraine's second wealthiest oligarch, Viktor Pinchuk, the conference was attended by, among others, Bill and Hillary Clinton, Dominque Strauss-Kahn, Gerhard Schroeder, Petro Poroshenko, Viktor Yanukovych, Lawrence Summers, Robert Zoellick, David Petraeus, and Bill Richardson, who touted the supposed benefits of fracking.

The goal of the meeting was breaking Ukraine's ties with Russia and planting it firmly in the EU/NATO camp. Also in attendance, however, was Putin's economic advisor, Sergey Glazyev, who tried to explain that the promises being made by the West to Ukraine amounted to a chimera. Glazyev pointed out that Ukraine had heavy foreign debts and that the increase in imports from the West that would result from the agreement would exacerbate the problem, necessitating either a default on its debts or a hefty bailout (Johnstone 2014).

In the same month, Polish Prime Minister Donald Tusk and his foreign minister, Radoslaw Sikorski, invited eighty-six members of Ukraine's Right Sector, a National Socialist political organization (neo-Nazis), to partake in a university exchange program at Warsaw's University of Technology (Meyssan 2014).

However, as acknowledged by their official schedule, the eighty-six Right Sector members, many of whom were over forty years of age, never went to the University of Technology. Instead they went to the police-training center in Legionowo, Masovia, Poland (Meyssan 2014). Over the course of the next four weeks, the Right Sector members received training in:

- crowd management
- person recognition
- combat tactics
- command skills
- behavior in crisis situations
- protection against gases used by police
- erecting barricades, and
- sniper shooting skills

The Polish newspaper, the *Polish Weekly*, has verified that the training took place via a number of photos that showed the Right Sector participants in full Nazi regalia and insignia taking instruction from their Polish trainers (Meyssan 2014).

In **October of 2013** Ukraine's negotiations with both the West, via the IMF, and Russia, via the Commonwealth of Independent States (CIS), would ultimately lead to its decision about what orbit it preferred.

The motivations of the West were manifold and predicated on the usual suspects—asset pillage (gas, shale, land, gold reserves), extortion, via IMF "austerity," a pliable West friendly "changed-in" regime and a geostrategic move via NATO boots in Ukraine to encircle or checkmate Russia, long a goal of Grand Chessboard fundamentalists.

The West presented a proposal to Yanukovych via the IMF, which called for the doubling of gas prices and electricity for both households and businesses, slashing state funds for school children and the elderly, devaluing the Ukrainian currency, and lifting the ban on the sale of Ukraine's rich agricultural lands, which would open them to outside investors. Ukraine was also informed that it would have to cut its ties with its major economic partners, Russia and other members (Armenia, Belarus, etc.) of the Commonwealth of Independent States (CIS) (Nazemroaya 2014). Ukraine was, in turn, promised for its concessions the sum of $4 billion. It was an offer that President Yanukovych couldn't refuse, despite the paltry amount offered to Ukraine. As outlined in the article, "Patriotic Heresy vs. the New Cold War," Professor Stephen Cohen (2014) lays out the reasoning behind the proposal put forth by the West:

> *Fact: The EU proposal was a reckless provocation compelling the democratically elected president of a deeply divided country to choose between Russia and the West. So too was the EU's rejection of Putin's counterproposal of a Russian-European-American plan to save Ukraine from financial collapse. On its own, the EU proposal was not economically feasible. Offering little financial assistance, it required the Ukrainian government to enact harsh austerity measures and would have sharply curtailed its longstanding and essential economic relations with Russia. Nor was the EU proposal entirely benign. It included protocols requiring Ukraine to adhere to Europe's "military and security" policies—which meant in effect, without mentioning the alliance, NATO. In short, it was not Putin's alleged "aggression" that initiated today's crisis but instead a kind of velvet aggression by Brussels and Washington to bring all of Ukraine into the West, including (in the fine print) into NATO.*

To make things even more interesting, the West asked for additional concessions, which were neatly contained within the "fine print." For example, Yanukovych and the various Ukrainian oligarchs quickly realized that the association agreement would give advantage to EU companies over their own companies. The EU companies (and oligarchs) would thus be able to dismantle, replace, or absorb the Ukrainian oligarch's companies. Further, Ukraine would have to soften or eliminate trade laws and regulations, which would be extremely disastrous to their continued survival. And lastly, and most interestingly, the West wanted the former prime minister, Yulia Tymoshenko, who had been convicted of embezzlement and abuse of power, released from jail. The combination of the various *wants* from the West would find Ukraine experiencing decades if not a half century of economic destitution and oblivion (Lendman 2014).

The motivations of Moscow were manifold as well. Moscow sought a relatively stable and East-leaning governing body in the Ukrainian border state. It also sought to keep the Ukraine neutral of any geostrategic military alliance (NATO) that would compromise its national security. Moscow was, of course, not keen on the idea of short-, medium- or long-range missiles on its border either. And the idea of losing Crimea—its only warm water port, an important naval asset, and part and parcel of Russia for nearly two hundred years—would be a clear redline.

Russia's proposal to Yanukovych would come in the form of a $15 billion dollar loan, the slashing of gas prices by one-third, increased trade, and continued integration via its various industrial and military manufacturing relationships.

The fine print on the Russian contract, if one has a fairly good imagination, may have read: sign with the West and there's a high probability that you will be freezing this winter; and NATO is a redline, beware.

On **November 20, 2013**—the day before the Yanukovych government decided not to sign the Association Agreement with the European Union, Ukrainian deputy Oleg Tsarov, an elected representative of the Regional Party gave a speech before Ukraine's Rada (Parliament)(Messay 2014).

Tsarov's three minute and forty-five second speech was heckled continually by other Rada members throughout. Nonetheless, Tsarov delivered his speech, which presaged events that would take place on February 21, 2014, almost three months to the date. Tsarov noted the following in his speech (full text below — original translation):

> *In my role as a representative of the Ukrainian people activist of the organization "Volya" turned to me providing clear evidence, that within our territory with the support and direct participation of the US Embassy [in Kiev] the "TechCmp" project is realised...under which preparations are being made for a civil war in Ukraine. The "TechCamp" project prepares specialist for informational warfare and the discrediting of state institutions using modern media. Potential revolutionaries for organising protests and for toppling the Stat Order. The project is currently overseen and under the responsibility of the US ambassador to Ukraine Geoffrey R. Pyatt. After the conversation with the organisation "Volya" I have learned they succeeded to access facilities of "TechCamp" disguising as a team of IT specialists. To their surprise, briefings on peculiarities of modern media were held. American instructors explained how social networks and Internet technologies can be used for targeted manipulation of public opinion as well as to activate protest potential, to provoke violent unrest on the territory of Ukraine, radicalisation of the population triggering infighting [sic]. American instructors presented examples of successful use of social networks used to organise protests in Egypt, Tunisia and Libya. "TechCamp" is currently holding conferences throughout Ukraine. A total of five events have been held so far. About 300 people were trained as operatives, which are now active throughout Ukraine. Recent conference too place Nov. 14-15 [2013] in the heart of Kiev on the Embassy of the United States of America! You tell me which country in the world would allow a NGO to operate out of the*

US Embassy? This is disrespectful to the Ukrainian government and against the Ukrainian people! I appeal to the constitutional Authorities of Ukraine with the following question: is it conceivable that representatives of the US Embassy which organise the "TechCamp" Conferences misuse their diplomatic mission? UN Resolution of 21 December 1965 regulates inadmissibility of interference in the internal affairs of a state to protect its independence and its sovereignty in accordance with paragraphs one, two, and five. I ask you to consider this as an official beseech to pursue an investigation of this case. Thank you. (Messayan 2014)

On **November 21, 2013**, perhaps after the stinging realization that he, the oligarchs, and the people of Ukraine would be targeted for IMF structural adjustments, and with Russian *soft pressure* (no gas, no trade), Yanukovych said no to the West and their IMF surrogate. What Yanukovych did not clearly understand, however, was that the offer was one that he could not refuse. However, as described by Robert Parry in the article, "NYT Is Lost in Its Ukraine Propaganda," it was also an offer he could not possibly accept:

In November 2013, Yanukovych learned from experts at the National Academy of Sciences of Ukraine that the total cost to the country's economy from severing its business connections to Russia would be around $160 billion, 50 times the $3 billion figure that the EU had estimated, Der Spiegel reported. (Parry 2015)

Yanukovych then signaled his intention to move east toward Russia and the Customs Union (which would later be transferred into the Eurasian Economic Union). Yanukovych's "no" would "strangely" coincide with the increasing violence of the Maidan protests.

On **November 24, 2013**, three days after Yanukovych gave his "no" to the West, the first direct clashes between the protestors and police began. It would also mark the first attempt by a small segment of the protestors to aggressively attack a police barricade with the aim of breaking into the Cabinet of Ministers of Ukraine building (Meyssan 2014). The group identified as responsible for the aggressive demonstrations, attacking the police with firecrackers, and also penetrating a police barrier, was the neo-Nazi, All-Ukrainian Union (AAU, Svododa) Party.

However, despite the violence of the protestors, the gutting of buildings, and the destruction of various monuments, the Obama administration and other Western leaders warned President Yanukovych not to use force against the now violent and destructive protestors, who had turned to Molotov cocktails in their *peaceful* protest.

November 26, 2013, Western leaders began their open and direct interference in the internal affairs of the sovereign state of Ukraine. The first state actor to abet the protestors was the speaker of the Lithuanian Seimas (parliament), Loreta Grauzhinene, who was accompanied by two vice-chairmen of the Seimas. During their uninvited appearance and presentation to the Maidan crowd, Grauzhinene urged the protestors to press their demand that the Ukrainian government sign the association agreement with the EU (Meyssan 2014).

On **December 1, 2013,** right-wing activists, supporters of the Pravyi Sektor and Svoboda, attempted to violently overthrow the Yanukovych government. They clashed violently with police and eventually took over the House of the

Trade Unions and the Kiev City State Administration building. The neo-Nazi youth group Sich/C14 then set up their headquarters in the Kiev City State Administration building.

On the same day, the deputy of the Polish Sejm (parliament), Jaroslaw Kaczynski, speaking from the Maidan stage, transmitted a message from the president of the European Parliament, Martin Schulz, while assuring the gathered crowd that their EU entry was a forgone conclusion (Meyssan 2014).

On **December 4, 2013,** the German Foreign Minister, Guido Westerwelle, visited the Maidan and met with leaders of the opposition, Vitali Klitschko (future Mayor of Kiev) and Arseniy Yatsenyuk (future Prime Minister).

On **December 6-11, 2013**, a number of uninvited foreign dignitaries visited the Maidan to rally on the protest that, at this point, had become decidedly violent.

US Assistant Secretary of State for European and Eurasian Affairs, Victoria Nuland, visited the Maidan and attempted to rally the protestors via the widely reported distribution of cookies (the truth is, indeed, stranger than fiction).

As outlined by Thierry Meyssan (2014) in the White Book report on the Ukraine, Nuland was but the visible tip of the iceberg of the State Department and various government controlled NGOs and private foundations:

> *According to some media and independent analysts, Euromaidan was directed by the US State Department through government-controlled NGOs and private foundations. The site of Ron Paul Institute for Peace and Prosperity (USA) published a study of the American political scientist Steve Wiseman, who provides specific information in this regard. According to him, the planning of events in Ukraine started in advance. A group of several dozen*

> Ukrainian opposition organizations was created, which received funds from the Soros Foundation and the Pact Inc. organization, working for the US Agency for International Development. Steve Wiseman cites a number of examples of how protests against the government of Viktor Yanukovych were held, using American technologies and new developments in propaganda and mass communications. The publication claims that the main coordinators in the US State Department for the organization of the coup in Kiev were the Assistant Secretary of State for European and Eurasian Affairs Victoria Nuland and the US ambassador in Kiev Geoffrey Pyatt [sic]. (Meyssan 2014)

The report goes on to say that then-US Ambassador to Ukraine Geoffrey Pyatt gave grants upward of $50,000 to newly created Ukrainian Internet TV channel Hromadske, while coordinating additional funds from the Soros Foundation ($30,000 US) and the Netherlands Embassy in Kiev ($95,000 US). As Meyssan (2014) reports:

> The newly created channel, according to the American political scientist, began to broadcast one day after the President of Ukraine Viktor Yanukovych suspended the signing of the Association Agreement with the EU on November 21, 2013 until analysis of its economic consequences [ ] is finalized. (Meyssan 2014)

A recording (Appendix I) between Nuland and Pyatt was then leaked to the internet. The conversation precisely detailed not only that the US was the major orchestrator of the coming coup, it also laid out who the successors of a new coalition would be once President Yanukovych had been illegally overthrown. An excerpt of the conversation follows; for a transcript of the full conversation please see Appendix I.

US Ambassador Pyatt: "I think we're in play. The Klitchko piece is obviously the complicated electron here. Especially the announcement of him as deputy prime minister and you've seen some of my notes on the trouble in the marriage right now so we're trying to get a read really fast on where he is on this stuff...and I'm glad you sort of put him on the spot on where he fits in this scenario."

Nuland: "Good. I don't think Klitsch should go into the government. I don't think it's necessary, I don't think it's a good idea."

Pyatt: "Yeah, I guess..in terms of him not going into the government, just let him stay out and do his political homework and stuff."

Nuland: "I think Yats is the guy who's got the economic experience, the governing experience. He's the...what he needs is Klitsch and Tyahnybok on the outside. He needs to be talking to them four times a week you know. I just think Klitsch going in...he's going to be at that level working for Yatsenyuk, its just not going to work."

Pyatt: "Yeah, no. I think that's right. OK. Good. Do you want us to set up a call with him as the next step?"

The US contingent was joined on the Maidan on December 7, 2013 by Jacek Saryusz-Wolski, a member of the European Parliament, who incited the crowd to believe that Russia was interfering with the decision of Ukraine to join the EU, while urging the Yanukovych government to release the protestors who were responsible for violence from prisons and to stop its own violence against the protestors.

On **December 15, 2014**, US Senators John McCain and Chris Murphy gave speeches at the Maidan, further claiming that the US supported their bid to join Europe, via the Association Agreement.

From **January 19–27, 2014,** the Pravyi Sektor engaged in violent clashes with security forces, where over 300 people (mostly police) were injured on Grushevski Street. On January 22, 2014, the Svoboda activists violently overtook the Brody State Administration in Lviv Oblast. During this time and under the supervision of Svoboda, the "People's Self-Defense" groups and the "People's Councils" were formed for the purposes of armed rebellion, the stockpiling of ammunition, and the seizure of power. Also during this time, the movement Obschee Delo attempted to violently seize the Ministry of Justice of Ukraine and the Ukrainian Ministry of Energy and Coal. The various opposition groups to Yanukovych would go on to seize regional administration buildings in all areas of Western Ukraine, except for the Transcarpathian region (Meyssan 2014).

Between **January 29–February 1, 2014**, further interference came from Elmar Brok, the Chairman of the European Parliament Committee on Foreign Affairs and Henri Malosse, President of the European Economic Social Committee. Brok called upon President Yanukovych to fulfill the demands of the protestors as he met with Victor Klitschko. Malosse, who visited the Maidan twice, called on his first visit for the Ukraine to focus on the EU; while on his second visit proclaimed to the Maidan crowd, "We will always be with you!" (Meyssan 2014).

From **February 14–19**, 2014, further violence ensued. Maidan opposition parties would set the house of A. Herman, Deputy Party of Regions,' on fire. Pravyi Sektor protestors would forcibly take over the Party of Regions in Kiev, while brutally murdering two men—one hit by a Molotov cocktail would die of burns and suffocation, while the other man's head was smashed in and he was thrown down a flight of stairs. Women, who happened to be in the building, were stripped naked to their waists while their backs were painted with symbols and slogans. They were then kicked into the street. A number of buildings in Kiev, including the Ukrainian Ministry of Health, Central House of Officers, House of Trade Unions, and others were burned and destroyed. The protestors then severely beat and publicly tortured the Governor of the Volyn Regional State Administration, A. Bashkalenko, in an attempt to force his resignation (Meyssan 2014).

On **February 21, 2014,** President Yanukovych and opposition leaders, Vladimir Klitschko (Udar), A. Yatsenyuk (AUU Batkivshchyna), and Oleg Tyagnibok (Svoboda), signed an agreement to end the crisis. Present at the signing were the Ministers of Foreign Affairs of France, Germany and Poland. The terms of the agreement were a—

> *[A] Return to the 2004 Constitution, constitutional reform (to be carried out before September 2014), the organization of early presidential elections no later than December 2014, the formation of a national unity government, the end of opposition occupation of administrative and public buildings, the surrender of illegal weapons, and the renunciation of the use of force on both sides. (Meyssan 2014)*

That very same day, representatives of the newly formed Maidan Self-Defense coalition rejected the agreement. One of the demands put forth by a representative of the Maidan Self-Defense force was the immediate resignation of President Yanukovych or else the Self-Defense coalition would storm the

Presidential Administration and the Verkhovna Rada. Dmitry Yarosh of the Pravyi Sektor, who had not been present at the agreement's signing, refused to abide by it.

It is important, however, to reflect upon these events in light of the September 2013 *trainings* in Poland, where members of the Pravyi Sektor were trained for the purposes of overthrowing Yanukovych's presidency.

So while President Yanukovych negotiated in good faith with opposition leaders, the various "self-defense" forces of the opposition leaders and their Western sponsors were in the process of overthrowing Yanukovych. Twelve hours after the agreement had been signed, the legally elected President of Ukraine, Viktor Yanukovych, would be illegally and unconstitutionally overthrown in a coup d'état and forced into exile.

February 22, 2014. Within twenty-four hours and amidst rising violence and a coup spearheaded by neo-Nazi militias, the US recognized the coup government as the *legitimate* government of the Ukraine. As detailed below—

> *The US announced the removal of the legitimately elected President of Ukraine as a fait accompli and recognized the legitimacy of the self-proclaimed authorities, headed by Oleksandr Turchinov and Arseniy Yatsenyuk. On March 4, 2014, the Secretary of State John Kerry arrived in Kiev to pay his respects and show his support. (Meyssan 2014)*

Upon the new coalitions' ascension to office, numerous acts of violence and intimidation continued in the face of the previous day's signed agreement. Nestor Shufrich, deputy from the Party of Regions, was captured by the Euromaidan activists as he was leaving the Verkhovna Rada and was nearly lynched. Only the intervention of Vitali Klitschko saved him.

R. Vasilko, first secretary of the city committee of the Communist Party of Lviv, was detained by EuroMaidan supporters, illegally sentenced, and tortured. As explained by Meyssan (2014):

> *According to eyewitnesses, he had needles pushed under fingernails, his right lung pierced, three ribs, nose, and facial bones broken. The rioters also threatened to destroy his family. After the severe torture, R. Vasilko was taken to hospital, where the threats continued. Eventually, Vasilko had to flee Ukraine with the help of his relatives. (Meyssan 2014)*

Vasilko would be one of the first members in the Communist Party to come under attack. Also targeted would be Communist newspapers and district and regional Communist committees that would be sacked, seriously damaged, and illegally occupied.

> *The Communist Party, remaining a legal parliamentary party, was actually forced to shut down. Given the threat of deadly violence a large majority of the Communist Party faction in the Verkhovna Rada of Ukraine moved to the Crimea or Russia. (Meyssan 2014)*

On the same day, V Rybak, the chairman of the Verkhovna Rada (Party of Regions), tendered his resignation as did I. Kaletnik, the first vice-speaker of the Verkhovna Rada (Communist Party). The reason for their resignations and the subsequent resignations:

> *It is significant to note that the entire subsequent period was marked by massive intimidation of Verkhovna Rada deputies from the ruling Party of Regions and the Communist Party members by the supporters of Euromaidan. (Meyssan 2014)*

On **February 23, 2014,** the Ukrainian Verkhovna Rada, purged of members from the Party of Regions and the Communist Party, voted to appoint O. Turchynov as interim President of Ukraine until May 25, 2014, despite the fact that President Yanukovych was still the democratically elected President of Ukraine, still in the country, and that the appointment of Turchynov was unconstitutional. President Yanukovych soon thereafter left the country.

On the same day, the deputy of the Verkhovna Rada and leader of the Radical Party, Oleg Lyashko, introduced a draft decree to ban both the Communist Party and the Party of Regions, in a clear violation of the law.

On **February 23, 2014,** Pravyi Sector members began to extort local shops in Kiev for "protection fees" and tied the regional administration head of customs, S. Harchenko, to a pole and threatened him with violence (Meyssan 2014).

On **March 4, 2014,** US Secretary of State John Kerry arrived in Kiev to show unconditional support for the newly elected coup-government, despite the fact that it was clearly unconstitutional by Ukrainian law.

On **March 5, 2014,** a leaked telephone conversation between Estonian Foreign Minister, Urmas Paet, and EU High Representative for Foreign Affairs and Security Policy, Catherine Ashton, appeared on the internet. The call found Minister Paet providing information to Ashton about his visit to the Ukraine regarding the information he had received from a Maidan doctor, Olga Bogomolets. Dr. Bogomolets stated that the people and police who were shot during the protest were shot by the same snipers. Paet then expressed his dismay to Ashton that the new coalition was unwilling to investigate the incident, which both Dr. Bogomolets and Paet believed pointed to the new coalition as responsible for the attacks. Paet also conveyed to Ashton that, "there is very strong pressure on the members of parliament." He told Ashton that journalists had witnessed armed men beating a deputy in broad daylight in front of the Verkhovna Rada.

From **March 6—31, 2014,** the new coalition and its various "security" and "self-defense" adjuncts participated in the following activities as reported by Meyssan (2014):

- The governor of Donetsk, Pavel Gubarev, was detained by Ukrainian security services and tortured in a prison in Kiev, where he subsequently fell into a coma, as detailed in reports by the prison's physicians.
- Pravyi Sektor activists gunned down E. Slonevsky, a local businessman, at a cafe in Kharkov.
- Thirty masked men with wooden sticks occupied the Sviatoshynskyi district prosecutor's office in Kiev and threatened the senior prosecutor to resign and, upon his refusal, he and a colleague were severely beaten.
- N. Naumenko, the director of the Migration Services of Ukraine, refused to give Pravyi Sektor activists the files of refugees and was subsequently beaten and stabbed in the face.
- In Uzhgorod, Maidan activists tortured the wife and son of a former regional official and robbed them. (Meyssan 2014)

On **March 21, 2014**, having been immediately recognized by the West as the legitimate government of

Ukraine, despite the unconstitutional succession of the new regime, Arseniy Yatsenyuk, acting Prime Minister (as selected by Victoria Nuland), signed the EU—Ukraine Association agreement much desired by the West.

Within weeks after being recognized by the West, the violence as directed by Kiev, would escalate markedly and the talk of civil war would soon begin.

NAZIS IN THE HOUSE

Though Western mainstream media has been loath to report on or to bring evidence forward of neo-Nazis serving in key positions in Ukraine's current ruling coalition, the facts are hard to ignore.

The main organizations from which the various neo-Nazis have come are Svoboda and the Right Sektor or the Pravyi Sektor parties.

Svoboda: The Svoboda party was founded in 1991 as the Social National Party of the Ukraine, a direct reference to Adolph Hitler's National Socialist party. It had even adopted the Nazi Wolfsangel logo, which closely resembles the swastika (Ryan 2014). In 2004, when Oleh Tyahnybok assumed the leadership, the party changed its name to Svoboda, presumably, an attempt to moderate its image, while maintaining its neo-Nazi heart and soul (Ryan 2014). As Professor John Ryan explains in his article, "The Media's Disinformation Campaign on Ukraine: There Are No Neo-Nazis in the Interim Government," the man long idolized by the Svoboda party, Stepan Bandera, was a Nazi Collaborator:

> *From its very beginnings as the Social National Party, Svoboda has idolized Stepan Bandera, a Nazi collaborator who formed the Organization of Ukrainian Nationalists (OUN) and organized the Ukrainian Waffen SS Galician Division—from 82,000 initial Ukrainian volunteers, the Nazis trained only 13,000 for battle. The division was then sent to fight the Russian and Ukrainian Soviet army, but this unit was decimated at the 1944 Battle of Brody, leaving only 3,000 who went on to form the nucleus of a further rebuilt SS division, later to become the core of the Ukrainian Insurgent Army. (Ryan 2014)*

The article goes on to mention an extremely brutal aspect of the Bandera-led division, when it came to the massacre of civilians and religious and ethnic minorities:

> *Aside from fighting the Soviet army, Bandera's forces assisted the Nazis by willingly killing off tens of thousands of Poles and Jews, and actively took part in the BabiYar massacre and the Holocaust in general. Although Bandera had some disagreements with the Nazis and was imprisoned for a while, he and his followers never disagreed with the Nazi Jewish policy in Ukraine, which eventually killed over 1.5 million Ukrainian Jews. (Ryan 2014)*

To date, the Svoboda leadership remains proud of Bandera's collaboration with the Nazis and the atrocities it inflicted. In a 2004 speech, Oleh Tyahnybok urged Ukrainians to fight against the "Muscovite-Jewish mafia" (Ryan 2014). Svoboda's ideologist, Yuri Mikhalchishin, a Tyahnybok deputy, has alluded to the Holocaust as a "bright period" in European history.

This is all especially interesting, in light of the current Western refusal to acknowledge that there are, in fact, neo-Nazi's serving in Ukraine's government.

The European Parliament passed a resolution (#8) in December 2012, which directly targeted Svoboda and which stated:

> *[The European Parliament] is concerned about the rising nationalistic sentiment in Ukraine, expressed in support for the Svoboda Party, which, as a result, is one of the two new parties to enter the Verkhovna Rada; [and] recalls that racist, anti-Semitic and xenophobic views go against the EU's fundamental values and principles and therefore appeals to pro-democratic parties in the Verkhovna Rada not to associate with, endorse or form coalitions with this party. (Ryan 2014)*

It would appear that memories in the West and in the European Parliament, in particular, are quite short when political expediency is required.

Right Sektor (Prayvi Sektor). The Right Sektor was formed in 2013 as an umbrella organization that included several paramilitary groups, including the Ukrainian National Assembly and the Ukrainian National Self Defense (UNA-UNSO) whose members dress in uniforms modeled on Hitler's Waffen SS and have been fighting Russia for years, including in Chechnya (Ryan 2014). As of March 22, 2014, these groups have formed a singular political party with Dmytro Yarosh as their lead candidate for president.

Recently, Yarosh was placed on an international watch list after being charged with inciting terrorism when he urged Chechen terrorist leader Doku Umarov to launch attacks on Russia over the Ukrainian conflict. Yarosh has also threatened to destroy Russian pipelines on Ukrainian territory (Ryan 2014).

Despite deafening silence and, perhaps, the willful ignorance of the West, members from both Svoboda and the

Right Sector hold, as of October 2014, key positions with the current Poroshenko Government, as detailed below. Whether they will still be serving in office as of the publication of this book will remain to be seen. However, when the coalition was formed the following neo-Nazis from Svoboda and the Right Sector rose to elected office, as documented by Richard Becker (2014):

- **Dmytro Yarosh,** a Right Sector neo-Nazi commander, became the second-in-command of the National Defense and Security Council (covering the military, police, courts and intelligence apparatus).
- **Andriy Parubiy,** the co-founder of the fascist Social National Party renamed Svoboda, became the top commander of the National Defense and Security Council.
- **Ihor Tenyukh** a member of Svoboda party, became the Minister of Defense.
- **Oleksandr Sych,** another member of the Svoboda, became one of the three vice prime ministers.
- **Oleg Makhnitsky,** yet another member of the neo-Nazi Svoboda organization, became Prosecutor-General (Attorney General)(Becker 2014).

Of course, the inability of the Western media to call into question the obvious—a Ukrainian regime topped with neo-Nazis at key defense and intelligence positions in the country—is, at best, troubling. At worst, it is damning for Western media, the self-styled arbiters of truth, transparency, and justice. It would appear on this fact alone that Western media have become little more than replanted organs of state propaganda.

CRIMEA

> *The ironies, contradictions and hypocrisies of Washington and its European allies towards the people of Crimea are staggering. Western standards are readily being seen to be nothing but empty, cynical rhetoric, used to conceal their own rapturous embrace of "law of the jungle."*
>
> —*Finian Cunningham*

> *Crimea is an autonomous region within Ukraine and seems to have the same rights as a Canadian province. So if it is perfectly legal for a province such as Quebec to hold a referendum on independence, why would it not be legal for Crimea to do the same? At no time did the USA object to Quebec holding a referendum on independence, so why the big brouhaha over Crimea? Moreover, what business would it be for the USA to have such objections – for Quebec or Crimea?*
>
> — *John Ryan, Ph.D., Retired Professor of Geography and Senior Scholar, University of Winnipeg, Canada*

There is, of course, a relatively recent example that provides a great deal of enlightenment with regard to how the West interprets matters of international law when it suits their best interest and the lengths to which they will go to *legitimize* the outcome.

On March 24, 1999, President Bill Clinton began an eleven-week "humanitarian" bombing campaign against the sovereign state of Yugoslavia, as governed by President

Slobodan Milosevic. There was no UN mandate and no referendums prior to or during the bombing campaign. The end goal for the West was an independent Kosovo.

The casus belli for the Yugoslavian bombing campaign was human rights. Allegations of atrocities at the level of genocide were being leveled by Clinton Administration officials, who claimed at the time that upwards of 100,000 Albanian refugees had been murdered by the Serbs (Scahill 2008).

The truth of the matter, however, would be something completely different, not unlike the cry of "WMDs" in the Bush Administration's run up to war with Iraq. As investigative journalist Jeremy Scahill points out in his article, "The Real Story Behind Kosovo's Independence," something else altogether was behind the seventy-eight day NATO bombing campaign:

> *A month before the bombing began, the Clinton administration issued an ultimatum to President Slobodan Milosevic, which he had to either accept unconditionally or face bombing. Known as the Rambouillet accord, it was a document that no sovereign country would have accepted. It contained a provision that would have guaranteed US and NATO forces "free and unrestricted passage and unimpeded access throughout" all of Yugoslavia, not just Kosovo. It also sought to immunize those occupation forces "from any form of arrest, investigation, or detention by the authorities in [Yugoslavia]," as well as grant the occupiers "the use of airports, roads, rails and ports without payment." Additionally, Milosevic was told he would have to "grant all telecommunications services, including broadcast services, needed for the Operation, as determined by NATO." Similar to Bush's Iraq plan years later, Rambouillet mandated that the economy of Kosovo "shall function in accordance with free market principles." (Scahill 2008)*

It was an offer that President Milosevic could not possibly accept, and simultaneously, it was an offer that he could not possibly refuse.

One month later, after Milosovic rejected Clinton's extortion demand, the bombing began. What followed on the ground in Yugoslavia as a result of NATO's "humanitarian" war:

> *So the humanitarian bombs rained down on Serbia. Among the missions: the bombing of the studios of Radio Television Serbia where an airstrike killed 16 media workers; the cluster bombing of a Nis marketplace, shredding human beings into meat; the deliberate targeting of a civilian passenger train; the use of depleted uranium munitions; and the targeting of petrochemical plants, causing toxic chemical waste to pour into the Danube River. Also, the bombing of Albanian refugees, ostensibly the people being protected by the US. (Scahill 2008)*

In the end, there had been no massacre of 100,000 Albanians or 50,000 or even 10,000.

> *The International Tribunal itself reported that just over 2,000 bodies were recovered from postwar Kosovo, including Serbs, Roma, and Kosovars, all victims of the vicious civil war in which we intervened on the side of the latter. The whole fantastic story of another 'holocaust' in the middle of Europe was a fraud. (Raimondo 2008)*

There had been no genocide at all. The "Albanian genocide" would be the precursor of Iraqi WMD's.

How then does the Crimean referendum compare to Kosovo's referendum and the West/NATO's involvement toward a sovereign Kosovo?

Crimea, officially an autonomous region formally within Ukraine, has had its own parliament and, up until 1995, its own President. The majority of Crimeans, Russian-speakers, had voted repeatedly for close relations with Russia in referendums in 1991, 1994, and 2008 (Raimondo 2014). It is also important to note that the Crimean region had been a part of Russia and then the Soviet Union from 1783 to 1954, until handed over to the Ukraine by Nikita Khrushchev.

In a 1994 referendum on closer ties with Russia, Crimeans voted overwhelmingly, nearly 80%, in favor of the referendum. And in 2008 the Crimean Parliament voted to rejoin Russia, while in the same year one million Crimeans signed a petition demanding that the Russian fleet be allowed to retain its presence in Sevastopol (Raimondo 2014).

Immediately after the new Kiev regime leaders assumed their respective offices, their first act was to outlaw the Russian language (the first language of a vast majority of Crimeans and Novorossiyans). What followed was the destruction of Russian war memorials that had been erected to celebrate Ukraine's liberation from the Nazi Third Reich. Then came the violent physical attacks on the Russian-speaking population of Ukraine and their various representatives in the Communist Party and the Party of Regions by the neo-Nazi security forces of the new regime.

The Crimeans, aware that the new coalition was composed of yet more corrupt oligarchs and now neo-Nazis working at the behest of the West, did not believe that the new regime in Kiev would "represent their interest or respect their rights" (Raimondo 2014). The Crimeans quickly sought an exit from the new Ukraine and the coup-installed government now in charge of the Ukrainian state and acts which, as we will detail later, had rendered the Ukrainian constitution null and void. As Justin Raimondo states in his article, "Crimea for the Crimeans:"

> With officials of the ultra-rightist Svoboda party – formerly the "Social National" party—in top positions in the new government in Kiev, and with the outright neo-Nazis of "Right Sector" being handed control of police and law enforcement bodies, Crimeans are refusing to recognize Kiev's authority. The Crimean Parliament has —once again—declared independence and appealed to Russia for security guarantees, while the head of the Ukrainian navy, which is stationed in Sevastopol, has defected to the Crimean side. (Raimondo 2014)

Unlike Kosovo (wherein no election was held and extortion led the day), Croatia and Slovenia (illegal referendum, 1991), Bosnia (referendum in violation of its own constitution, 1992) Scotland (2014), or Quebec (1980, 1995), all of which the West immediately recognized or ignored, the Crimeans, in the opinion of the West, were not entitled to the same rights and privileges. However, the Crimeans weren't listening.

On **March 6, 2014**, the Supreme Council of Crimea decided to join the Russian Federation. On March 11, the Parliament voted for a declaration of independence, as legally required, to underpin the current referendum (Cunningham 2014). On Sunday, **March 16, 2014**, roughly 82% of Crimeans participated in the referendum with approximately 96% voting to join Russia.

ODESSA

> *This action [in Odessa] was not prepared at some internal level, it was a well-planned and coordinated action in which some authorities' representatives have taken part.*
>
> —*Oleh Makhnitsky, acting Attorney General, Ukraine*

On May 2, 2014, in the city of Odessa, Ukraine, a horrific massacre was about to take place between those aligned to the coup-installed government in Kiev and ethnic Russians who did not approve of either the coup and or the neo-Nazis that had consequently risen to power.

Resistance to Kiev's coup-installed new government was not only being witnessed in Eastern Ukraine, but it was rising in the South as well. And when coup leaders found themselves unable to press the Ukrainian troops to fire on civilians, they sought other ways of suppressing dissent.

The coup leaders turned to Andriy Parubiy, a self-described neo-Nazi and the founder of Svoboda, for solutions. Parubiy had become Ukraine's National Security Chief as a result of the coup. His solution to the growing resistance was to employ the neo-Nazi shock troops, formerly the Maidan self-defense forces: the same troops that had proven themselves so valuable in the violence that had led to the coup.

As detailed by Parry (2014) in the article, "Burning Ukraine's Protesters Alive. Neo-Nazi 'Shock Troops' Supported by US," the National Guard units:

> *Were drawn primarily from well-organized bands of neo-Nazi extremists from western Ukraine who hurled firebombs at police and fired weapons as the anti-Yanukovych protests turned increasingly violent. (Parry 2014)*

These were the units that the new coup-installed government "dispatched to the east and south to do the dirty work that the regular Ukrainian military was unwilling to do" (Parry 2014).

On May 2, a soccer game had been scheduled between Odessa's local soccer club, FC Chernomorets Odessa, and Kharkov's FC Metallist.

The train from Kharkov arrived in Odessa at 8:00am that morning. The Kharkov soccer fans then made their way to the soccer stadium. As the Kharkov soccer fans reached the "Afina" shopping center at the intersection of Greek Street and Vice Admiral Zhukov, they were attacked by balaclava clad (a common accessory of neo-Nazi attire) gunmen, who were wearing St. George ribbons, a symbol adopted by Russian Separatists, and red armbands, perhaps, as an additional more clandestine identifying mark (Valiente 2014).

After a short bout of fighting, the balaclava clad "Russian Separatists," responsible for the violence then directed the Kharkov soccer fans to Kulikovo Field, while they subsequently fled into the Afina shopping center under police protection.

In late February, Kulikovo Field had become home to a tent camp of Odessa residents who opposed the new coup-installed regime in Kiev. Over the ensuing months, thousands of like-minded Odessa residents would visit the tent city in a show of support.

As the soccer fans made their way to Kulikovo Field, it appears that balaclava clad "Russian Separatists" sped ahead to warn the Kulikov Field residents that the "Right Sektor" was on its way to kill them. And as reported in the article,

"Odessa Massacre Planned and Executed by the Fascist Rulers of Ukraine" (Valiente 2014):

> *Led by the provocateurs [balaclava clad "Russian Separatists"], many activists entered the House of Trade Unions instead of scattering throughout the city. Some of them went down to the basement from which no one emerged alive – there they were tortured, killed, and butchered with machetes. Others headed upstairs. Gasoline was mixed with napalm to form deadly, acrid carbon monoxide. The recipe for these deadly cocktails was created by chemists from Independence Square, but they were not used there. In Odessa, the mixture was employed for the first time and this was no accident: a massacre with a large number of fatalities was needed in order to terrorize the entire country. (Valiente 2014)*

The massacre that took place at the House of Trade Unions in Odessa lasted several hours and would result in the horrific deaths, officially, of some 46 people, whose bodies had been horribly charred from the fires that raged within.

Yet even more horrific was the fate of the Odessa residents who managed to escape the burning building, only to be strangled, shot, and beaten to death.

It is believed that the unofficial death toll of the Odessa massacre is between 120 and 130 people.

Perhaps the Crimean people were prescient when they voted to separate from the Ukraine and join the Russian Federation.

WAR BY ANY OTHER NAME: EASTERN UKRAINE

> *Who in their right mind would allow the US to "assist" in restoring stability, unity and political and economic health? It has*

> set out to [sic] destabilize, divide and cripple Libya, Syria, and Iraq by military means and continues to terrorize civilian populations with drone attacks in Pakistan and Afghanistan. It has been responsible for millions of deaths as a result of its military [escapades]. Time and again, the US-led alliance has violated international laws and demonstrated no respect whatsoever for any notion of national sovereignty or territorial integrity with its invasions as well as its illegal mass surveillance courtesy of the NSA and Britain's GCHQ.
>
> —*Colin Todhunter, Global Research*

When Novorossiyans, a majority of whom are Russian speakers and of Russian heritage, realized that the Western supported coup had, indeed, brought a coalition of oligarchs and neo-Nazis to power, they too sought independence. And as their suspicions were verified—their language threatened, violence against Ukraine's Russians rampant, the Party of Regions members intimidated and forced to resign, and the Communist Party outlawed—they too sought to distance themselves from the new coup-installed coalition. It was, however, a move that would find every man, woman, child, and infant designated as terrorists for seeking to escape a growing tyranny spreading from Kiev and set in motion by the West. Perhaps in this same light the founding fathers of the US might have themselves been considered terrorists by Kiev's coup-installed government for seeking to distance themselves from Great Britain.

However, despite the various events taking place across the country documented by numerous sources, US Secretary of State John Kerry provided an alternative explanation for the events on the ground, free from facts or a scintilla of actual documented or forensic evidence. This would serve as the framework for Secretary Kerry's future statements to the Western media:

> *It's an incredible act of aggression. It is really a stunning, willful choice by President (Vladimir) Putin to invade another country. Russia is in violation of the sovereignty of Ukraine. Russia is in violation of its international obligations. (Dunham 2014)*

Given the Secretary's preceding statement, one questions if Secretary Kerry is (or was) in full possession of all of his faculties, if he has no memory, whatsoever, of the recent past (Afghanistan, Iraq, Pakistan, Libya, Somalia, Yemen, Syria, etc.), or if duplicity reins supreme in the US State Department. The charge would amount to breathtaking hypocrisy, given the facts on the ground, finding the Secretary's statement, at best, a grim fairytale.

With Crimea now firmly in the Russian camp, the Novorossiyans in defiance of the illegally-installed oligarch and neo-Nazi controlled regime, and Kiev threatening to silence the "terrorists," war would not be far off.

In early **April 2014**, a "full-scale anti-terrorist operation" by Ukraine's coup-installed, acting president, Oleksander Turchinov, was launched against every man, woman, and child in the Donbas region.

Interestingly, the newly designated "terrorists" of the Eastern Ukraine would not elicit the same sympathy as had the Maidan protesters, despite the fact that they would be on the receiving end of civil war and bombarded by armaments ranging from white phosphorous to cluster bombs to ballistic missiles.

It is important also to note, given Secretary Kerry's earlier quote regarding one country violating the sovereignty of another country, that Ukraine's civil war began immediately after the departure of CIA chief John Brennan (who traveled to Ukraine under a false name). The trip was later verified by former Ukrainian President Viktor Yanukovych who stated that the CIA Director had ordered the "crackdown" on pro-Russian activists (Durden 2014):

> *Part of the responsibility for dragging the country into domestic war lays on the US, which brutally interfere[d] in the situation and to point out what to do, Yanukovich said. The ousted president declared that CIA chief John Brennan visited Ukraine and it was after the meeting that the coup-imposed authorities in Kiev ordered a military operation in the country's east. (Durden 2014)*

While initially denying the report regarding CIA Director Brennan's visit to the Ukraine, White House Spokesman Jay Carney later confirmed that Brennan had indeed visited Kiev (RT 2014).

The irony, of course, is that during Yanukovych's term in office, never had war been waged against civilians. The newly installed coup-government, enthusiastically backed by the US, however, was about to do just that: execute a war against its own people.

By early April, not long after the departure of CIA Director Brennan, acting, coup-installed, Ukrainian President Turchinov mobilized the Ukrainian army to launch a "full-scale anti-terrorist operation" against the Novorossiyans. Turchinov gave the Novorossiyans (his own countrymen and women) an ultimatum: if they did not leave the occupied buildings and give up their weapons, a war would be launched against them.

On Wednesday, **April 16**, three Novorossiyan "separatists" were killed by the Ukrainian National Guard in the Black Sea port city of Mariupol (Reynolds 2014).

The following day, **April 17**, in an attempt to head off further escalation, the EU, Russia, Ukraine, and the US came to terms in the 2014 Geneva Agreement, the text of which stated:

- All sides must refrain from any violence, intimidation or provocative actions. The participants strongly condemned and rejected all expressions of extremism, racism, and religious intolerance, including anti-Semitism.
- All illegal armed groups must be disarmed; all illegally seized buildings must be returned to legitimate owners; all illegally occupied streets, squares and other public places in Ukrainian cities and towns must be vacated.
- Amnesty will be granted to protestors and to those who have left buildings and other public places and surrendered weapons, with the exception of those found guilty of capital crimes.

However, immediately after the Geneva Agreement had been signed, the coup-installed acting foreign minister, Andrey Deshchytsa, stated that the agreement would not affect the anti-terrorist operation in Eastern Ukraine as, "the troops in the east of the country are carrying out a special operation and can remain where they are." The statement would be in direct contrast to an earlier statement issued by Deshchytsa, during the meeting held in Geneva, which stated that:

> *All sides have pledged to refrain from any form of violence, intimidation or provocative actions. The participants of the meeting strongly condemned and rejected all forms of extremism,*

> *racism and religious intolerance, including manifestations of anti-Semitism. (RT 2014)*

US Secretary of State John Kerry also weighed in on the Geneva agreement stating:

> *All of this, we are convinced, represents a good day's work, but on the other hand, this day's work has produced principles, and it has produced commitments and it has produced words on paper. And we are the first to understand and agree that words on paper will only mean what the actions taken as a result of those words produce. (RT 2014)*

Secretary Kerry's rambling statement would turn out to be prophetic with regard to "words on paper" and the required action to end the violence. But no such action would be forthcoming on the part of Ukraine's coup-installed, Western-enabled government.

On Saturday, **April 19, 2014**, a raid by the neo-Nazi Right Sektor paramilitary unit killed six people in Ukraine's Donetsk region, in the city of Slavyansk. Not long thereafter the Geneva Agreement would be in shreds (Chossudovsky 2014).

The following week (**April 21–25**), acting coup-installed Ukrainian Prime Minister Arseniy Yatsenyuk ordered a full military offensive against the Novorossiyan protestors.

By **April 26**, satellite images from the Russian Defense Ministry showed 15,000 Ukrainian troops and National Guards, approximately 160 tanks, 230 Armored Personnel Carriers (APCs) and 150 mortars, howitzers and multiple launch rocket systems (Grads and Smerch) being amassed for war.

On **May 2**, Kiev's coup-installed government pressed the military into battle as they began shelling the town of Slavyansk. Over the course of the next ten days Donetsk Oblast would also be under siege, while unarmed Ukrainian civilians in Mariupol would be gunned down on the orders of the Yatsenyuk regime (Chossudovsky 2014).

May 12, a day after the eastern cities of Donetsk and Lugansk held successful referendums on their independence from Kiev, the newly formed army of the Donetsk People's Republic provided the Ukrainian army with its own ultimatum, which gave the Ukrainian army 48 hours to leave the Donbas region. The Ukrainian army, however, pressed on (Lendman 2014).

On **May 17**, the next phase of the war began as indiscriminate attacks and civilian casualties escalated across the Donbas.

After the election of Ukrainian President Poroshenko on **May 25, 2014**, and despite his campaign promises to scale back the violence and sue for peace, he escalated the war.

The civil war now raged, pressed by the Ukrainian forces in Slavyansk, Andreevka, and across the Donetsk region. The Ukrainian army's modus operandi consisted of shelling civilian homes, hospitals, daycare centers, schools, nursing homes and industrial centers with rockets, heavy artillery, various illegal armaments (white phosphorous, cluster bombs), and even ballistic missiles. Kiev's military jets and attack helicopters also took to the operation and indiscriminately strafed and fired missiles into civilian areas. Civilian casualties quickly began to mount across the Donbas and a mass exodus to Russia began.

June, July. For the next two months the regime in Kiev would wage full-scale war against the entire population of Eastern Ukraine's Donetsk and Lugansk regions and would commit numerous war crimes and crimes against humanity, killing upwards of several thousand civilians. Some of the crimes committed during Kiev's military operation against Eastern Ukraine were documented in a white paper subsequently listed on the website Voltaire (Messayan 2014) which, detailed the following, to name just a few:

- The dropping of white phosphorous incendiary bombs on civilian populations (illegal)
- The dropping of cluster bombs on civilian populations (illegal)
- Military jets and attack helicopters being deployed against civilian populations (war crime)
- Artillery bombardment of entire civilian-inhabited towns (war crime)
- Bombing of churches, hospitals, schools (war crime)
- Refusal to provide escape corridors for civilians (war crime)

President Poroshenko, with US backing and encouragement, would press his advantage, eschewing Russia's (Sergey Lavrov) as well as France's (Laurent Fabius) and Germany's (Frank-Walter Steinmeier) calls to quell the violence and renew the ceasefire (McGovern 2014). President Putin would weigh in on the matter, stating:

> *Unfortunately, President Poroshenko has resolved to resume military action, and we failed – when I say "we," I mean my colleagues in Europe and myself – we failed to convince him that*

> *the road to a secure, stable, and inviolable peace cannot lie through war. (McGovern 2014)*

It is odd in the extreme that, while President Putin and Secretary Lavrov had pressed continually for peace, ceasefires, and an end to the Ukrainian civil war during this time, the West and Western media continued to portray Russia and President Putin as the aggressor and to level sanctions. The US role, however, which had been to push the coup-installed government and then Poroshenko's government to war against its own people, was ignored almost completely by the mainstream media. Of this, Secretary Lavrov on Russian TV had the following to say: "Peace within the warring country [Ukraine] would be more likely if negotiations were left to Russia and Europe," adding, "Our American colleagues… according to a lot of evidence, still favor pushing the Ukrainian leadership towards the path of confrontation" (McGovern 2014). Needless to say, this speech, which spoke to US aggression in the pursuit of reengaging war, was not a speech that found its way into the Western mainstream media.

August. By the end of July and early August the momentum of the war began to shift dramatically. The militia, though decidedly smaller in number and poorly armed, began to rout the Ukrainian army at nearly every battle. There is some evidence that the turning point of the Ukrainian civil war came in the town of Ilovaisk, where the Ukrainian troops suffered a "disastrous defeat at the hands of the Novorossiyan forces" (Petro 2014).

> *The exact details of what went wrong have not been made public. According to Semen Semenchenko—the commander of the*

> volunteer "Donbas" battalion that led the assault on Ilovaisk—after having taken the city center, Ukrainian forces were surrounded by the rebels and totally cut off. Russian media sources suggest that as many as 7,000 Ukrainian soldiers were trapped, along with several hundreds of military vehicles. (Petro 2014)

It was a scenario repeated time and time again by the Novorossiyan forces. As the Ukrainian army advanced, the Novorossiyan forces retreated, only to later strategically surround Ukrainian forces, creating what is known as a "cauldron," in which the Ukrainian forces were totally cut off. The Novorossiyan forces then systematically routed or destroyed the Ukrainian brigades (Ukrainian 79th Airborne Brigade, 72nd Brigade, 51st Brigade, 30th Brigade, 24th Brigade) and captured their weapons. The weapons captures would further the ability of Novorossiyan forces to defend themselves and eventually to go on the attack.

In terms of the number of casualties:

> It is likely that between 8,000 to 12,000 Ukrainian troops were killed in a period of around 2 months from 5th July 2014 until the announcement of the ceasefire on 5th September 2014. If so this would mean the Ukraine was losing during this period men at a rate of roughly 129 to 190 a day. Nothing comparable has happened in Europe since the German surrender on 9th May 1945. (Mercouris 2014)

Other reports estimate total Ukrainian troop casualties as high as 32,692 (20,274 dead and wounded; 12,418 POWs, deserters, missing).

By late August, the Ukrainian army, as a result of mounting desertions and massive battlefield losses, was in full retreat. The Novorossiyan army was now on the offensive and had advanced on the town of Mariupol, long held by the Ukrainian army (Saker 2014). The Novorossiyan army encircled Mariupol, cut off its supply routes, and placed it under siege. President Poroshenko's promise of a military victory in "hours" was is in complete shambles as his numerically superior and more heavily-equipped army was being daily routed by Novorossiyan forces. It was this turn of events that finally brought Poroshenko to the negotiating table, a decision that had long been encouraged by Russian, French, and German diplomats.

On **September 5, 2014**, a ceasefire was signed between Ukrainian government representatives and Eastern Ukraine's Novorossiyans. The Novorossiyan forces halted their assault on a surrounded Mariupol. The Ukrainian forces organized what had been a haphazard retreat on virtually all fronts and a demilitarized zone was set up between the factions.

In early September, after the ceasefire had commenced, an assessment of the casualties was summarily provided by the United Nations, which estimated that:

> Over 2,249 people have been killed so far and more than 6,033 wounded in the fighting in eastern Ukraine. The number of internally displaced Ukrainians has reached 190,000, with another 207,000 finding refuge in Russia, the UN said. (RT 2014)

Currently the ceasefire holds (with sporadic and continued bouts of shelling by the Ukrainian army) and there has been speculation that Poroshenko may be using the ceasefire to regroup. There has also been speculation that, should the civil war reengage, the probability of World War III would increase dramatically (Cohen 2014).

This is, of course, the fate the Crimean people escaped when they decided to "annul the Soviet decision to lump them into Ukraine" and then voted overwhelmingly to rejoin Russia (Orlov 2014). The Crimean referendum, what the West deemed an invasion, was, perhaps, the first bloodless *invasion* (not a single bullet being fired, nor a single death, a single building destroyed, bombed or pock-marked) ever witnessed by the West, whose invasions have been of a decidedly different nature.

THE END GAME

> *Globalist elites design their policies according to the classical maxim of divide et impera [divide and rule], yet its esoteric corollary is solve et coagula [concentrate and dissolve] the alchemical process applied to entire societies. Behind inane sloganeering on freedom, democracy, and human rights lies a relentless desire to destroy. Sovereignty must be ended, sex and the family distorted unto grotesquery, and God usurped by Mammon. The nation – the great extended family—must be annihilated. What the Brave New World needs are neither Russians nor Ukrainians, but demographic biomass engineered for exploitation.*
>
> —Mark Hackard, Oriental Review, 19 June, 2014

The past twenty years, as previously discussed, have seen the West and its military adjunct, NATO, seeking to execute the Grand Chessboard strategy in an attempt to encircle and then isolate Russia. The endgame is to render it a vassal state to the

West's New World Order, to extract its various resources for consumption by Western multinationals and oligarchs, and to spread the New World Order to every nation, city, town, and hamlet across the world.

Ukraine has always been considered by Neoliberals and Neocons alike, the defining piece of the Grand Chessboard strategy.

The strategic targets and interests identified by the West in relation to the Ukraine are outlined below.

MILITARY

Several of the military objectives long associated with shifting the Ukraine into the Western geostrategic orbit include:

- The expansion of NATO and the continued military encirclement of Russia with a ring of bases stretching from the Ukraine and tying those to the Baltic states and the Balkans and from Turkey to the Caucasus (Petras 2014)
- The eviction of Russia from its centuries-long military and naval base in the Crimea and the subsequent leasing of that base to NATO
- The conversion of Ukraine into a springboard for penetrating southern Russia and the Caucasus; a forward position to politically manage and support liberal pro-NATO parties and NGOs within Russia (Petras 2014)

- The termination, retooling, and evisceration of Ukrainian factories purposed with supplying key sectors of the Russian military (Petras 2014)

And, perhaps, the most significant reason militarily for what now transpires in Ukraine (and around the world), as summed up by Peter Koenig in his article, "Civilization of the Neocons":

Wars must go on. The US neoliberal economy depends on them. The war machine and its ramifications contribute more than 50% to the US GDP. Without wars, the country would collapse. All peace talks and negotiations initiated or feigned by Washington are fake, a deception, propaganda for the goodness of the naked emperor. Kudos for the exceptional nation. World peace would mean a black hole for the United States, demise. (Koenig 2014)

ECONOMIC

The economic objectives for the West associated with the Ukraine are varied and many, as Western *rescue* events are generally predicated on enriching numerous factions (energy companies, the military-industrial complex, other corporate multinationals, banking concerns, foreign policy objectives of aligned countries, geopolitical enrichment, etc.).

However, another parallel facet of the Chessboard Strategy regarding Russia's military isolation is its economic isolation from the world, witnessed by successive sanctions leveled by Western countries.

Economically, what might be considered a rather brazen and telling geopolitical enrichment maneuver, heavily seasoned with nepotism, is the appointment of Hunter Biden, son of Vice President Joe Biden, to Burisma Holdings, Ukraine's largest private gas producer, on May 13, 2014 (Messayan 2014). Mr.Biden, however, will not be lonely as he will be joined by Devon Archer, the chair of the support committee for the 2004 presidential campaign of current Secretary of State John Kerry (Messayan 2014).

Also missing entirely from the Western narrative was one of the first official acts of welcoming Ukraine into the Western sphere of influence, the stealth removal of thirty-three tons of Ukraine's gold reserves (Kranzier 2014). Other financial objectives include:

- Control (and or cessation) of the energy transport corridor which crosses Ukraine and links oil and natural gas reserves from the Caspian basin to European markets
- Sabotage of overall trade relations between Europe and Russia, in order to disempower both Europe and Russia
- A $10 billion shale gas deal with Chevron, that would allow Chevron to explore the Olesky deposit in western Ukraine that Kiev estimates holds 2.98 trillion cubic meters of gas (Ahmed 2014) *(Chevron has announced in December that it will be pulling out of this deal)*
- An IMF Austerity plan which will facilitate the "financial robbery of public goods, reduction of pensions, minimum wages, social services, privatization of education and health, expropriation

and privatization of natural resources by foreign corporations" (Koenig 2015)

As Naomi Klein points out in her book *The Shock Doctrine*, the West has made quite a profitable business out of destroying other nation-states, privatizing resources, stripping assets, and then "attempting to rebuild" the destroyed infrastructure while murdering millions, in the process, to feed, what can only be labelled, sociopathic avarice. To date, it has been a very profitable gambit.

However, US *exceptionalism* may yet be imperiled, as Damoclesian swords fall earthward toward Neocons, Neoliberals, and us all. As summed up by Mr. Orlov (2014):

> *...the US is a dead man walking: unless it can continue rolling over trillions of dollars in short-term debt every month at record-low interest rates, it won't be able to pay the interest on its debt or its bills. Good-bye, welfare state, hello riots. Good-bye military contractors and federal law enforcement, hello mayhem and open borders. (Orlov 2014)*

So great is the voraciousness among the world's 1 percent for money and power that they now appear to imperil the world and themselves by the serial ruination of nation-states, planned chaos, and the subsequent economic maelstrom that even now continues to build in the Ukraine.

PLANNED CHAOS

> *In order to stop, or at least forestall this downward slide into financial/economic/political oblivion, the US must move quickly to undermine every competing economy in the world through whatever means it has left at its disposal, be it a bombing*

> *campaign, a revolution or a pandemic (although this last one can be a bit hard to keep under control). Russia is an obvious target, because it is the only country in the world that has had the gumption to actually show international leadership in confronting the US and wrestling it down; therefore, Russia must be punished first, to keep the others in line.*
>
> —Dmitri Orlov, Author Reinventing Collapse

Another strategic aspect of the Western endgame and, in particular, the US's endgame in the twenty-first century (and, no doubt, long before) is the policy objective of *planned chaos*. It is a policy inextricably linked to the debt situation in the US, which some believe equals no less than $220 trillion dollars and is mathematically incapable of being paid down (Lawler 2012). Thus, it is imperative to stave off the final reckoning, the any-second-now *margin call*, by systematically destroying economically viable nations and their economic systems, plundering any and all assets (to pay the pushers of banking), and then instilling planned chaos to keep said nations and their economic systems perpetually nonviable (Afghanistan, Iraq, Libya, Syria, Somalia, Yemen, etc.).

And in the case of rising countries that are competitive and also not bereft of teeth (an actual military—air force, navy, special forces, medium-/long-range ballistic missiles, associated attack craft, and other viable means of defense) warfare is waged via economic sanctions, color revolutions, military encirclement, extensive propaganda campaigns, and various other isolation mechanisms.

And though "terrorism," "freedom," "democracy," and the "Right to Protect (R2P)" have long served as the cover story for US imperialism/adventurism/gangsterism abroad, planned chaos is consistently the desired end result. In this scenario, the least chaotic and most heavily armed nation is king; and, of course, able to extort, plunder, and propagandize at will.

In other words, chaos seems to provide the heavily armed, sclerotic, and declining US empire with the means to appear dominant among economically crippled nations. It is this selfsame policy that allows the US to strategically pillage, asset strip, "color revolutionize," terrorize, and pauperize via economic warfare as waged by the banking programs of the IMF and World Bank. And their victims are legion. The Ukraine currently serves as testament to the policy objective of planned chaos as witnessed by asset pillage (gold reserves appropriation), wanton death and destruction, ethnic and ideological division (divide and conquer), lickety-split pauperization (IMF Austerity Plans), and war—chaos. Of course, the icing on the cake for the US is that the chaos is all happening on Russia's border.

CHAPTER 6

PROPAGANDA & UKRAINE—AMERICAN STYLE

> *Consider the world of mainstream journalists, in particular TV news anchors. There we have a world with echoes of 1984, where what is said must conform to the party line. Any thoughtcrime—such as an anchor commenting onscreen that he doesn't buy the official story of 9/11, or he thinks Russia isn't an aggressor—would be quickly punished by the equivalent of death—expulsion from the world of journalism. Thus for the majority of the population we have a tightly controlled, two-tier, mind-control regime. The thoughtcrime dynamic governs what the media says, and the conspiracy-theory dynamic immunizes people against other views. For the majority, the party line (either CNN or FOX) is "truth" as in Orwell's world, but without the need for Big Brother's extreme methods.*
>
> —Richard K. Moore, *Mind Control: Orwell, Huxley, and Today's Reality*

Prior to discussing the propaganda campaign now being waged by the Western mainstream media with regard to the Ukraine, it is necessary to understand what mainstream media is and the optic by which it both views and reports the news.

The mainstream media's overlord is corporate America. A total of five corporate giants, Time Warner, Disney, Murdoch's News Corporation, Bertelsmann of Germany, and Viacom (formerly CBS), control 90% of what is watched, listened to, or read.

The upshot of the above is that if a story, facts, forensic analysis, or the truth, is bad for business—whether business is selling bombs, fighter jets, advanced weaponry (and thus war) or selling advertising (and all the attendant products) — then truth will be victim number one. The truth has been buried so deeply across the corporate media landscape that the current state of affairs has been deemed a "Truth Emergency" (Phillips and Huff 2010).

As reported by Peter Phillips and Micky Huff (2010) of Project Censored with regard to the Truth Emergency:

> *In the United States today, the rift between reality and reporting has peaked. There is no longer a credibility gap, but rather a literal Truth Emergency in which the most important information affecting people is concealed from view. (Phillips, Huff 2010)*

Thus the overarching goal of the various corporate, media, and political *elite* is to control the narrative of any given topic, situation, and desired result via censorship and propaganda. As a result, a war for resources, regime change, power projection, plunder, and privatization (Iraq), will have a well-defined propaganda and censorship campaign (WMDs, democracy, etc.) to achieve its unstated goals and hide its true purpose via a mountain of lies. The current campaign *du jour* brings us to the Ukraine.

Over the course of the past several months, with regard to Ukraine, one is continually reminded of the run up to the Iraq war. The glaring lack of actual un-embedded reporters, the absence of substantiated facts or forensic data: the unabashed parroting of White House, State Department, and intelligence agency talking points, and the non-stop parade of retired Generals across the mainstream news circuit, has been *déjà vu* all over again.

And when war finally did come to Iraq, the various talking points that had been disseminated by the White House,

State Department, and subsequently TV anchors, one by one, were exposed for the baseless lies that they were.

The primary and much celebrated cause for going to war with Iraq, Weapons of Mass Destruction (WMDs), became the first victim as the white-hot projectiles of facts on the ground exploded that canard. The thrilling performance of the secretary of state brandishing a vile of soap powder in the UN Assembly and declaring with absolute certainty that Saddam Hussein, Hitler 9.0, had chemical and nuclear weapons was, in fact, a lie. A lie celebrated at the time by literally every news anchor, pundit, radio commentator, newspaper, and shock jock in America's mainstream media.

The inevitability of a mushroom cloud rising over some part of the American landscape as launched by Saddam Hussein, Hitler 9.0, as told in the form of a campfire horror story by Bush, Rice, Cheney, Blair et al., was, in fact, the mother of all lies. As were the roving chemical weapons factories, installed within minivans and motorhomes, and the air conditioned, vacation bunkers with satellite TV, shopping malls, and all-you-can-eat cafeterias that were *supposedly* buried deep within the Afghan mountains.

The experts of the day informed us that the Iraq war would cost us a nifty $50 billion (actually upwards of $3 trillion) and we the people, who ultimately pay for all wars against our will, would be paid back by the revenues from Iraqi oil. Lies, again, that had been parroted non-stop by the mainstream media and, in some cases, so effectively that devotees of certain news networks to this day believe that WMDs were, indeed, found in Iraq. And the payback from Iraqi oil reserves? Well, if you remember the record profits of the various oil companies during that time, you will know exactly who got paid back.

As the lies quickly unraveled, there was always a ready source of new lies—freedom and democracy, women's rights, etc. The various freedoms would, of course, be instituted at the barrel of a gun, attack helicopters, F-16s, depleted uranium munitions, cruise missiles, predator drones, predawn home invasions, and curfews. It appears that Saddam Hussein's fault was not imposing democracy forcefully enough upon the citizens of Iraq.

A little more than a decade from the onset of the war in Iraq, the democracy graft has not only failed to take hold, it has violently and, perhaps, terminally infected the host (planned chaos).

Now, as the crisis in the Ukraine unfolds and the mainstream media's modus operandi becomes eerily reminiscent of its performance in the Iraq war, two questions arise. Have the media learned anything from "carrying water" for the White House and the State Department? Or is Pravda on the Potomac a more fitting descriptor for the US mainstream media of today?

For the past several months the mainstream media has again marched in lockstep with Official Government Sources (White House, State Department, Pentagon, etc.) with regard to the demonization of Russian President Vladimir Putin (the new Hitler 10.0), Russian "meddling" and "aggression," and Putin's vile intentions to reconquer the world or, at least, Western Europe.

The White House, State Department, and their attendant spokespeople, all of whom have professed to mountains of evidence to substantiate their claims, have, to date, relied exclusively on social media. Social media, in the form of Facebook and Youtube clips, has been offered up as "common sense" verifiable proof to document Russian troop movements, missile launches, artillery fire, and Russian Special Forces penetration. What need then is there for sixteen intelligence agencies with $100 billion plus budgets?

Save for a comedy, any serious movie script that had the White House and State Department Officials offering up social media as an intelligence gathering apparatus, capable of providing evidence in a war zone, would be regarded as amateurish and laughable, at best. Yet with the seriousness of a guilty child standing beside a broken vase and lying to her parents, saying that she "didn't do it," government spokespersons have offered up as definitive proof Facebook pictures and Youtube videos, while exclaiming, "Duh, it's like, common sense."

A clip from a March 6, 2014 CNN interview, pitted Christiane Amanpour, CNN "investigative" reporter and Wolf Blitzer, CNN news anchor, against Professor of Russian Studies, Stephen Cohen, a noted scholar and author of numerous books on Russia since the Bolshevik Revolution. Professor Cohen had, ostensibly, been invited on Wolf Blitzer's CNN show to discuss the situation unfolding in the Ukraine.

Ms. Amanpour, completely bereft of evidence and facts, lectured and berated Professor Cohen with regard to what was transpiring in the Ukraine. She then went on to predict the intentions of the newly coup-installed, unelected government in Kiev regarding Russia's Black Sea Fleet and what she believed the intentions of Putin—whom she openly called a thug—to be. Ms. Amanpour blamed Russia for "trumping up" Crimea's referendum to join Russia, as they were not (yet) being attacked by Kiev. She further berated the entirety of the Russian media claiming that they were the party responsible for the hate speech, nationalistic rhetoric, and incitement to war.

In the 50 seconds Professor Cohen was given to put his point forward, he spoke clearly to the facts on the ground by stating:

> *The extremism didn't come from Russia. It was coming from Western Ukraine. There's a small but resolute and determined right-wing nationalist movement in Ukraine. It's quasi-fascist, and it is dictating terms to the parliament in Kiev which is not legitimate in law, international or constitutional. This parliament which is a rump parliament, because they banned the two majority parties that represented the East and have been passing anti-Russian legislation. They banned the use of Russian as an official language. It isn't Russia that's been spewing this ideological destabilizing message. It's been coming from the West. And here the worst part is that has been—that hatred has been supported by Washington and Brussels in embracing this west Ukrainian movement. That will—that must stop. (CNN 2014)*

Given less than a minute to respond to Ms. Amanpour's prolonged attack, Mr. Blitzer interrupts Professor Cohen, to inform him and Ms. Amanpour that the time is up. However, for the remaining portion of the show, almost double the time awarded to Professor Cohen, Mr. Blitzer and Ms. Amanpour continue their attack on Professor Cohen's position, claiming that Nazis and Anti-Semites are not an integral part of the new Kiev government. Ms. Amanpour qualifies the presence of Nazis in Kiev's government as "the Russian position," despite clear and extensively corroborated evidence from multiple sources—*Telelgraph* (UK), NBC, *The Guardian* (UK), Huffington Post, BBC, MSNBC—to the contrary.

Perhaps if Ms. Amanpour were to actually report on the happenings in Donetsk, Lugansk, and other areas in the east of Ukraine, emotions and gut-feelings would be underpinned by something more closely resembling the truth. Her reporting might even speak to the fact that the Svoboda Party and the Right Sector are, indeed, fascist organizations. Further, investigative reporting would uncover the fact that these parties have intimidated, threatened, beat up, tortured, and murdered various members of the state parliament, and may well be responsible for the deaths of 40 Ukrainians in Odessa alone. Perhaps Ms. Amanpour would also discover, with a bit of diligent research (an internet search), that former Ukrainian Presidential candidate Yulia Tymoshenko had professed in a leaked conversation, "It's about time we grab our guns and go kill those damn Russians together with their leader" and that "they [the Russians] must be killed with nuclear weapons." Perhaps these were pieces of news that escaped the self-acclaimed *investigative* reporting skills of Ms. Amanpour.

Of course, whether Ms. Amanpour knew it or not, her talking points were the exact same talking points that had been consistently broadcast by White House and State Department officials regarding the Ukraine.

A short time later, Professor Cohen appeared with John Mearshiemer on an April 28, 2014 episode of *CrossTalk*, a current affairs program on Russia Today (RT), a state-sponsored Russian television channel. The program featured intelligent discussion, historical perspective, insight, real politick, a complete lack of ad hominem attacks (no "thugs" here), and irrational grandstanding. It appears that American intellectuals from Professor Cohen and Mearchiemer to Noam Chomsky and other noted scholars, exiled from mainstream western media, have found an alternative and ostensibly more free press, of all places, on Russian TV.

In a case that can best be described as classic psychological projection, Secretary of State John Kerry called

RT "a state-sponsored propaganda bullhorn." Of course, the lockstep narrative of the American mainstream media, which continually echoes the talking points of Secretary Kerry, his State Department minions, and the White House, must represent to Secretary Kerry the "free press." Needless to say, mainstream media is doing its best to accept without question or actual reporting the narrative fed to them by "official government sources."

PROPAGANDA IN UKRAINE

> *In Washington DC, one feels the rarefied air of a Himalayan peak. Seen from the grandiose palaces of the administration, where the fate of the world is decided, foreign people look small, primitive and largely irrelevant. Here and there some real experts are tucked away, but nobody really consults them.*
>
> —Uri Avnery

Imagine, if you will, the president of the United States addressing US citizens and conveying horror stories of some distant, terrifying threat, anathema to freedom, democracy, and the American way. Ostensibly, the innocent God-fearing subjects of this land are being chemically gassed (often made available from the West), bombed, and massacred and are under the foot of some maniacal madmen who is up for the year's Hitler Award.

The president then further laments that "we (the US) are a peace-loving nation and while we abhor violence—order and democracy must be (violently) implemented/restored and the innocent rescued (killed, uncounted, and forced to emigrate)."

In quick order the war machine is geared up, the coalition of the willing (bought, bribed, coerced, threatened) is assembled, and the bombs and missiles—cruise, smart, bunker-buster, DU, cluster, phosphorous, neutron—are unleashed. Unfortunately, of course, the bombs are unable to discern the innocent, poor, terrorized masses from the maniacal madmen, and tens to hundreds of thousands to millions of those we intended to *free* are, indeed, *liberated* from their mortal coils. In fact, the US tends to be much more efficient at this than the long line of maniacal madmen yearly auditioning for the year's Hitler Award.

In the former Yugoslavia, the *script* we were treated to, as described by Caleb Maupin (2014), was the following:

> *Bill Clinton claimed to be stopping "mass rapes" and "concentration camps." After the smoke had cleared, and thousands had been killed, the truth came out. The United Nations admitted that no "genocide" had taken place. The talk of mass rapes and concentration camps had been hype. (Maupin 2014)*

There is, however, an interesting irony that is seemingly ever-present in "so-called" endeavors launched by the US. Again, as stated by Maupin (2014):

> *While the alleged crimes used to justify destroying Serbia had been exaggerated, the crimes of the US-funded Kosovo Liberation Army were very real. The Balkans have never recovered from the bombing and destruction and the funding of ethnic hate groups. The "rescue mission" resulted in deeper misery than ever before.*

The script for Libya was, of course, the same—planned chaos, with a few names substituted here and there:

> *Obama told horror stories about Gaddafi. As US-backed insurgents were defeated on the battlefield, the US and NATO unleashed a horrific bombing campaign. Now Libya, once the wealthiest country on the African continent, is in ruin. The country has been destroyed, and rival factions battle for power surrounded by poverty. (Maupin 2014)*

And Syria, again with a name change here and there and a few of the *reasons* for the US intervention recycled from the previous heroic mission:

> *In Syria, propaganda about alleged crimes by President Bashar Assad have been used to justify western support for an ugly civil war. Syria had been one of the more prosperous and peaceful countries of the region, but the US and its allies continue to funnel money to armed terrorists. A war that would have ended in a few months has dragged on for four years, with nearly 150,000 dead, and millions forced to become refugees. (Maupin 2014)*

And in the Ukraine, where the various justifications for freedom, democracy, and EU candidacy have again been recycled, a new candidate for the Hitler Award is developed by specious claims and outright propaganda.

When Edward Herman, Professor Emeritus of MIT and expert on mass media and propaganda, was asked about what was missing in the US mainstream media's news coverage of Ukraine, his response was:

> *What is missing, first of all, is a minimum of objectivity. The media are functioning more than ever as a propaganda machine for the State Department. One thing missing—and being suppressed —is the important role of neo-Nazi elements both in the Kiev government and in the forces they have fielded in their war against East Ukraine. The media are eager to find Russians in Ukraine,*

but will not even recognize neo-fascists staring them in the face, but working on our side. (Falcone 2014)

Addressed below are a number of critical points regarding Western propaganda, which range from the Maidan revolt to the claims of Russian aggression to the Crimea "Invasion" to Malaysian flight MH17.

PEACEFUL VIOLENCE ON THE MAIDAN

The US-based Occupy Movement, by and large a peaceful movement, which objected to the growing disparity between the 1 percent and everyone else and the $22 trillion bailout of the "Banksters " was violently crushed, via police raids, in the US. Its analogue in the UK, the 2010 anti-austerity and student protests, was also violently dealt with by the British authorities (Melendez 2013). However, had the violence of these protests risen to the level of the Maidan — fire-bombing buildings and policemen, relentlessly attacking the security forces with Molotov cocktails, dangerous homemade implements and guns, and destroying national monuments — the Western response would have been the overwhelming use of deadly force (consider the West Philadelphia Bombing, Waco, Ferguson).

Michael Hudson (2014), distinguished research professor of economics at the University of Missouri — Kansas City, describes how the US treated its peaceful protestors:

Remember how brutally US dispersed the Occupy Movement and destroyed their camps in many US cities? Remember that policeman who was going in circles calmly spraying with a very powerful pepper spray the defenceless, sitting on the ground, students in California? All those students could do was to cover their faces and try to protect their lungs and eyes from damage. (Hudson 2014)

Yet, the West demanded that President Yanukovych deal peacefully with the violent and armed protestors on the Maidan (Meyssan 2014). Other violent actions of the Maidan groups known to be associated with neo-Nazi organizations (Trident, White Hammer, Right Sector, etc.) included the violent seizure and setting ablaze of homes, the injuring of nearly 200 security officers, and numerous human rights violations. Yet, Yanukovych was threatened with violent retaliatory action, "all cards on the table," should he seek to utilize Western methods for dealing with armed and violent protestors.

President Yanukovych's reply is described below by Michael Hudson (2014), and can be viewed via raw videos posted to YouTube:

> *Berkut [Ukrainian Police] was given a new order not to respond, but just stand there – per reports – WITHOUT DEFENDING THEMSELVES, while their eyes were being poked at with metal spears, while they were burned with Molotov cocktails, taken hostage, and shot. (Note, I am not the biggest fan of police in any country, but the truth is glaring.) This order was given to them by Ukrainian President Yanukovych in response to the threat of sanctions by the EU and US if Yanukovych tried to restore order in the country he was supposed to govern. (Hudson 2014)*

The violence by the protestors continued as buildings were seized and looted. Several of the buildings destroyed by the *peaceful* Maidan protestors were the Kiev, Lviv, Ternopil and Rivne City-State Administration Buildings, the Lviv Interior

Ministry and four Central District Police Departments (looted of nearly 1,300 firearms). The Ministry of Internal Affairs, the Ministry of Health, the Central House of Officers, the House of Trade Unions, and the Lviv home of Party Regions deputy, A. Herman were all set ablaze.

Numerous human rights abuses took place in the Party of Regions building that was taken over by Right Sektor militants of the Maidan. As mentioned previously, two men were brutally murdered in the Party of Regions building.

Other quite horrific acts of the Maidan militants were the public torture of the governor of the Volyn Regional State Administration, A. Bashkalenko; the firing at tour buses, and a particularly brutal event against Anti-Maidan protestors:

> *Near the town of Korsun-Shevchenkovsky (Cherkassy region), several buses with passengers, who were returning to Crimea from protests against European integration at St. Michael's Square in Kiev, were fired upon and stopped at the barricades, where the flags of the UPA, the Udar (Strike) party, and AUU Svoboda were flying. The people, both men and women, were dragged out of the buses through a corridor of militants who beat them with bats and entrenching shovels. Then the passengers were knocked down in a heap on the roadside, doused with gasoline, and threatened to be set on fire. According to witnesses, militants from the crowd shouted: "Just wait, we're going to come and get you in Crimea. We are going to stab you and shoot you, that is, those of you who we haven't already beaten to a pulp and shot up yet." After that, many Crimeans were forced to take off their shoes for the needs of Maidan soldiers, and they were driven around the buses like cattle and forced to pick up the broken glass. The humiliation and abuse continued for several hours. There were casualties among the victims. Most of the buses were burned. (Voltaire 2014)*

Another severe human rights violation undertaken by the Right Sektor militants of the Maidan, deemed freedom fighters by the West, was the torture of the first secretary of Lviv's Communist Party, R. Vasilko. According to the Voltaire White Paper:

> *Euromaidan supporters detained, illegally sentenced and tortured the first secretary of the city committee of the Communist Party of Lviv R. Vasilko. According to eyewitnesses, he had needles pushed under fingernails, his right lung pierced, three ribs, nose, and facial bones broken. The rioters also threatened to destroy his family. After the severe torture, R. Vasilko was taken to hospital, where the threats continued. Eventually, Vasilko had to flee Ukraine with the help of his relatives. (Voltaire 2014)*

Yet, the West turned a blind eye to these extremely violent acts and the various human rights abuses of the Maidan militias, while repeatedly saluting their actions and referring to them as "freedom fighters."

However, the most violent acts perpetrated, which now appear to also be linked to the Maidan militia, were the sniper attacks that took place in late February of 2014.

THE MAIDAN SNIPERS

On Thursday, February 20, 2014, the demonstration in Kiev's Maidan Square would become dramatically more violent. The violence resulted in the combined deaths of nearly 100 protestors and police officers and death threats against President Yanukovych, who would soon flee the country for fear of his life.

The tragic day began as the Maidan demonstrators made their approach to the government building, along Institute Street, in small coordinated groups. Their goal was to occupy the building. However, before they could reach the building, sniper fire began to rain down upon them from the roofs of nearby buildings, striking both Maidan protestors as well as the security police. When the sniper fire ended, approximately 94 people, policemen and protestors, had been murdered.

The massacre would lead to a public ultimatum issued from a Maidan security-forces commander, who called for President Yanukovych to resign by 10:00am on February 21 or face an armed assault (Katchanovski 2014). On February 23, the democratically elected president of Ukraine, Viktor Yanukovych, fled the same day for fear of his life.

The charges issued against President Yanukovych were leveled without evidence, forensic data, or any kind of a thorough investigation to ascertain his guilt or innocence. The coup-installed government, which was immediately recognized by the US as a legitimate governing body, had "democratically" adjudged President Yanukovych guilty until proven innocent.

However, actual evidence was about to rear its ugly, contravening head, and that evidence pointed in an entirely different direction.

The evidence from Maidan eyewitnesses, police snipers, TV news crews, and Maidan doctors rendered dubious the claims made by Maidan leaders that the Yanukovych government was responsible for the sniper attacks. And further actions—the loss of evidence, doctored evidence, and the failure to follow incriminating leads also pointed to possible Maidan involvement. Additionally, the fact that no Right Sektor members, commanders, etc. were targeted, killed, or wounded, despite their broad visibility (on a raised stage) is yet another piece of circumstantial evidence suggesting an altogether different responsible party.

A report entitled, "The Snipers Massacre on the Maidain in Ukraine," by Dr. Ivan Katchanovski, School of Political Studies and Department of Communication at the University of Ottawa, has also identified alternative parties responsible for the massacre.

The explanation to date as provided by the West, its attendant media, and the coup-installed Ukrainian government, is that "the massacre was perpetrated by government snipers on a Yanukovych order" (Katchanovski 2014). However, Professor Katchanovski (2014) states clearly that:

> ...analysis of a large amount of evidence in this study suggests that certain elements of the Maidan opposition, including its extremist far right wing, were involved in this massacre in order to seize power and that the government investigation was falsified for this reason. (Katchanovski 2014)

Critically important was the fact that the buildings from which the sniper fire came—the Trade Union building, the Kozatsky Hotel, the Hotel Ukraina, the October Palace, the Main Post Office building, and the Philharmonic Hall were all under the control of Maidan security forces.

A German *Sixty-Minutes*-type news program, *ADR Monitor*, televised a report on April 10, 2014, corroborating the information concerning the direction of the sniper fire via a series of interviews. The *ADR Monitor* reporter interviewed the former head of Ukraine's security services, Major General Aleksandr Yakimenko; a Maidan protestor named Mikola, who was on Institute Street the day of the sniper attacks; an amateur radio enthusiast who recorded conversations between the government snipers; and Oleksandr Lisowoi, a doctor from Hospital No. 6 in Kiev. Additionally, the *ADR Monitor* team, with the help of a weapons specialist, undertook its own forensic investigation.

Aleksandr Yakimenko, a witness to the Maidan shootings, had been put on the Maidan hit list while he was still in office as Ukraine Chief of Security. As Mr. Yakimenko recalls with regard to the sniper shootings:

> *First shots were fired from the Philharmonic building. Maidan Commandant Parubiy was in charge of the building. On February 20, this building was used as a base by the snipers and people with automatic weapons. They basically covered those who were attacking the demoralized policemen running in panic, hunted down like animals. They were followed by armed people with different kinds of weapons. At that point, somebody opened fire at those who attacked the police, and some of them were killed. All this fire was coming from the Philharmonic building. After this first round of fire, about 20 people came out of this building – this was witnessed by many. These people wore special combat clothes and carried sniper rifle cases, as well as AKMs with scopes. There were witnesses, and not just our operatives, but also Maidan activists from Svoboda, Right Sector, Batkivshchyna, and UDAR. (ADR Monitor 2014)*

Commandant Parubiy, as mentioned in Mr. Yakimenko's recollection, is the cofounder of the fascist Social National Party renamed Svoboda. The Philharmonic building had long been under Commandant Parubiy's control. Commandant Parubiy would subsequently become the top commander of the National Defense and Security Council for Ukraine (Becker 2014).

Mr. Yakimenko then recounts what happened immediately after the initial rounds of sniper shots were fired in to the crowd:

> *The snipers split into two groups—10 men each. The Security Service lost track of one of the groups. The other group took a position at the Ukraine hotel. Killings continued. In the beginning, when the shots were scattered, I was asked by Right Sector and Svoboda to mobilize a Special Forces unit and remove the snipers from the buildings. (ADR Monitor 2014)*

When Mr. Yakimenko was asked to mobilize a Special Forces unit to find the snipers, ironically, it would be Commandant Parubiy whose permission he would need before entering the Philharmonic building. Yakimenko's fear was that entering the building without the Commandant's permission would have left his team open to attack by Maidan self-defense forces that had taken up position in the back of the building. As Yakimenko explains:

> *Parubiy didn't give such permission. No weapons could be brought to Maidan without Parubiy's permission. Hand guns, rifles, scopes —he had to agree to all of that. We had some intel about discharged Ukrainian army special forces participating in those activities. Some reports claimed that these were fighters from former Yugoslavia, as well as mercenaries from other countries. (ADR Monitor 2014)*

Yakimenko explained the pervasive foreign presence of State Department and CIA agents in the Security Services building and that they had been responsible for the coordination of weapons and money that fed the Maidan rioters. He then provided a window into the events, which ultimately led to Yanukovych's ouster, even as he conducted "good faith" negotiations with the Maidan opposition:

> *They [American Intelligence] sought to delay the negotiations and prevent the incumbent president from striking a deal with Russia and Russia from helping to prop up the social and economic order in Ukraine. After that they were planning to depose the president and integrate Ukraine into Europe, using Russian money. Who was troubled by the victory of the EU and the pro-integration forces? Only the US. It was the only country concerned over a possible alliance of Europe, Russia and Ukraine. The Customs Union and the connection between Russia and Ukraine did not sit well with their plans, either. (ADR Monitor 2014)*

Mikola, a Maidan activist, participated in the demonstrations on February 20 and is pictured in *ADR* footage taking sniper fire like other Maidan protestors. In Mikola's words, "Yes, on the twentieth, we were shot at from behind, from the Hotel Ukraina, from the eighth or ninth floor" (ADR Monitor 2014).

On February 20, an amateur radio operator recorded the conversations between President Yanukovych's snipers, who were trying to identify the *other* snipers. As detailed in the *ADR Monitor* program the radio traffic between Yanukovych's snipers show them discussing the fact that someone is shooting at unarmed people (ADR Monitor 2014). The taped conversation between Yanukovych's snipers follows below:

1st government sniper: Hey guys, you over there, to the right from the Hotel Ukraina.

2nd government sniper: Who shot? Our people do not shoot at unarmed people.

1st sniper: Guys, there sits a spotter aiming at me. Who is he aiming at there – in the corner? Look!

2nd sniper: On the roof of the yellow building. On top of the cinema, on top of the cinema.

1st sniper: Someone has shot him. But it wasn't us.

2nd sniper: Miron, Miron, there are even more snipers? And who are they? (ADR Monitor 2014)

To date, the snipers potentially responsible for the massacre have not been identified or even tracked down, much less brought to justice.

Dr. Oleksandr Lisowoi, a doctor from Hospital No. 6 in Kiev, responsible for treating the various people, protestor, and police who were shot by the snipers. He confirmed the fact that, "the wounded we treated had the same type of bullet wounds, I am now speaking of the type of bullets that we have surgically removed from the bodies — they were identical" (ADR Monitor 2014).

The German reporter from *ADR Monitor*, with the help of an independent weapons specialist, then conducted his own investigation. Utilizing film footage from February 20, the *ADR Monitor* reporter and the weapons specialist determined that the direction of sniper fire, which had killed both protestors and police, had come from behind the protestors and not from the government's snipers that were positioned in front of the protestors. The weapons specialist, utilizing a device which emitted a green laser, traced the path of the fired bullets directly to the Hotel Ukraina. The Hotel Ukraina on the day of the sniper attacks was also under the control of the Maidan security forces.

Dr Katchanovski's (2014) report would corroborate the direction of the sniper shots as coming from behind the Maidan protestors, via the following eyewitness accounts:

- A Swedish neo-Nazi volunteer confirms that the police units on the Maidan were shot with live ammunition from the Conservatory and the Trade Union buildings before 9:00am

- Maidan eyewitnesses among the protesters said that organized groups from Lviv and Ivano-Frankivsk regions in Western Ukraine arrived on the Maidan and moved to the Music Conservatory on the night of the February 20, massacre, and that some of them were armed with rifles

- The head of the medical service of the Euromaidan and other medics reported that both protesters and the police were shot by similar ammunition, specifically 7.62mm caliber bullets and buckshot (pellets), and that they had similar types of wounds

On March 5, 2014, a recording of a telephone conversation between Estonian Foreign Minister Urmas Paet and EU High Representative for Foreign Affairs and Security Policy Catherine Ashton dated February 26, 2014, was released by unknown parties, to the internet. The leaked conversation corroborated the charge that Ukraine's coup-installed government was possibly behind the sniper shootings. The leaked recording reveals that Paet had received information from the chief Maidan doctor, Dr. Olga Bogomolets, who was deeply troubled by the results of her surgeries.

Dr. Bogomolets, formerly the personal physician to the Orange Revolution's first President, Viktor Yushchenko, and who had received an award from the CIA and the George Soros-funded Radio Liberty, had passionately urged her students to take part in the Euromaidan protest (Madsen 2014). Dr. Bogomolets had volunteered her medical services for the Maidan activists and, after the sniper shootings, performed surgery on the victims and examined the bodies. Dr. Bogomolets discovered upon extracting the snipers' bullets that the same bullets that had killed protestors had also killed police. Dr. Bogomolets conveyed to Paet that she believed Maidan elements were directly responsible for the sniper attacks and as the coup-installed government refused to follow up on the sniper attacks, she grew more suspicious.

The leaked conversation between Paet and Ashton had Paet conveying his concern about the snipers:

> *Paet: All the evidence shows that people who were killed by snipers from both sides, policemen and people from the streets, that they were the same snipers killing people from both sides. . . . Some photos that showed it is the same handwriting, the same type of bullets, and it is really disturbing that now the new coalition they don't want to investigate what exactly happened. So there is now stronger and stronger understanding that behind the snipers, it was not Yanukovych, but it was somebody from the new coalition.*
>
> *Ashton: "I think we do want to investigate. I mean, I didn't pick that up, that's interesting. Gosh.*

Paet: "It already discredit[s] this new coalition."

The leaked conversation was later confirmed by Estonian Foreign Minister Paet, but Ms. Ashton and other EU representatives have, to date, refused to comment.

Dr. Katchanovski's explanation for what seemed like irrational shootings on the Maidan, when viewed through the optics of *Cui Bono*, however, turn out to be quite rational. Dr. Katchanovski's (2014) observations were that:

- Snipers killed unarmed protestors and targeted foreign journalists but did not kill or shoot at Maidan Leaders, Maidan Self-Defense and Right Sektor headquarters or the Maidan spokespeople who were on stage and thus the most visible
- The police retreated as a result of the shootings
- President Yanukovych and his other top government officials fled Ukraine as a result of the shootings
- Maidan leaders, in fact, rose to power after the shootings
- The EU subsequently got its Association Agreement

Katchanovski (2014) concludes based upon the findings of his report:

> *The evidence indicates that an alliance of elements of the Maidan opposition and the far right was involved in the mass killing of both protesters and the police, while the involvement of the special police units in killing of some of the protesters cannot be entirely ruled out based on publicly available evidence. The new government that came to power largely as a result of the massacre falsified its investigation, while the Ukrainian media helped to misrepresent*

> the mass killing of the protesters and the police. The evidence indicates that the far right played a key role in the violent overthrow of the government in Ukraine. (Katchanovski 2014)

Russian Foreign Minister Sergei Lavrov also stated that Moscow had gathered evidence, that pointed to Ukraine's Right Sector and neo-Nazi organizations as the parties responsible for the sniper shootings on the Maidan, as well as numerous violent clashes that took place in Kiev. Further, Foreign Minister Lavrov stated that Moscow had made its findings known to its Western counterparts. Mr. Lavrov was quick to add, "I cannot say I'm 100 percent sure, but there are a slew of facts that indicate just as much. Of course, they should be double-checked."

The Russian authorities and members of parliament have also called for the EU to create a commission to investigate the killings on the Maidan and possible Ukrainian opposition involvement. Vitaly Churkin, Russia's UN envoy, further encouraged an investigation, calling on UN Deputy Secretary Jan Eliasson and Human Rights Commissioner Ivan Simonovic to persuade authorities in Kiev to conduct a thorough investigation.

As of the publication date of this book, the new Ukrainian government has conducted an investigation charging three members of the Ukrainian police force for the massacre with no evidence of their guilt. Further, the Ukrainian government has consistently failed to investigate Right Sector and Maidan security forces involvement, despite overwhelming evidence. Oddly enough, one of the accused Ukrainian police officers charged with the sniper shooting is missing one of his hands. Reuters has also questioned the investigation.

Additionally, the US, EU, and the United Nations have all failed to press Ukrainian authorities for a thorough investigation. To date, only the Russian authorities have continued to call for a thorough investigation of this tragic incident.

Nonetheless, evidence continues to mount that places responsibility for the massacre of nearly 100 people on Right Sektor and various Maidan security forces.

RUSSIAN AGGRESSION?

> *It is astounding that all the militarist hype surrounding the NATO conference, along with bombastic declarations of collective security and vows to [protect] "[NATO's] members in Eastern Europe," has been invoked with absolutely no credible proof, such as satellite images of Russian troop and tank movements, missile launches or aircraft incursions of Ukrainian territory. It's like policy is being made on the basis of fantasy and preconceptions.*
>
> —Finian Cunningham, Strategic Culture Foundation

Russian aggression? It is difficult, if not impossible to fathom a mainstream media anchor or foreign or domestic news correspondent not entirely under the spell of Western propaganda, who could utter the phrase "Russian aggression" without an iota of actual evidence not reliant upon social media.

In one of President Putin's yearly press conferences, he answered questions from a variety of the world's reporters. President Putin was bereft of a teleprompter or a secret earpiece sprouting from a black box *stealthily* attached to his back. It is a feat that no Western leader, in the modern era, appears to have replicated.

One of the questions fielded by President Putin concerned Russia's pursuit of aggressive policies. President Putin was quick to point out that not only was the US's military budget 10 times that of Russia's (Russia at $50 billion versus the US's at $575 billion), but that while Russia only had two military bases outside of its borders (Kyrgystan, Tajikistan), the US had as many as 1,000 military bases spread throughout the world (Hitchens 2014). Of course, President Putin might have also mentioned serial and continuing breaches by NATO of the 1997 NATO Russia Founding Act, wherein it was agreed that the "permanent stationing of substantial combat forces to Eastern and Central Europe would be avoided."

A further point with regard to Russia's "imperial ambitions" relative to NATO's would be Russia's peaceful ceding of control of over 180 million people and roughly 700,000 square miles of valuable territory since 1989. NATO, on the other hand, has gained control of over 120 million people in the lands ceded by Russia, and roughly 400,000 square miles since 1989 (Hitchens 2014). So with many opinions to the contrary abounding in the West, the fact is that Russia has withdrawn into Russia, while the West—US and NATO, have steadily and aggressively moved to the Russian border.

As writer and geopolitical researcher Tony Cartalucci (2014) sums up:

> *The term "Russian aggression" has been inundating headlines across the Western media and even graces the title of a US Senate bill introduce this year—S. 2277—Russian Aggression Prevention Act of 2014. But what "aggression" is the West*

referring to? A cursory look at Russian history over the past 500 years compared to say, Britain, France, or even America and its "Manifest Destiny," portrays Russia as a nation preoccupied within and along its borders, not in hegemonic, global expansion. The idea of far-flung former colonies is one unique to the British, French, Dutch, and Spanish. Even today geopolitical, socioeconomic, and even outright military intervention in these former colonies is exclusively the pursuit of the United States and Europe. (Cartalucci 2014)

In the twenty-first century, it is not Russia whose military bases can be found in 150 of the world's 200 nations (Russian bases can only be found in 2 countries). It is not the Russians who annually spend nearly one trillion dollars on defense (though it could be much more, given the various black budgets). It is not the Russians whose drones daily murder innocent men, women, children, the aged, wedding party and funeral attendees, or those who hide in bomb shelters. It is not the Russians who have serially invaded and destroyed nation-states thousands of miles from its borders, under some Orwellian pretense always found lacking an iota of truth or, simply, based upon a pack of lies. It is not the Russians who imprison and torture men, women, and children at black sites across the world and keep international citizens imprisoned for years with no evidence or trial. No, it is the US that is responsible and guilty in each of the aforementioned cases for its relentless, serial aggression abroad these past fifty years and for the deaths of countless millions. Russian aggression?

A 2013 Gallup poll administered to people in sixty-eight countries asked, "Which country do you think is the greatest threat to peace in the world today?" The results should give the mainstream media, all organs of the US government, and

US citizens pause. The replies to the Gallup poll were (Gallup 2013):

1. United States 24%
2. Pakistan 8%
3. China 6%
4. Afghanistan, Iran, Israel, North Korea, each 5%
5. India, Iraq, Japan, each 4%
6. Syria 3%
7. Russia 2%
8. Australia, Germany, Palestinian territories, Saudi Arabia, Somalia, South Korea, UK, each 1%

Yes, it is US aggression that the world truly fears, while "Russian aggression" is at a distant seventh place with a mere 2 percent of the vote.

What might you ask is the probable basis for such a response? In an article entitled, "US Empire Reaches Breaking Point: Greatest Threat to Humanity, Time to End It," authors Kevin Zeese and Margaret Flowers (2014) recount some of the possible determinants as outlined by author and historian William Blum, in his book, *Rogue State: A Guide to the World's Only Superpower*, published in 2000. Blum's account points to the following reasons why the US has attained the mantle of "greatest threat to peace":

- The attempted overthrow of more than 50 foreign governments, most of which were democratically elected
- The dropping of bombs on people of more than 30 countries

- The attempted assassination of more than 50 foreign leaders
- The attempt to suppress populist or nationalist movements in 20 countries
- The gross interference in democratic elections in at least 30 countries (Blum 2000)

In light of the above, one is hard pressed to come to terms with what is now termed "Russian aggression." Is this a claim based upon psychological projection, Machiavellian duplicity, or, perhaps, mass hysteria resulting from prolonged mis/disinformation and propaganda campaigns? Certainly historians, if we should survive this current period, will be curious to uncover the reason for this colossal disconnect from reality.

Of course, there are a multitude of other factors that count the term "Russian aggression" as an enormous red herring. The Obama Administration's Eastern Pivot, which has prodded the sleeping Japanese military machine awake in order to aggress China, is, as Zeese and Flowers (2014) point out, one such indication:

> *Already there have been tense moments between China and Japan with its ally, the US. Last November there were multiple challenges as Japan and the US violated the "Air Defense Zone" of China resulting in China scrambling fighter jets over the East China Sea in response. Tensions will likely rise as the US has now brought drones into the Asian Pacific which are housed on military bases in Japan. (Zeese 2014)*

Other nation-states that have been enlisted for what can be clearly described as US aggression directed at China—a country deemed far less aggressive than the US—are Australia, South Korea, and the Philippines.

In a truly disturbing turn of events, the US is seeking to station yet another military base on South Korea's "Peace Island," Jeju, in order to more effectively *pivot* towards China. Why disturbing? The single greatest massacre in Korean history took place on Jeju Island, where sixty thousand Koreans were killed by forces allied to a Korean Strong Man (military dictator) under US command (Zeese et. al 2013). A total of four million Koreans and one million Chinese would be killed over the course of the Korean War, June 1950—July 1953. As S. Brian Willson (2013) writes:

> *This was a staggering international crime still unrecognized that killed five million people and permanently separated ten million Korean families. (Willson 2013)*

Russian aggression? Perhaps a clear indication of who's been aggressing whom is best represented by a twenty-first century map of Europe with regard to NATO countries. On such a map one would see NATO bases at or quite near the Russian border. These are the former Soviet satellites and Warsaw Pact countries, that have been gobbled up and then excreted as NATO forward operating bases.

On April 10, 2014, NATO released satellite images that clearly showed Russian "aggression" with troops massing on Ukraine's border. As stated by NATO's top military commander, General Philip Breedlove, "There is evidence of 40,000 Russian troops on the Ukrainian border."

The images depicted Russian tanks, helicopters, fighter jets, and special-forces brigades. However, the images were satellite photos of the Combat Commonwealth exercises held in the south of Russia in 2013, eight months "before" the stated date of the NATO satellite photos (Zeese 2014).

This allegation begs the larger question, regardless of its inaccuracy does not a state have the right to amass military resources on its territory in response to a potential threat?

Next there was the allegation of Russian special forces' involvement in Eastern Ukraine, based upon a picture supplied by the government in Kiev. The pictures supplied by Kiev found wide use in the mainstream media, appearing on channels from NBC to CNN to the BBC and to the pages of the revered *New York Times*.

The pictures were purported by Western governments and attendant media to show clear evidence of a particular member of the Russian special-forces, who had been active in Georgia, and by association his comrades, as the same soldier deployed in Eastern Ukraine. However, the soldier identified in the photos was a different man entirely. He was not a Russian special-forces member and his name was Alexander Mozhaev, a Cossack and a member of the "rapid reaction force of the local Novorossiya militia" (Human Rights Investigation 2014). There has been no critical examination, no forensic investigation of any kind, regarding the supposed photos of Russian special-forces.

On July 24, 2014, during her press briefing, State Department Spokesperson Marie Harf presented the story that Russian artillery strikes were taking place against Ukrainian military bases along the border. Of course, Ms. Harf's evidence was *secret* and her sources were not to be revealed.

In Ukraine, however, the situation was not as Ms. Harf had described. Jason Ditz (2014) writes in his article, "US Invents Report of Russia Attacking Ukraine Bases: No Reports Out of Ukraine on Any Such Incidents":

> *During the past several days, there has not been a single report out of Ukraine of an artillery strike against any of their military bases, anywhere in the country. The last such incident was <u>two weeks ago, when rebels fired a BM-21 grad</u> at a military base. (Ditz 2014)*

As the story failed to gain traction in light of the missing *secret evidence* and with no other corroborating sources, it became imperative to serially invent numerous and undocumentable cases of aggression, that would each have ever diminishing half-lives.

In closing this section, there is a a question that must be asked. Does an aggressive country deemed a threat to the world, hell-bent on increasing its empire, call continuously for, and embark on missions of shuttle diplomacy for peace between warring parties (Geneva, Minsk)? Further, are the parties who continually eschew, completely ignore, serially violate, or demonize peace plans actually non-aggressors?

RUSSIA INVADES (AGAIN)

> *The Washington hawks still hope to force Putin to intervene militarily, as it would give them the opportunity to isolate Russia, turn it into a monster pariah state, beef up defence spending and set Europe and Russia against each other. They do not care about Ukraine and Ukrainians, but use them as pretext to attain geopolitical goals.*
>
> —*Israel Shamir, "The Ukraine in Turmoil"*

To read or listen to the mainstream media with regard to Russian "invasions" in the Ukraine is, as we have outlined above, Orwellian in all respects and reflects psychological projection, psychological warfare, or perhaps collective insanity.

The statements of various leaders in the West, from Obama to Kerry to Hollande to Merkel to Cameron to various NATO officials, have been warning that Russia will not only invade Ukraine, but that it may soon be invading the whole of Western Europe (and maybe even Kansas). It does make one curious as to whether or not the latest crop of speech writers have been "renditioned" from Hollywood's "B" movie ranks to the various Western capitals. After all, how does one explain the "unreality of phantom Russian subs in Swedish waters, invading Russian armored columns that journalists inexplicably fail to photograph, and BUK missile launches whose existence Western security services refuse to prove by making their intelligence public?" (Byzantium 2014)

After weeks and then months of waiting for the Russians to invade Ukraine and Western Europe, and with nary a Soviet tank on the horizon, the West decided to take things into its own hands. Indicative of this has been the State Department's propensity to utilize images lifted directly from video games, satellite pictures (apparently illustrated by children), and social media as "common sense" proof of a Russian invasion.

In an article entitled, "Russia Has Already Invaded Ukraine," Strobe Talbott, President of the Brookings Institution, found it "Maddening and incomprehensible how governments and the media keep talking about the possibility, the danger, the threat of Russia invading," as he believed that Russia had indeed already invaded (Gardels 2014). Mr. Talbot's proof:

> *Russia invaded Ukraine early in the spring. They started with the so-called "little green men"—Russian soldiers without insignia on their green uniforms—then proceeded with uniforms with epaulets and the annexation of Crimea. Russia has been the force behind, and on the ground, with the separatists in eastern Ukraine. (Gardels 2014)*

Mr. Talbot's proof was, unfortunately, without forensic data—radar, satellite imagery, on the ground photographs, video of Russian tank columns crossing into Ukraine or, as has been the case with the State Department et al., not even "common sense" social media.

Mr. Talbot, however, did wax romantic for former Soviet leaders Mikhail Gorbachev and Boris Yeltsin, who he believed:

> *In these back-to-back tenures of the last president of the Soviet Union and the first president of post-Soviet Russia, Gorbachev and Yeltsin, over a period of 20 years, put Russia on a new and promising track—promising for Russia itself. (Gardels 2014)*

The final point in Mr. Talbot's quote is quite interesting, however, in that he feels it necessary to emphasize how good these leaders were for Russia, though all evidence is to the contrary.

What Mr. Talbot considered a "promising track" for the Russian state after the fall of the Soviet Union was, instead, economic implosion, abject ruination, and the carving up, plundering, and privatizing of Russian resources, all of which, it is estimated, led to the deaths of millions of Russians (Strelkov 2014).

One of the leaders that Mr. Talbot hails, Boris Yeltsin, is universally despised by the Russian people for the hardship his polices leveled and for literally giving away the family jewels (oil, gas, industry, and banking). Mikhail Gorbachev, on the other hand, is believed to have simply capitulated to the West, which led to the "destruction and dismemberment" of the USSR. As Dmitry Orlov (2014) notes, the Russian people refer to Gorbachev as *Mishka mécheny* as ('Mickey the marked— marked by the devil, that is'). Is it possible that Mr. Talbot is being a bit disingenuous about this promising track "for Russia itself?"

In the balance of the article Mr. Talbot makes several interesting points that appear to march in lockstep with the West. Mr. Talbot believes:

- The Russians and the Chinese fixate on what they see as American "hegemonism" as the great danger. That is not the danger.
- The danger for both Russia and China is a future in which they isolate themselves (see $400 billion gas contract, BRICS bank, BRICS investment fund, Shanghai Cooperation Organization, CTSO).
- Putin is looking to the past for a model for the future. That is unwise in the extreme, for Russians —and for the rest of us (see Grand Chessboard Theory).

It is important to note that Mr. Talbot was President Clinton's right hand man during the time when President Clinton was offering, "more shit for Yeltsin's face," which translated to more orders for Yeltsin to parcel off all Russian assets to US Oligarchs and multinationals and to impoverish the Russian people.

On August 28, 2014, a *Washington Post* article claimed that, "Russian soldiers, tanks and heavy artillery began rolling into southeastern Ukraine (in earnest this time)" (Gowen and Gearen 2014). And though the "US officials" considered the "escalation" a de facto Russian invasion, "President Obama stopped short of using the term *invasion* at a news conference."

The evidence for the invasion was a satellite image dated August 21, 2014, that showed Russian self-propelled artillery units at an "undisclosed" location inside Ukraine. Why an "undisclosed location"? Certainly, if they were Russian artillery units, the Russians knew where they were. Then it became clear: the current administration has learned not to tie their "evidence" to specific geographic locations that can subsequently be verified (in contrast to Rumsfield's allegations of WMD in the area around Tikrit, Baghdad).

However, the *evidence* would later be disproved (again) by the OSCE, who has been monitoring the border between Russia and Ukraine since the end of July (2014). The OSCE's monitoring chief, Paul Picard, confirmed, "that since the beginning of its observer mission at the end of July to present, it had not recorded any movement of military equipment or units from Russia into Ukrainian territory" (Cunningham 2014). Journalist Finian Cunningham writes:

> *Tellingly, the OSCE assessment nullifying Washington and NATO claims of Russian invasion and infiltration of Ukraine was given negligible reportage in the Western media, which persists with the anti-Russian narrative that seems to operate on the basis of not letting the facts intrude on a convenient storyline.* (Cunningham 2014)

In an article written by Dmitry Orlov, "How Can You Tell Whether Russia Has Invaded Ukraine?" it became quite clear of what the evidence would be for a Russian invasion. With this caveat, "If Russia invaded on Thursday morning, this is what the situation would look like by Saturday afternoon (Orlov 2014)," Orlov lays out that evidence:

- Ukrainian artillery would sit destroyed, smoldering, and very quiet (after having been pinpointed by the Russian Military and silenced).

- Battalions of Russian soldiers, their attendant armored vehicles—tanker trucks, communications, field kitchens, and hospitals would be plainly visible and photos taken of them easy to upload to social media (with verifiable time stamps, etc.).

- The Ukrainian military would vanish into thin air, with nothing left but more abandoned military hardware.

- There would be Russian checkpoints everywhere, where war criminals would be promptly scooped up.

- Most of Ukraine's borders would be under Russian control and backed up with artillery systems, tank battalions and air defense systems.

- There would be a no-fly zone imposed over the Ukraine and the cancellation of civilian flights, which would provide for a lot of nervous US State Department staffers, CIA and Mossad agents, and Western NGO people stuck in airports across the country.

- The current Ukrainian leadership would follow the lead of the Ukrainian soldiers and thereby vanish into thin air.

- The various refugees, now numbering at close to 1 million would start returning to their homes from Russia (not Europe).

- There would be Russian tanks on the Maidan and the various National Socialists (read Nazis) on the run.

- There would be intense diplomatic and military maneuvering around the world in the US and NATO.

After reading through Dmitry's list, it seemed like "common sense". And the world wouldn't be continually subjected to evidence-free assertions, mountains of secret never-to-see-the-light-of-day evidence, video game excerpts of troop movements, children's illustrations on satellite overlays, and "common sense" social media.

Perhaps the various intelligence personnel or more accurately, the careerists within these organizations who apparently do not hold to the line that politicians and mainstream media pundits hold, would themselves be relieved. As ex-CIA agent, Philip Giraldi (2014) states in the article, "Does the CIA Believe Obama?":

> *Within the intelligence community memories of Iraq and the prefabricated judgments made regarding Syria's alleged use of sarin gas last year are still fresh among both analysts and information collectors, requiring the political leadership to make its case unambiguously. Intelligence work makes one naturally cynical, but*

the rank and file are now becoming generally suspicious of and even hostile to what is going on. (Giraldi 2014)

It would appear that the pragmatists, those who hold to a policy of realpolitik within the intelligence community (past and present), see the Administration's and thus NATO's policy with regard to the Ukraine and confronting Russia as "bordering on the incomprehensible" (Giraldi 2014).

It does strike one as disturbing that the West—US and its NATO allies—having serially invaded (under false pretexts), destroyed, and murdered hundreds of thousands to millions of innocent civilians across Afghanistan, Iraq, Pakistan, Somalia, Libya, Syria, and Yemen, directly and indirectly, in the past decade alone. Yet now they are incensed over a Russian invasion that remains unverifiable, forensically-evidence and fact free, and hush-hush.

There appears to be a pattern building across the various topics as relates to Western propaganda or psychological projection.

PUTIN IS MAD, CHANNELING HITLER... A THUG AND LIVING IN ANOTHER WORLD

> *When figures from the Western elite talk of "Russian aggression" what they really mean is that Russia is checking Western aggression. When Putin is compared to Hitler — it is because he is standing in the way of the real heirs of Adolf Hitler, the war lobby in the West, who like the mustachioed one, have an insatiable appetite for attacking and threatening to attack independent sovereign states.*
>
> —Neil Clark, *Putin Demonized for Thwarting Neocon Plan for Global Domination*

The list is long for those guilty of being crowned with the various epithets above now being leveled at President Vladimir Putin. If memory serves, President Noriega of Panama was one of the first crowned with the yearly award "World Leader Channeling Hitler, who is a Thug, Mad as a Hatter, and Openly Living in Another World." The yearly award would then pass on to a number of other heads of state from Slobodan Milosevic to the Taliban (who would collectively win the award), to Saddam Hussein, who would win the award twice, to Mahmoud Ahmadinejad, who would hold on to the award for several years, to Mohamar Khaddafiy to Bashar al-Assad. It is now, however, President Putin's year to be nominated for the award.

It is curious, however, that the award has not gone to a Western leader, whose never-ending crimes would show the other awardees as trifling, shiftless impostors. And given the criteria necessary to be nominated for the award, one comes perilously close to the idea that the awards judges are showing favoritism and prejudicially overlooking a host of quite worthy Western leaders.

But let us first look at the various criteria that have been utilized to evaluate President Putin for the year's honor, "World Leader Channeling Hitler, who is a Thug, Mad as a Hatter and Openly Living in Another World."

President Putin's first so-called act on the world stage, responsible for his nomination, was interfering in the geo-politics of another country, Ukraine. It is said that President Putin instigated the turmoil in these ways:

- Facilitating the violent overthrow of the Ukrainian government of President Yanukovych, who was ideologically aligned to Russia's geo-strategic

concerns regarding NATO and who had just decided to forego the European Union (and ostensibly NATO) agreement and to sign with the Customs Union, Russia's equivalent to the EU
- President Putin has further been nominated for sending snipers to the Maidan and positioning them inside buildings occupied and controlled by self-identified neo-Nazis' from the Right Sektor and the Svoboda parties, who hate Russians and just about everyone else, who then subsequently killed innocent protestors and police (In an interesting turn of events, President Putin seems to be the only world leader who continually calls for an investigation of his own crime. Machiavellianism at its finest?).
- This act, of course, would be material in the downfall of his geo-strategic ally and soon to be Custom Unions signee and associate, President Yanukovych, via a violent coup, while initiating chaos and turmoil on Russia's border and sending upwards of a million refugees into Russia.
- Further, President Putin, after a unanimous referendum by the citizens of Crimea, overwhelmingly ethnic Russians, who decided to opt out of Ukraine when a toxic combination of oligarchs and neo-Nazis violently took over, decided to welcome them into the Russian Federation (another Machiavellian masterstroke).
- Additionally, President Putin has serially invaded Ukrainian territory with major troop and armor

movements and so stealthily, it seems, that the US State Department, the various intelligence agencies, NATO, and the White House have been forced to enlist patrons of social media in order to ascertain troop movements, Russian Special Forces penetration and missile launches.

- President Putin is also quite guilty for turning off the gas spigot to Ukraine, which has been historically late in paying its gas bill to the tune of several billion dollars, while also siphoning off (stealing and extoring) gas belonging to other Western European countries that had actually paid for it.

- And most diabolically, President Putin has been deemed responsible for the downing of Malaysian Flight MH17 and the killing of its nearly 300 passengers and crew, without the burden, it seems, of any actual forensic evidence or data, and before an investigation, though the West is currently in possession of the flight's black box recorders, military and satellite intelligence data, and Kiev Air Traffic Control tapes, but has refused to make the information public and in several cases has gone as far as signing Non-Disclosure Agreements (NDAs) to prevent said leak of information (on this one, Putin is brilliant!).

- And in a truly Machiavellian turn of events the Master, President Putin, has consistently called for an immediate end to the conflict in the Ukraine, has orchestrated two peace conferences (Geneva, Minsk) and has been the only state player to deliver humanitarian aid to the civilians in the affected regions.

I can see how the nomination committee may have reacted to the above, though it seems a host of more appropriate candidates for the award were closer to home than realized. Putin's super-majority-referendum re-snatching of the historically Russian state of Crimea saw not a single shot fired or a single innocent citizen killed, or a building pockmarked by depleted uranium munitions or ballistic missiles. This seems, well, rather banal and completely lacking in imagination when compared to Western "shock and awe."

How truly unfair that the nations responsible for Yugoslavia, Afghanistan, Iraq, Pakistan, Somalia, Libya, Syria, Yemen, Lebanon, and the deaths of literally millions of their citizens were unable to secure their bid for "World Leader Channeling Hitler, Who is Mad as a Hatter and Openly Living in Another World." One certainly doesn't wish to name names as that would be impolitic, pedestrian, and gouache, but maybe the nominating committee should be looking to other candidates for the coming year.

Despite his nomination, President Vladimir Putin is currently more popular in Russia (80 percent approval rating) than any Western leader in the US or Europe, where leaders are hopelessly stuck in just barely double-digit approval ratings. And the recent events have found President Putin's popularity rising not only at home, but around the world. This, in turn, has led to more and more countries looking to drift into Russia's increasingly "isolated" orbit (BRICS, SCO, EEC, Customs Union, etc.).

It does appear that the judges are puffing up President Putin's actions in a bid to nominate him over more worthy nominees. Favoritism? Perhaps.

In truth, and as spoken to in Chapter 4, President Putin is the mirror opposite of what he is portrayed to be by the West. Perhaps this is the greatest case of Western psychological projection in the world today.

As Neil Clark (2014) states in his article, "Putin Demonized For Thwarting Neocon Plan For Global Domination":

> *By any objective assessment, it's the Western elites – and in particular the neocon faction within that elite – who are the biggest dangers to world peace, not Putin. Look at the havoc their policy of endless war, whether waged directly or through terrorist proxies, has caused in Iraq, Libya and Syria.*

These serial warmongers are particularly angry that Russian foreign policy has thwarted their plans for "regime change" in Syria, a key strategic objective. They're also angry that Putin clamped down on oligarchs whose role it was to help Western plutocrats get control of Russia's natural resources.

Additionally, President Putin has rebuilt Russia, (resurrected it from the ashes of the West's exploitation, austerity, and dismemberment), increased the standard of living of ordinary Russians, grown the Russian economy by 7 percent from 2000–2007, reached out to countries large and small for constructive engagement and returned to the practice, now long abandoned by the West, of realpolitik.

WESTERN PROPAGANDA AND THE CRIMEA

> *The US and EU supported the coup d'etat in Ukraine, and reverted to outright justification of any acts by the self-proclaimed Kiev authorities that opted for suppression by force of the part of the Ukrainian people that had rejected the attempts to impose the anti-constitutional way of life to the entire country and wanted to defend its rights to the native language, culture, and history. It is precisely the aggressive assault on these rights that compelled the population of Crimea to take the destiny in its own hands and make a choice in favor of self-determination. This was an absolutely free choice no matter what was invented by those who are responsible in the first place for the internal conflict in Ukraine.*
>
> —Sergei Lavrov, September 27, 2014 United Nations Speech

While breaking down the West's argument regarding Russia's illegal annexation of Crimea, it is important to establish a baseline definition of annexation and then to follow the trail of events:

> *Annexation - the formal act of acquiring something (especially territory) by conquest or occupation; "the French annexation of Madagascar as a colony in 1896"; "a protectorate has frequently been a first step to annexation." (Webster Online)*

As mentioned earlier, on March 11, 2014, the Crimean Parliament voted for a declaration of independence as a first step in formally separating from the Ukrainian state. The referendum (Quebec, Scotland, etc.), a democratic vote by the people to determine their future, was then undertaken on March 16, 2014, which garnered a super majority of the votes, 96 percent for re-unification with Russia.

For those who have stated that the referendum was illegal, as it violated the Ukrainian constitution (despite its clear legality under international law per the Kosovo advisory opinion), it is important to establish, if, indeed, there was a viable and functioning Ukrainian constitution in place.

One of the major arguments put forth for the legality of the Crimean vote is that the violent overthrow, *coup d'état*, of President Yanukovych was itself illegal, as the constitutional process for impeachment was never followed. Thus the coup that had *illegally* removed the *legally* elected President, Yanukovych, from office, invalidated the Ukrainian constitution. The referendum, therefore, could not have violated an instrument that had been rendered null and void by a violent *coup d'état*.

Other arguments presented against the validity of the Crimean referendum are:

Russian troops intimidated voters, so the process was not free and fair.

Ewald Stadler, a member of the European Parliament, dismissed the myth of a referendum at gunpoint when he stated, "I haven't seen anything even resembling pressure. People themselves want to have their say" (RT 2014).

Russia bussed in larger numbers of native Russians to stack the deck.

Like the Western allegations of serial Russian invasions and the shoot down of Malaysian Flight MH17 that are completely free of an evidentiary trail to back Western charges, there is not a single shred of evidence, even in terms of social media, to back these allegations.

The referendum was inconsistent with the Ukrainian constitution, which says that all Ukrainians would have to vote on Crimea's secession.

As mentioned above, the violent coup, which removed from office the legally elected President of Ukraine, Yanukovych, rendered the constitution a dead letter.

The Russian proposal was based on an outdated theory of secession.

In terms of the law—the United Nations International Court of Justice handed down an advisory opinion in 2010 saying unambiguously that a unilateral declaration of independence is in accordance with international law (Mezyaev 2014).

Additionally, the conditions and legitimacy of the Crimean referendum was overseen by 135 international observers from 23 countries (Austria, Belgium, Bulgaria, France, Germany, Hungary, Italy, Latvia, Poland, etc.). Among those monitoring the referendum were members of the EU and national European parliaments, international law experts and human rights activists (RT 2014).

It's a matter of international law: territory cannot be annexed simply because the people who happen to be living there today want to secede.

By virtue of the principle of equal rights and self-determination of peoples enshrined in the Charter of the United Nations, all peoples have the right to freely determine, without external interference, their political status and to pursue their economic, social, and cultural development, and every State has the duty to respect this right in accordance with the provisions of the Charter (Declaration on Principles of International Law 1970).

And finally, as discussed by Alexander Mezyaev (2014), a Russian lawyer and chief of the Department of the Constitutional and International Law of the Public Management University of Tatarstan:

> *It should be noted that no way could Russia's actions be compared with what the West does – Russia acts upon the invitation of the Ukraine's legal authority. Here is the mismatch between the international law and what Western politicians say and do. They realize well that the authority which has invited Russia is legal. That's why the discussion is adroitly made [to] slide to the issue of "legitimacy" which is not a legal, but rather a scientific notion. (Mezyaev 2014)*

Mr. Mezyaev (2014) then goes on to hypothesize, given the above, what Western lawyers truly mean by the pronouncements of "violation of international law":

> *So what do Western governments and their lawyers mean when they say the Crimea referendum is "in violation of international law"? The lack of clear-cut definitions and weighty legal arguments is egregious. It proves that they understand well the referendum in Crimea does not violate any whatsoever international legal norms. To the contrary, it's an example of*

compliance with international law by the people of Crimea. (Mezyaev 2014)

Over the course of the referendum the various international observers believed the referendum credible and free of violations. One of the lead international observers, Mateus Psikorkski, reported that, "Our observers have not registered any violations of voting rules." And international observer, Pavel Chemev, stated:

> The lines are very long, the turnout is big indeed. Organization and procedures are 100 percent in line with the European standards.

With regard to the right of the Crimeans to hold a referendum, a number of the observers had the following to say:

> Our opinion is – if people want to decide their future, they should have the right to do that and the international community should respect that. There is a goal of people in Crimea to vote about their own future. Of course, Kiev is not happy about that, but still they have to accept and to respect the vote of people in Crimea.
>
> — Johann Gudenus, member of the City Parliament of Vienna,

> The view we get from the American and European media is very distorted. You get no objective information. So we decided to come here to have a look at what's really going on and see if this referendum is credible.
>
> — Johannes Hübner, an Austrian MP

> Yes, I think the referendum is legitimate. We are talking about long-term history. We are talking about the Russian people, about

the territories of the former USSR with artificial borders. So, I think it's a legitimate referendum that will give opportunity for this Russian population's reunification with Russia.

— *Aymeric Chauprade, a political scientist and geopolitician from France*

At the end of the day, the Crimeans had decided their own fate through a legal referendum overseen by 135 international observers; yet the hypocritical cries from the West of an "illegal Crimean annexation" flowed readily.

Despite an overwhelming response by the Crimean peoples to distance themselves from the illegal junta in Kiev stacked with oligarchs and neo-Nazis, the West, at the behest of the United States, decided to levy sanctions against the Russians. Perhaps future historians will wonder who indeed was responsible for the geopolitical actions of the West.

To compare for a moment Kosovo versus the Crimea, it is important to take note of the differences.

The Russians, for instance, did not rain bombs on an entire population for eleven weeks. The Russians did not unleash cluster bombs on densely crowded marketplaces or target civilian passenger trains and petrochemical plants or use depleted uranium munitions. The Russians did not recklessly kill the exact people that they were supposed to have been protecting. The Russians did not fire a single round of ammunition, did not kill a single person, and did not drop a single bomb. No one died. The Russians simply waited for Crimeans to conduct and conclude their referendum, for which over 90% voted in favor. Russia then welcomed Crimea into the Russian Federation.

The Western strategic goal to evict Russia from its Crimean military and naval bases was thus in tatters.

MALAYSIAN AIRLINE FLIGHT MH17

> *"There's a Mountain of Evidence Linking Russia to the Downing Of The Malaysia Airliner."*
>
> —*Pau Szoldra, Business Insider*

On July 17, 2014, Malaysian Flight MH17 on route from Amsterdam to Kuala Lumpur was shot down over eastern Ukraine, which resulted in the deaths of 298 passengers.

Less than twenty-four hours later, lacking an official investigation, the presentation of any forensic evidence, the examination of Flight MH17's flight data recorder (black box), and/or actual reporting boots on the ground, a blizzard of propaganda raged in the Western mainstream media and from Western capitals. Blame was immediately assigned to Putin, Russia, and the Eastern Ukraine separatists. They were solely to blame for the malicious and calculated downing of Malaysian Flight MH17 and the cold-blooded murder of the 298 innocent people who happened to be aboard the plane that day. And any actual evidence supporting this claim was irrelevant and immaterial.

It was a troubling but familiar pattern for the West, reminiscent of "Saddam's weapons of mass destruction (and the inevitable "mushroom cloud")," the Serbian "Massacre of the Albanians," Assad's "gassing of his own people," the "Tiananmen Square massacre," and Iran's possession of or soon-to-be possession of "nuclear-armed Intercontinental ballistic missiles (ICBMs)."

The various headlines that filled Western airwaves and print media within hours of the downing of flight MH17 were unanimous:

"Here's The Ridiculous Way Russia's Propaganda Channel Is Covering The Downed Malaysian Airliner."

—Pau Szoldra, Business Insider

"Hillary Clinton: Putin 'bears responsibility' in downing of MH17."

—Jason Miks, CNN

"Miscalculation. Failure. Escalation—Why Putin Shot Down MH-17."

—Greg Satell, Forbes

"Web evidence points to pro-Russian rebels in downing of MH17."

—Arthur Bright, The Christian Science Monitor

US State Department Spokesperson Marie Harf in a July 22, 2014, press conference presented the US argument and her "strong assessment" why the "Russian-backed separatists" were responsible for the downing of Flight MH17. During Harf's address she stated that, "We saw videos on social media," that provided a "preponderance of evidence," which was "backed by a lot of information," and that that information was "common sense." Further, Harf noted that should there be any alternative explanations as to the downing of Flight MH17, that those explanations would simply "defy logic." It is also rather interesting that Harf's "broad assessment" and her "host of information" had not taken into account the Russian Defense Ministries' press conference wherein actual forensic data—satellite and radar data—were presented to the world. It is a press conference that must be seen to be believed, for the sophomoric assertions that Harf makes entirely free of logic or actual intelligence data. Nor does Harf appear to be embarrassed by the above.

Nearly seven months later Ms. Harf's "preponderance of evidence" and her "host of information" remains top secret, invisible, and hush-hush. In the meantime there have been bushels of information, reports, and investigations that all point to a dramatically different conclusion than that preemptively reached by the West and spokesperson Harf's State Department bosses.

THE FLIGHT

At approximately 10:30 a.m. (GMT) on Thursday, July 17, 2014, Malaysia Airlines flight MH17, a Boeing 777, departed Amsterdam's Schiphol airport on route to Kuala Lumpur. The flight carried a total of 298 passengers and crew members. The pilot of MH17 had filed a flight plan, requesting to fly at 35,000 ft. throughout Ukrainian airspace, which was considered close to the optimum altitude.

The path that MH17 flight crew took on July 17 was a familiar one that had been traversed fourteen times over the course of the past two weeks. This path drew out a southeasterly diagonal across the length of Ukraine to the Sea of Azov, just east of Crimea (Pegues CBS Online 2014). On this day, however, flight MH17's path was diverted from its normal route along the international air corridor, known as L980, some 300 miles north of its usual route, which would bring flight MH17 directly over a war zone. It is not clear as to why the route was changed or who was responsible for changing the route, though it is clear that Eurocontrol (European Organisation for the Safety of Air Navigation) was not responsible. To date, Kiev Air Traffic Control (KATC) has not been cleared of responsibility as the Air Traffic Control tapes were immediately confiscated by the Kiev military authorities at the time of the downing and have not been released.

The flight path, however, was only one of two crucial changes that may have led to the downing of the flight. Malaysian Airlines has confirmed that KATC instructed the pilot to fly at a lower altitude upon its entry into Ukrainian airspace (Chossudovsky 2014). The original flight plan called for a cruising altitude of 35,000 ft. KATC, however, ordered the pilot to lower flight MH17's cruising altitude to 33,000 ft., directly over the Ukrainian war zone. It was an area where military planes, transports, and helicopters had all been shot down in the preceding days and weeks.

At 13:20, literally minutes before flight MH17 was shot down from the sky, the plane made an unscheduled "left turn," that resulted in a 14km deviation from its already altered flight plan and a reduction in cruising speed from 580mph (933 kmph) to 124mph (200 kmph). The turn took MH17 directly over the Donetsk area, before the pilots attempted to realign with their altered flight plan. However, before the pilots were able to reestablish their flight path, MH17 dropped from altitude and disappeared from radar. The time was 13:23.

Immediately after flight MH17 crashed, Ukrainian officials of the coup-installed Kiev government confiscated the audio and all records of flight MH17.

Approximately two hours later, at 15:40, the Ukrainian government officially announced the downing of Flight MH17.

Nearly half an hour later, Ukraine's Prime Minister Arseniy Yatsenyuk ordered an investigation of MH17.

Approximately three hours later, 18:28, East Ukrainian freedom fighters located Flight MH17's flight data recorders, black boxes.

At approximately 23:30, Malaysian Airlines confirmed that 298 passengers had been killed as a result of the downing of Flight MH17.

As mentioned earlier, blame was cast before the bodies of the men, women, and children had been removed from the crime scene, before the gathering of any evidence and prior to a forensic investigation or receipt of the plane's black boxes.

Below are a number of events and factors that may shed some light on the downing of flight MH17.

THE LAY OF THE LAND

At the time of flight MH17's downing in Eastern Ukraine, the area was rife with various Western militaries undertaking exercises that were premised on gathering intelligence and monitoring in real-time the events unfolding on land, air, and sea.

NATO, on that day, was conducting Operation Sea Breeze 2014 in the Black Sea approximately 40 miles from the Russian border. The operational mandate of Sea Breeze 2014 was to monitor commercial airline traffic throughout the region.

The military assets that NATO had employed for Operation Sea Breeze 2014, ranged from aircraft such as the Boeing EA-18G Growler and the Boeing E3 Sentry Airborne Warning and Control System (AWACS) to electronic warfare and intelligence aircraft, to the AEGIS-class guided missile cruiser and the USS Vela Gulf. Between the AWACS and the AEGIS's AN/SPY1 radar NATO had the ability to track aircraft over the whole of Ukrainian airspace and well into Russian Territory (Madsen 2014). Additionally, Flight MH17 would have appeared across multiple radar screens of NATO's various intelligence assets.

Also on that day, 200 US Army personnel were participating in a second NATO led exercise, Rapid Trident II, in conjunction with Ukraine's Ministry of Defense, during the downing of flight MH17.

It was also pointed out, during a Russian military press conference, that at the precise time flight MH17 was downed, a US experimental spy satellite was positioned directly overhead. And using measurement and signature intelligence, or MASINT, the satellite would have easily been able to detect the heat signature of a missile launch or the missile's internal search and tracking system as it sought to engage the intended target (Vartabedian 2014).

In addition to all of the above, the US Air Force continually maintains a fleet of listening and early warning satellites that would have easily identified both the location of the missile launch site as well as its trajectory (Vartabedian 2014).

Further, Kiev's commercial and military radar systems should have also easily been able to identify missiles rising to 33,000 ft. as well as a second aircraft trailing flight MH17 (which will be discussed later in detail).

Russia, of course, would have also been able to track flight MH17's flight path via civilian and military radar and satellite telemetry.

To date, however, only the Russian military has shared with the world its forensic evidence and satellite data on flight MH17 in a military press briefing. It is the only such press briefing by any country on flight MH17, as of the date of this book's release.

As of the release of this book, the US, NATO nor any EU country has held a press briefing or shared a scintilla of forensic data—satellite telemetry, radar images, black box data, ATC tapes, or any data—that may have been gathered by its various intelligence assets in the area on the day of the downing of flight MH17.

THE RUSSIAN POSITION

On July 18, the Russian Defense Ministry held a press briefing on Malaysian Flight MH17 that was conducted by Russian Minister of Defense, Andrey Karatopolov, and Russian Defense Minister of General Staff Air Force, Igor Makushev. It would be the first and only such press conference that provided a worldwide audience with radar and satellite data on the various movements of flight MH17 until it was downed.

Also uncovered during this press briefing, as seen on radar-tracking tapes, was the appearance of a second plane—a military plane (as it did not have a secondary identification device), an SU-25, which the Ukrainian authorities have continually denied. The SU-25, visible as a radar blip, appeared to be in hot pursuit of Flight MH17.

At no point during the Russian Defense Ministry press conference was there any sign of a launched missile on their radar or satellite telemetry data.

After the press conference, Defense Minister Karatopolov, without placing blame, simply asked the Ukrainian authorities for clarification on ten questions, which he believed they'd be able to answer given ATC tapes (RT 2014):

> 1. Immediately after the tragedy, the Ukrainian authorities, naturally, blamed it on the self-defense forces. What are these accusations based on?
>
> 2. Can Kiev explain in detail how it uses BUK missile launchers in the conflict zone? And why were these systems deployed there in the first place, seeing as the self-defense forces don't have any planes?
>
> 3. Why are the Ukrainian authorities not doing anything to set up an international commission? When will such a commission begin its work?
>
> 4. Would the Ukrainian Armed Forces be willing to let international investigators see the inventory of their air-to-air and surface-to-air missiles, including those used in SAM launchers?
>
> 5. Will the international commission have access to tracking data from reliable sources regarding the movements of Ukrainian warplanes on the day of the tragedy?
>
> 6. Why did Ukrainian air traffic controllers allow the plane to deviate from the regular route to the north, towards "the anti-terrorist operation zone?"

7. Why was airspace over the war zone not closed for civilian flights, especially since the area was not entirely covered by radar navigation systems?

8. How can official Kiev comment on reports in the social media, allegedly by a Spanish air traffic controller who works in Ukraine, that there were two Ukrainian military planes flying alongside the Boeing 777 over Ukrainian territory?

9. Why did Ukraine's Security Service start working with the recordings of communications between Ukrainian air traffic controllers and the Boeing crew and with the data storage systems from Ukrainian radars without waiting for international investigators?

10. What lessons has Ukraine learned from a similar incident in 2001, when a Russian Tu-154 crashed into the Black Sea? Back then, the Ukrainian authorities denied any involvement on the part of Ukraine's armed forces until irrefutable evidence proved official Kiev to be guilty.

The Russian deputy defense minister refused to assign blame until an investigation was undertaken and more evidence found. This despite the fact that less than twenty-four hours earlier Western governments and Western media, with no evidence and prior to an official investigation or forensic press briefing, were placing the blame on Russia, the Eastern Ukraine, and President Putin.

THE KIEV AND US POSITION

> *We know, we saw in social media afterwards, we saw videos, we saw photos of the pro-Russian separatists bragging about shooting down an aircraft that then they then...excuse me, took down once it became clear that it may have been a passenger airline... Based on open information which is basically common sense, right, we know where it was fired from, we know who has this weapon.*
>
> —*Marie Harf, US State Department Spokesperson*

Again, less than twenty-four hours after the downing of Malaysian Flight MH17, prior to an investigation, an examination of the flight data recorders, or the presentation of any forensic evidence, the West made its case against Russia and the Novorossiyan Separatists. The case made by US Secretary of State John Kerry alleged that:

- A SA-11 surface-to-air missile system, BUK, was in the vicinity, under the control of East Ukrainian Separatists
- A launch was detected and its trajectory vector verified to have intercepted Flight MH17 (Corbett 2014)

The data verifying the launch and its trajectory, however, seems to have disappeared with Harf's mountain of evidence, as, to date, neither have seen the light of day.

The Kiev regime for its part attempted to substantiate the points made by Secretary Kerry by providing 1) an intercepted conversation between an Eastern Separatist and a colonel from Russian military intelligence and 2) by showing a video of a BUK missile system, without two of its missiles, supposedly heading back across the Russian border.

However, within twenty-four hours the intercepted conversation that had been uploaded by Ukrainian Security Services (SBU) was discovered to have been pieced together from disparate, unrelated conversations.

A Russian expert in sound and voice analysis, Nikolai Popov (2014), after studying the tapes, confirmed that the recording that had been submitted by the SBU was, "Not an integral file and made up of several fragments."

In the first fragment a Ukrainian Separatist Commander, Igor Belzer, talks about shooting down a plane. He does not, however, mention anything about the type of plane or the name of the town. The tape's second fragment, the experts discovered, was composed of three disparate pieces that are presented as a single conversation. This was discovered using a spectral and time analysis of the recordings. As Popov notes:

> *Short pauses in the tape are very indicative: the audio file has preserved time marks which show that the dialog was assembled from various episodes. But the most indicative moment is that the audio tape clearly shows that it was created almost a day before the airliner crash (ITAR-TASS 2014)*

The video showing a BUK missile system being driven back across the Russian border was quickly debunked during the Russian military press conference. During the conference, Defence Minister Karatapolov pointed out that a billboard in the background of the supposed BUK missile system headed to Russia, was, in fact, shot in Krasnoarmeisk, Ukraine, which had been under Ukrainian military control since May 11, 2014.

The Western "evidence," upon examination, had once again become non-evidence, and was never to be discussed again in polite circles.

One month and a day after the downing of Flight MH17, Russia formally asked the United Nations Security Council, "Where are the ATC records?"

Several months after the downing of Malaysian Flight MH17, the West has barely uttered a word about flight MH17 and the ATC records have still not seen the light of day. Given the tendency of the West to continually blare unsubstantiated and false accusations against Putin, Russia and the Novorossiyans, the silence in the West is deafening. Deafening because of the lack of continuing accusations, given that the West now has actual data sources. This on its face appears quite damning. If the West was, indeed, in possession of forensic evidence that pointed to the culpability of Russia or of the Novorossiya freedom fighters, its reportage would be ceaseless. However, "all is quiet on the Western Front." But there's more.

Imagine a scenario wherein the countries conducting the investigation—Ukraine, the Netherlands, Australia and Belgium—sign an agreement wherein any of them can veto the results of the investigation, should they disagree with its conclusion. Further imagine that the country to whom the plane belongs and that is legally responsible for conducting an investigation, Malaysia, is actually denied participation for the first several months of the investigation.

An online article published by Live Journal titled, "The Causes of the MH17 Crash are Classified: Ukraine, Netherlands, Australia, Belgium Signed a Non-disclosure Agreement," states that any one of the signatories to the non-disclosure agreement (NDA) can actually veto the publication of the black box investigative results of Flight MH17 (Magnay 2014). This should, of course, be troubling to anyone interested in an honest and open investigation.

In direct relation to the Live Journal article, an article in *The Australian* entitled, "Russians Push Flight MH17 Crash Conspiracy" quoted Russian Foreign Minister, Sergei Lavrov, who stated:

> *We must not allow the investigation of the MH17 crash to be manipulated into oblivion. No one has told us anything coherent about the reasons why the recordings of the black boxes cannot be released fully. The truth must be revealed. (Magnay 2014)*

Why would the West allow countries responsible for investigating the MH17 crash to execute and sign a non-disclosure agreement? What have they to hide? Would they be hiding Russian culpability or, perhaps, their own?

And yes, the Malaysians were, indeed, denied a role in the investigation of the downing of one of their own planes. In the article, "A View from Australia: Why the Secrecy on the MH17 Investigation?," James O'Neill, an Australian barrister and former academic describes the situation:

> *Under International Air Transport Association rules, the parties responsible for the investigation would be the Malaysians, as owners of the plane and home country of the airline, and the Ukrainians, over whose territory the atrocity occurred. It was the Dutch, however, who took the lead role, citing two facts: the plane had departed from Amsterdam; and they had suffered the largest number of their nationals as victims. The Malaysians were initially excluded from the inquiry for reasons that have never been satisfactorily explained. They were finally invited to join the Joint Inquiry on 2 December 2014. (O'Neill 2014)*

How does the denial of participation of the country, Malaysia, legally responsible for the investigation of MH17's downing square?

THE TRUTH OUTS

> *"The Western intelligence and the Americans are very well aware of all the details: who shot [flight MH17] down, why and what for, but manipulate this information and this incident for their own benefit. This provocation was organized to lay [the blame] on Russia and force it into sending troops to Ukraine, officially, but the Russian government did not succumb to this provocation,"*
>
> —Retired Lt. Gen. Nikolai Pushkarev, formerly of the Russian Armed Forces' Main Intelligence Directorate (GRU)

There now appears to be a trail of evidence, that points to alternative culprits responsible for the downing of Flight MH17.

Leaked reports and private testimonies from Western intelligence agents have long pointed to the following scenario, but now there is further proof. An article published August 3, 2014 in ConsortiumNews entitled, "Flight 17 Shoot-Down Scenario Shifts," by Robert Parry (2014) states:

> *Contrary to the Obama administration's public claims blaming eastern Ukrainian rebels and Russia for the shoot-down of Malaysia Airlines Flight 17, some US intelligence analysts have concluded that the rebels and Russia were likely not at fault and that it appears Ukrainian government forces were to blame, according to a source briefed on these findings. This judgment—at odds with what President Barack Obama and Secretary of State*

> John Kerry have expressed publicly—is based largely on the
> absence of US government evidence that Russia supplied the rebels
> with a Buk anti-aircraft missile system that would be needed to hit
> a civilian jetliner flying at 33,000 feet, said the source, who spoke
> on condition of anonymity. (Parry 2014)

The interesting parallel here is that this same intelligence community had long discounted the fact that Saddam Hussein had rebuilt his weapons programs or that Iraq had in its possession any Weapons of Mass Destruction (WMDs). The intelligence community's information was quickly validated, however, as the Iraq war was enjoined.

A little over a decade later, history repeats itself via the divergent narratives of Western governments: their attendant media versus their own intelligence communities.

According to Michael Bociurkiw, a monitor with the Organization for Security and Cooperation in Europe (OSCE), who was one of the first investigators to reach the crash site and to begin a forensic examination:

> There have been two or three pieces of fuselage that have been
> really pockmarked with what almost looks like machine-gun fire,
> very very strong machine-gun fire. (CBC News 2014)

Mr. Bociurkiw's response when asked if he had uncovered any signs of a missile hitting MH17 during the investigation was, "No, we haven't" (CBC News 2014).

Additional confirmation of machine-gun fire being used to bring down MH17 was provided by Peter Haisenko, a retired Lufthansa pilot, who, after viewing the high-resolution images of the holes in the fuselage, concluded that:

> You can see the entry and exit holes. The edge of a portion of the
> holes is bent inwards. These are the smaller holes, round and clean,

> showing the entry points most likeley [those] of a 30 millimeter caliber projectile. The edge of the other, the larger and slightly frayed exit holes showing shreds of metal pointing produced by the same caliber projectiles. Moreover, it is evident that these exit holes of the outer layer of the double aluminum reinforced structure are shredded or bent—outwardly!.. It had to have been a hail of bullets from both sides that brought the plane down. (CBC News 2014)

The positioning of the round entry and exit holes, on the left and right side of MH17's cockpit would appear to establish, at the very least, another cause responsible for MH17's downing.

Interestingly, this evidence is missing entirely from all Western narratives.

But from where would the machine gun fire have come? And if it were possible for ground based machine-gun fire to reach MH17, at 30,000 feet, would it have been possible for ordnance to breach the left and right sides of the flight's cockpit?

The physics of a single BUK missile or its shrapnel penetrating from above the left and right sides of the cockpit would also appear highly improbable. As described by Major General Mikhail Krush, chief of the Russian Land Forces' tactical air defense troops, "The [BUK] missile strikes the target from above covering it with a thick cloud of fragments" (GlobalResearch 2014). Krush also mentioned in his interview with Voyenno-Promyshlenny Kuryer military weekly that:

> ...a guided missile launched by a Buk missile system leaves behind a specific smoke trail as it flies, like a comet. In daylight this trail can be clearly seen within a radius of 20-25 kilometers from the

missile system. It cannot remain unnoticed. There are no eyewitnesses to confirm there was any. No one reported a launch. This is one thing. Second. The holes left by the strike elements on the Boeing's outer skin indicate that the warhead blew up from below and sideways. A Buk missile strikes the target from above. (GlobalResearch 2014)

This begs the question, where would this type of ordnance have originated? Interestingly, the forensic radar and satellite data from the Russian press conference of July 21, 2014 provides a clue to this.

The data pointed to, at least, one unidentified aircraft trailing flight MH17 immediately prior to its downing. The aircraft was unidentified, as it was without a secondary or commercial transponder. This, however, led the Russian General to believe the plane to be of military design and possibly an SU-25 (equipped with 30mm cannons). Corroboration of the Russian general's claim would come from a most unlikely place — Kiev Air Traffic Control (KATC).

Minutes after MH17's downing on July 17, 2014, Spanish air traffic controller, Jose Carlos Barrios Sanchez, who was working contractually at Kiev's Borispol airport, tweeted via his Twitter Feed, @spainbuca, the following information with the associated timeline, translated from Spanish by Luis Lopez (GlobalResearch 2014):

- 10:21 - 17 July 2014: "Kiev Authorities, trying to make it look like an attack by pro-Russians"

- 10:24 - 17 July 2014: "warning! It can be a downing, Malaysia Airlines B777 in Ukraine [sic], 280 passengers

- 10:25 - 17 July 2014: "Warning! Kiev have what they wanted"

- 10:25 - 17 July 2014: "[Military] has taken control of ATC in Kiev"

- 10:30 - 17 July 2014: "The Malaysia Airlines B777 plane disappeared from the radar, there was no communication of any anomaly, confirmed"

- 10:35 - 17 July 2014: "they will take from our phones and others stuff at any moment"

- 10:38 - 17 July 2014: "Before They remove my phone or they break my head, shot down by Kiev"

- 11:13 - 17 July 2014: "What are doing foreigners with kiev authorities in the tower? Gathering all the information"

- 11:48 - 17 July 2014: "The B777 plane flew escorted by Ukraine jet fighter until 2 minutes before disappearing from the radar"

- 12:01 - 17 July 2014: "all this is gathered in radars, to the unbelieving, shot down by kiev, here we know it and military air traffic control also"

- 13:38 - 17 July 2014: "The fighters flew close to 777, up to 3 minutes before disappearing from the radar, just 3 minutes"

- 16:06 - 17 July 2014: "Military commanders here (ATC) control tower, confirm that the missile is from the Ukrainian army"

To summarize, the downing of flight MH17, as documented by Spanish air traffic controller, identified as "Carlos," documented via his Twitter account 1) that there were two Ukrainian military jets trailing flight MH17, 2) that it was the Ukrainian authorities, who were, in fact, responsible for the downing of flight MH17, and 3) that they sought to pin its downing on the Ukrainian rebels. Carlos's Twitter account was immediately terminated after the tragedy.

Though all of "Carlos's" claims have not been verified by a secondary source, to date, Russia's release of radar and satellite data appears to verify the presence of, at least, one Ukrainian SU-25 warplane trailing flight MH17.

Additional confirmation, however, comes from several eyewitnesses in the Donetsk area that verified a second plane trailing flight MH17 immediately before its downing. The BBC reporter, Olga Ivshina, interviewed eyewitnesses in Donetsk, who had also seen the second plane. In her report, Ivshina related the claims of residents:

> *The inhabitants of the nearby villages are certain that they saw military aircraft in the sky shortly prior to the catastrophe. According to them, it actually was the jet fighters that brought down the Boeing. (Uhler 2014)*

Ms. Ivshina's report was subsequently, and without explanation, withdrawn from the BBC's website, but it can still be found if one searches the web.

An article in Malaysia's *New Strait Times*, an English language newspaper, entitled "US Analysts Conclude MH17

Downed by Aircraft," charged that the US and European-backed regime in Kiev was responsible for shooting down Malaysian Airlines Flight MH17 in Eastern Ukraine in July (Hussain 2014). The article went on to state that this charge corroborated the initial analysis put forward by OSCE investigators that:

> *The Boeing 777-200 was crippled by an air-to-air missile and finished off with cannon fire from a fighter that had been shadowing it as it plummeted. (Hussain 2014)*

Further reference was made concerning the analysis of the plane's fuselage. Experts described:

> *...blast fragmentation patterns on the fuselage of the airliner show[ing] two distinct shapes—the shredding pattern associated with a warhead packed with "flechettes," and the more uniform, round-type penetration holes consistent with that of cannon rounds. (Hussain 2014)*

Additionally, it is necessary to rule out the scenario even now pressed by Western mainstream media, that a BUK missile brought down Flight MH17.

In a Russian documentary, *MH-17: The Untold Story* presented by RT, which aired on October 27, 2014, an altogether overlooked, but critically important factor of the vapor trail of a BUK missile as it launches and then flies to its target was once again brought to light.

The vapor trail of a BUK missile, as reported in the documentary, is large and very noticeable. In this particular case the vapor trail would be white and up to 10,000 meters in length, remaining visible for up to ten minutes. And despite this fact, there is not one reported account of anyone seeing the vapor trail, not one.

Talk regarding the downing of Malaysian Flight MH17 has all but disappeared. Western mainstream media and Western Leaders with "mountains of evidence" linking the Novorossoyia Forces and thus Russia to the downing have fallen uncharacteristically silent, while their evidence appears deathly allergic to sunlight. And four months after Western countries (Netherlands, Denmark) received the flight data recorders from Flight MH17, their lone report could best be characterized as purposely vague and inconclusive.

The Dutch Safety Board's report on Flight MH17's flight data recorder, as aired on *Democracy Now*, determined that Flight MH17 had been hit by "high-energy objects" and broke apart in the air over Eastern Ukraine (Democracy Now 2014). The report, however, failed to assign responsibility or hypothesize the source of the "high-energy objects."

Elephants appear to be wandering around US, EU, and NATO conference rooms, as eyes continually divert from the elephantine facts in the room, on the ground, and apparently in all of the various datasources—black boxes, radar, satellite, etc. There is, indeed, another culprit.

Again, if one were to judge solely on the deafening silence and evasion of the West, the Novorossiyans, Russia, and President Putin would be innocent of any and all responsibility for the downing of Malaysian Flight MH17.

CUI BONO

> *There is no such thing, at this date of the world's history, in America, as an independent press. The business of the journalists is to destroy the truth, to lie outright, to pervert, to vilify, to fawn at the feet of mammon, and to sell his country and his race for his daily bread. We are the tools and vassals of rich men behind the scenes. We are the jumping jacks; they pull the strings and we dance. Our talents, our possibilities and our lives are all the property of other men. We are intellectual prostitutes.*
>
> —*John Swinton, Chief of Staff New York Times at New York Press Club, 1953*

In the end, the phrase *cui bono*—who benefits—appears to set a reasonable expectation for determining, at the very least, the probability of the "who" responsible for the MH17's downing.

The Novorossiya Separatists, Russia, and President Putin stood to gain nothing. Unless, of course, world condemnation, attempted isolation, infamy, an invigorated civil war, crippling sanctions, and the beginnings of a new cold war are considered strategic benefits.

On the other hand, if the Kiev regime, which as detailed above, was losing battle after battle to the Novorossiya Separatists and was poised to potentially lose the war, this incident would have been a benefit to them. It would be a benefit in terms of rallying the West, in the form of NATO, to their cause, and to rallying world opinion.

The US stood to gain (and did) with regard to forcing additional sanctions on Russia, from an increasingly recalcitrant (and financially susceptible) Europe, as well as maintaining dominion over Europe (via NATO). And lastly, NATO would now have a new casus belli (reason for being) to validate its continued existence and to increase its funding.

As of the publication date of this book, the tragic events surrounding Malaysian Flight MH17 have virtually disappeared from discussion in the Western Media. The White House, State Department, the Pentagon, and NATO have not held a press conference and brought to light their findings from the flight data recorder, their various satellites in position at the time, Kiev ATC tapes, or data from NATO's Black Sea operations, in regard to the MH17 downing. Despite military and intelligence budgets collectively approaching $1 trillion, not a single shred of forensically verifiable evidence has been brought forth to substantiate Western claims. To date, videos from social media have been the only form of evidence used to underpin State Department and White House claims. Facebook, Youtube, and Twitter, it appears, have become the de facto sources of intelligence gathering by the West.

The truth, despite the red-hot wave of high-energy propaganda, which has bombarded us daily, across a range of areas regarding Ukraine and Russia, is easily obtainable. Simply reverse any negative geopolitical statement uttered by Western politicians, pundits, and mainstream media newspersons meant to demonize a group or person, as merely propaganda, psychological projection, or both. This will, of course, have the effect of neutralizing propaganda campaigns large and small, while providing a clear picture of reality and thus reducing the need for mind/mood-altering legal and illegal drugs.

CHAPTER 7

RUSSIA CHECKMATES

> *US President Barack Obama, or at least the warhawk neoconservatives pushing him to war everywhere, are beginning to get hit with the boomerang of their stupid economic sanctions against Putin's Russia. A few days ago, Russia's largest oil company, state-run OAO Rosneft, headed by close Putin ally, Igor Sechin, announced discovery of a giant new oil field in Russia's Arctic north of Murmansk. The stupid part comes from Obama's decision to agree to impose sanctions on Sechin and his company and to prohibit US companies from doing business with them.*
>
> —*William Engdahl, Obama's Stupid Sanctions Give Putin New Oil Bonanza*

What the West sought for Russia, via its reckless incursion into Ukraine, was Russia's isolation from the world and from Europe and its dispossession from its long-standing military and naval bases in the Crimea. The Ukraine was to be a chaotic nation used as a NATO forward operating base on Russia's border. The added benefit, however, would be the privatization and plunder of Ukraine, with the loved ones of US government officials sitting on Ukrainian boards of directors and fast-tracked Ukrainian citizenship for US citizens in order to head key government posts in Ukraine.

To this end, the imperial West has chased conquest and plunder across a Grand Chessboard much like Don Quixote chased and fought windmills.

In the past decade this has become apparent to the world, as serial failures in Iraq, Afghanistan, and Georgia and unintended consequences in Libya, Somalia, Yemen, and

Ukraine offer stark proof. The West with its ungodly military budget and destructive apparatus has been proved a paper tiger. As Dmitri Orlov states of the US military:

> *While one might naively assume that the rest of the world is quivering before such overwhelming military might, nothing of the sort is occurring. There is a little secret that everyone knows: the United States military does not know how to win. It just knows how to blow things up. (Orlov 2011)*

What, in fact, the West has come away with is failure so absolute as to have imperiled its near-term existence, financially and politically, as well as its ability to project power across the world. The lone hegemon has stumbled and now falls face forward of its own accord.

Yet the West still seeks to challenge rising powers China and Russia, who have been forced into each other's arms by the West itself. And this newly minted pair, with a combined military capability to literally destroy the West, is rising quickly.

How has the West precipitated its own inevitable checkmate?

CRIMEA

> *"Our western partners created the "Kosovo precedent" with their own hands. In a situation absolutely the same as the one in Crimea they recognized Kosovo's secession from Serbia legitimate while arguing that no permission from a country's central authority for a unilateral declaration of independence is necessary....And the UN International Court of Justice agreed with those arguments. That's what they said; that's what they trumpeted all*

over the world and coerced everyone to accept—and now they are complaining about Crimea. Why is that?"

—Vladimir Putin

In the context of the West/NATO's End Game, as mentioned above, Crimea was, no doubt, a major prize sought by the West in order to deprive Russia of its only warm water port in Sevastopol, Crimea. Russia's Black Sea Fleet would have been banished from a port it had held for over two centuries, which would have proved a key strategic blow to Russia and a proverbial checkmate.

However, several failed moves made by Western pawns in Ukraine telegraphed the West/NATO's forthcoming moves:

- A violent *coup d'tat* that displaced the democratically elected government and installed unelected leaders
- Washington's newly installed government in Kiev featured ultra-nationalists and neo-Nazis (consider historical Nazi atrocities against the Soviet Union) in key ministry posts
- The first act of the newly appointed government was to override the country's constitution
- The newly appointed government then banned Russian as an official language in the Ukraine
- Former Ukrainian Prime Minster Yulia Tymoshenko's leaked phone call hits the internet: "It's about time we grab our guns and go kill those damn Russians together with their leader." And when asked what to do with the 8 million Russians currently living in the Ukraine, Madame

Tymoshenko had this to say, "They must be killed with nuclear weapons."
- The fear that the newly appointed government in Kiev would not recognize the East or their rights, based upon the above

On March 16, 2014, perhaps as a direct result of the above and other provocations, 82 percent of the Crimean population went to the voting polls, 96 percent of whom answered "yes" to the referendum to join the Russian Federation.

The legitimacy of the referendum was also validated by 135 international observers from 23 countries, which included members of the EU, international law experts, and human rights activists.

Of course, the West/NATO and their attendant media were up in arms over the Crimean referendum. Western leaders from the US, UK, France, Germany, and Poland were unanimous in their condemnation of the Crimean referendum and Putin's acceptance of Crimea into the Russian Federation. Without exception, the various Western leaders immediately deemed the move "a violation of international law," "unacceptable by the international community," "illegal and illegitimate."

Yet as Alexander Mezyaev (2014) pointed out in his article, "Is the Crimean Referendum Legal?":

> *The United Nations International Court of Justice handed down an advisory opinion in 2010 saying unambiguously that the unilateral declaration of independence is in accordance with the international law. A referendum-based decision is not a "unilateral declaration of independence". The Court's ruling was related to the unilateral declaration of independence by the illegitimate government of Kosovo and Metohija. In the case of*

> *Crimea the government is democratically elected and legitimate. There are no international norms to be violated; such norms simply do not exist. (Mezyaev 2014)*

The Western strategic goal to evict Russia from its Crimean military and naval bases was thus neutralized, another piece from its chessboard rendered to the side: captured, if you will, by Russia.

Sanctions Backfire

The West, led by Washington, has leveled several rounds of sanctions at Russia for *invading* and *annexing* Crimea (despite a democratic referendum) and destabilizing Ukraine (though there appears to be quite a bit of evidence to the contrary). Sanctions were first aimed at individuals in the Russian government, Russian oligarchs, and select Ukrainians. Later rounds of sanctions targeted Russian industry—banking, oil, gas, and technology.

The intended purposes of the West's, and specifically US-inspired sanctions against Russia were three-fold. The sanctions had been leveled to 1) exclude Russia from international markets (isolation), 2) inhibit the growth of Russia's domestic economy (economic strangulation), and 3) block the development of Russia's South Stream pipeline project and thus further European and Russian integration.

These, of course, have long been the tactics associated with the Grand Chessboard strategy and have little to do with Russia's phantom destabilization/aggression campaign in the Ukraine. As described by geopolitical analyst Eric Draitser (2014) in the article, "Waging War Against Russia, One Pipeline at a Time":

> There have been a number of attempts by the US and its partners to derail Russian pipeline development, and, as a corollary, to continue to promote projects that undermine Russia's position in the energy market of Europe. Indeed, it seems that Europe, and by extension the US, is attempting to leverage their political clout in Eastern Europe to block Russian development and, simultaneously, keep those countries subservient to the West. (Draitser 2014)

However, it appears that the various sanctions leveled at Russia have indeed backfired.

Russia did not immediately retaliate against sanctions by the West, however, when it did retaliate its sanctions were targeted to economically and politically disrupt the sanctioning countries. Russian sanctions targeted agricultural products from the EU, Australia, Canada, Norway, and the US. As noted by Tyler Durden (2014) in the article, "Europe Furious That Putin Dares to Retaliate to Sanctions, Blames Economic Slide on Kremlin":

> Either Europe is run by a bunch of unelected idiots, or... well, that's about it. After blindly doing the US' bidding over all propaganda matters Ukraine-related, and following just as blindly into round after round of US-inspired sanctions, sanctions to whose retaliation Europe would be on the frontline unlike the largely insulated US, Europe appears to be absolutely shocked and is apoplectic that after several rounds of sanction escalations, Russia finally unleashed its own round of sanctions and yesterday announced a 1 year ban on all European food imports, something which will further push Europe into a triple-dip recession as already hinted by Italy yesterday. (Durden 2014)

It is, indeed, interesting that Europe neglected to consider that after several rounds of politically motivated sanctions, Russia might level its own sanctions.

However, the longer-term implications of the Western sanctions will be the growth and revitalization of Russia's domestic produce markets, which will replace the banned goods. Additionally, Russia seeks to diversify imports from other nations—Latin America, China, etc., in order to meet its domestic needs (Durden 2014).

Russia quickly realized that the only way to free itself from future rounds of sanctions-as-economic-warfare was to quickly leave the Western economic universe. The steps taken to date:

- Russians have en masse sold off their dollar holdings and repatriated their money from US banks back to Russia.
- Russia has sold or reallocated $105 billion in Treasury notes from the Fed's custody accounts (Durden 2014).
- Gazprom, a Russian gas company, will only accept payments for its gas in rubles and yuan (Durden 2014).
- Russia and China are moving to create an alternative to the international banking transaction system, Society for Worldwide Interbank Financial Telecommunications (SWIFT), while China's UnionPay payment system, a version of Visa and MasterCard, is ready to provide the infrastructure for Russia to establish its own payment system (RT 2014).

- Russia and Iran have banded together to strategically outmaneuver Western sanctions
- Finance is rapidly moving from the Western world to a non-Western world, de-dollarization model (Simha 2014).
- Russia and China have agreed to a joint venture to produce wide-body aircraft, while Russia and India seek to come to terms on mid-sized aircraft (Simha 2014).
- Russia, as allied to the BRICS founded a new $100 billion Development Bank and a $50 billion infrastructure fund in July, as an alternative to the World Bank and IMF, free of austerity devices (Ford 2014).
- Russia and China have developed closer ties economically, politically, and militarily.
- Chinese banks are stepping in to finance projects and provide development capital that Western sanctions have banned, which completely defeats Western oil/gas funding sanctions (Durden 2014).

As a result of the above and as stated in the sections "No Gas for The EU?" and "The Dollar Falls" EU gas security and the US Dollar as the world's reserve currency have both been dealt a devastating blow.

And a final, no doubt, unintended consequence of Western sanctions, was President Putin's approval rating which has soared to over 80 percent.

Despite these facts, there are yet other glaring sanctions backfires that would not be deemed a viable plot for a straight-to-video film, as it would be considered too unbelievable.

In 2011, Rosneft, Russia's largest state run oil company, and ExxonMobile entered into a joint venture to drill in Russia's Arctic North Murmansk region. The projections were that a discovery of between 750 million to 1 billion barrels of oil would be found at a gross dollar amount equal to $7.5 to $10 trillion (Engdahl 2014). On September 27, 2014, Rosneft and ExxonMobile announced the discovery of a massive new oil field in the Kara Sea (Engdahl 2014). The oil field is estimated to contain more than 9 billion barrels of oil or 9 times the maximum amount projected in 2011. And as part of its agreement with Rosneft, ExxonMobile spent $600 million to drill the first well, which would represent the most expensive drilling operation in ExxonMobile's history.

However, as a result of economic sanctions leveled by the US and, as explained by Mr. Engdahl (2014) in his article, "Obama's Stupid Sanctions Give Putin New Oil Bonanza":

> *Because of the economic sanctions drafted by the US Treasury Undersecretary for Terrorism and Financial Intelligence, David S. Cohen, as of October 10, ExxonMobil will be forced to withdraw from the Russian project and incur huge losses or violate the US Government sanctions and face severe penalties. (Engdahl 2014)*

In an odd twist of fate and what amounts to a reverse telling of the "Little Red Hen" story, ExxonMobile and Morgan Stanley (financier of the project) helped Russia to plant the oil-seeds, cut and mill the oil-wheat, and bake the oil discovery bread, metaphorically speaking, but ExxonMobile and Morgan Stanley will not be able to enjoy a single bite of the baked oil discovery bread, of course, through no fault of

Russia's. Thus the potential $90 trillion loaf of oil-discovery-bread will have to be shared with someone else.

Enter China. To continue the metaphor, President Putin has asked Chinese state oil companies to take a stake or a bite that is, in a major onshore subsidiary of Rosneft, Vankor (Engdahl 2014):

> *It will be the largest Chinese equity deal in a Russian oil company to date. Until the Ukraine crisis and sanctions, Russia had jealously limited foreign share-holding in its state-owned oil and gas companies. That deal deepened the growing energy ties between China and Russia, ironically, the opposite result of what Washington geopolitical Eurasia strategy is intended to achieve. (Engdahl 2014)*

As of October 31, 2014, Halloween, the EU received its "tricks" and Russia received a few "treats" after the EU, Russia, and the Ukraine finally signed a gas deal.

The gas deal will find the EU paying Russia for Ukraine's several billion-dollar gas debt and prepaying Russia for all new Ukrainian gas purchases. Thus, Russia will no longer be responsible for continuing to fund a bankrupt Ukraine—it will finally have the Ukrainian debt cleared from its balance sheet—and the recession-stricken, heavily indebted EU will assume Ukraine's full financial burden, as related to gas purchases and, no doubt, a good deal more.

It appears that the leverage responsible for the EU stepping up to the plate was Ukraine's threat to steal the EU's gas, as Ukraine had done in the past, and Russia's threat to turn off the flow of natural gas entirely, should that happen.

In a recent RT article entitled, "Europe to Pay for the Whole Mess in Ukraine (RT 2014)," economist and Wall Street analyst, Michael Hudson made the following statement:

> *Europe realized that it wouldn't get the gas if it didn't step behind Ukraine and all of a sudden Europe is having to pay for Ukraine's war against Russia. Europe is having to pay for the whole mess in Ukraine so that it can get gas, and this is not how they expected it to turn out. (RT 2014)*

And a final "treat" for Russia on Halloween 2014, as described by Michael Hudson:

> *The sanctions are hurting Europe, they are turning out to be a great benefit for Russia because finally Russia is realizing: "We can't depend on other countries to supply our basic imports, we have to rebuild our industry." And the sanctions are enabling Russia to give subsidies to its industry and agriculture that it couldn't otherwise do. So Russia loves the sanctions, Europe is suffering and the Americans are finding that the Europeans are suddenly more angry at it than they are at Russia. (RT 2014)*

It would appear that there is nothing more *Keystone Copish* or more tragic than the "geostrategy" of the West.

Eastern Pivot—Bear & Dragon

> *What's been clear at the meeting is that there's a coming together between China and Russia. And this has been just exactly the opposite of what American foreign policy has been trying to push for ever since the 1980s. So what is ironic, if we get to irony, is that where the United States thought that it was putting pressure on Russia and sanctions by the adventure of NATO in the Ukraine, what it's actually done is bring Russia and China together.*
>
> —Michael Hudson, RNN, 2014

"Go east bad bear!" said the recalcitrant, oblivious, intellect-starved, and heavily indebted West. And so the resource-rich, heavily-armed, technologically sophisticated, flush bear turned eastward and into the hug of a friendly, welcoming resource-starved, heavily-armed, increasingly technologically savvy, and very well-to-do dragon. On their way to the "Rising Eurasian Pole" they encountered a stately Bengal Tiger (India), a savvy Honey Badger (South Africa), and a powerful Jaguar (Brazil). The end.

A fairytale to some, a nightmare to others, "The West," as written, produced, and published by none other than—the West.

What happens when the scholars, the diplomats, and the adherents and practitioners of realpolitik and diplomacy leave the various government buildings? See above.

Whether one loves them or hates them, the old-school diplomats of yesteryear knew better than to force a heavily-armed bear into a political, economic, and military alliance with a heavily armed dragon. This, however, is the current reality of the day.

It is safe to say that based upon Western/NATO extortive tactics (sanctions), resource wars, encroachments, serial provocations, and the chronic interference in the domestic affairs within both Russia and China (and numerous other nations), that the two have been moving closer and closer together over the course of the past two decades. Militarily, at least, a touchstone may have been reached between the two Eastern nations in September 2013, when the West/NATO sought to call the bluff of Russia and China with respect to Syria.

The US/NATO was about to begin yet another campaign of regime change via the violent removal of another elected leader and the murder of countless innocent civilians in an attempt to "free" those same civilians. This time, however, Russia and China had had enough of US/NATO regime change campaigns and were about to put their proverbial foot down. It would be a show of force against the West not witnessed for at least a quarter of a century.

With Russian, Chinese, and NATO fleets staring each other down in the Eastern Mediterranean, the possibility for World War III was the highest it had been since the Cuban Missile Crisis. As Israel Shamir points out in his article, "The Cape of Good Hope: American Hegemony is Over":

> *The chances for total war were high, as the steely wills of America and Eurasia had crossed in the Eastern Mediterranean. It will take some time until the realisation of what we've gone through seeps in: it is normal for events of such magnitude. The turmoil in the US, from the mad car chase in the DC to the shutdown of federal government and possible debt default, are the direct consequences of this event. The most dramatic event of September 2013 was the high-noon stand-off near the Levantine shore, with five US destroyers pointing their Tomahawks towards Damascus and facing them—the Russian flotilla of eleven ships led by the carrier-killer Missile Cruiser Moskva and supported by Chinese warships. Apparently, two missiles were launched towards the Syrian coast, and both failed to reach their destination. (Shamir 2013)*

The reason the expensive GPS-guided missiles failed to reach their targets, says Shamir, is that "they are relatively easy to subvert with the proper, cost-effective technology" (Shamir 2013).

Perhaps the most important consequence to the West, besides their defeat and capitulation on Syria, was the military alliance forged in a war setting between Russia and China. The Russian bear had begun its own eastern pivot.

Since the beginning of the crisis in the Ukraine, the Western demonization, Congressional posturing, threats, and sanctions, continuously leveled at Eastern Separatists, Putin, and Russia have had a most unintended consequence—they have backfired and, it appears, that they will all fail miserably, in the near-term.

Below please find a point-by-point breakdown of how the Western geopolitical and strategic campaign, aimed at isolating Russia, via an ideology frozen in time, has failed.

Russia China Gas Deal. On May 20, 2014 shortly after the first wave of Western sanctions had taken affect, Russia and China signed a $400 billion natural gas deal, the largest international deal in the history of mankind. The deal purportedly involves Russia supplying 38 billion cubic meters of gas per year to China via a Siberian pipeline project, Altai, and a new eastern pipeline, "Power of Siberia," for the next thirty years.

For Russia, with an increasingly hostile West leveling round after round of sanctions, this deal represented a diversified market partner and nearly a quarter of Europe's combined yearly gas imports of 160 billion cubic meters. Should sanctions persist, when the Russian-Chinese gas deal commences in 2018, 38 billion cubic meters of gas will be a powerful bargaining chip.

The deal represents for China, currently the world's largest oil importer, a stable energy source via two secure pipeline routes, a future potential replacement for coal (its number one source of energy), and imported oil, which has been problematic for China *vis-a-vis* US disruption.

China's String of Pearls, the importation route that brings oil to China from Middle Eastern and North African (MENA) suppliers, has been particularly vulnerable via a strategically developed scheme by the US to disrupt Chinese energy security (Gunnar 2014). As stated by geopolitical analyst Ulson Gunnar (2014):

> *The United States, in a bid to reassert itself in the Pacific and maintain both regional and global hegemony, has committed to years of disrupting China's oil lifeline and in theory, strangle China's growth. The US has sown chaos across MENA and attempted to carve off the entire Pakistani province of Baluchistan. (Gunnar 2014)*

Natural gas, a cleaner source of energy that is proximate and relatively free from the disruptive polices of the West is, of course, a precious commodity for China.

However, the larger geostrategic and financial implications is that the deal was conducted in yuan and rubles. Further, it is not only the size of the deal struck between two rising powers, one a resources superpower and the other a manufacturing and economic hegemon, it is what this deal symbolizes to the world—an alternative global currency and a multipolar world. All, of course, turbo charged by Western geopolitical blundering, short-sightedness, and a fundamentalist ideology run amok.

Iranian Oil Deal, etc. In August of 2014 Russia and Iran agreed to a $20 billion five year trade deal that encompassed not only oil-gas sales, but the "construction of power plants, energy grids, heavy machinery, consumer goods, and agricultural products," as stated by Moscow's Energy

Ministry. The deal speaks to the exportation of 500,000 barrels of oil per day to Russia.

The immediate implications of this deal between Russia and Iran represent, among other things, an about-face of Russia's prior willingness to work with Western imposed sanctions on Iran—in fact, a direct thwarting of those sanctions has begun. Additionally, the Iran—Russian reproachmont signals the beginning of another strategic eastern military, political, and economic partnership, a blow to petrodollar dominance, and the near-term demise of the dollar as reserve currency. And, interestingly, the aforementioned events have been turbo charged by Western geopolitical blundering, shortsightedness, and adherence to a dated ideology run amok.

MULTI-POLES

There are now numerous geopolitical poles rapidly taking shape and solidifying, in direct response to the long established *order* represented by the West as a direct result of the current Ukrainian crisis.

The various rising poles of influence, with Russia part and parcel of nearly every one, is, of course, a clear repudiation of Western boasts of an isolated Russia. It also speaks volumes to another failed Western policy and to a world that has grown tired of the "New World Order" as nations are determinedly seeking something else. Several of the counter-organizations currently growing and solidifying are:

THE SCO

The Shanghai Cooperation Organization (SCO) began as the Shanghai Five in 1996 and it represented three-fifths of Eurasia and 25 percent of the world's population (Hallinan 2014). In 2001, its member states included China, Russia, Kazakhstan, Kyrgyzstan, Tajikistan, and Uzbekistan.

Its major focus is the security of member states, and many recognize the SCO as a counterbalance to NATO. The SCO has also held annual military drills.

> *The SCO has consistently rebuffed US requests for observer status, and has pressured countries in the region to end US basing rights. The US was forced out of Karshi-Khanabad in Uzbekistan in 2006, and from Manas in Kyrgyzstan in 2014. (Hallinan 2014)*

As of today, the SCO has grown to also include new members India, Pakistan, Iran and Mongolia. This represents the single largest expansion of a group dedicated to economic cooperation and security in SCO history (Hallinan 2014).

THE BRICS

BRICS is an acronym for Brazil Russia India China South Africa. The term, interestingly enough, was first used in an article written by Jim O'Neill of Goldman Sachs. The article outlined the various synergies—product manufacturing, services exports, raw materials, population size, market demographics, and growth rates—between the countries and how these factors would catalyze by 2050 to make the BRICS the dominant power bloc (Ghosh 2013).

Interestingly, the BRICS countries came together as a result of Mr. O'Neill's article or, as Jayati Ghosh, economics professor at Jawaharlal Nehru University in New Delhi, states:

> *Strange things happen in the world. Imagine a grouping of countries spread across the globe, which gets formed only for the simple reason that an analyst for an investment bank decides that these countries have some things in common, including future potential for growth, and then creates an acronym of their names! Bizarre but true. (Ghosh 2013)*

Eight years later in June of 2009 the group had its first official meeting in Yekaterinburg, Russia. Since then, the BRICS have met every year. In terms of what this collection of nation-states brings to the table, Ghosh summarizes:

> *The BRICS now cover 3 billion people, with a total estimated GDP of nearly $14 trillion and around $4 trillion of foreign exchange reserves. Each country is effectively a sub-regional leader. (Ghosh 2013)*

Whether or not the initial impetus of the BRICS countries was to move out of the Western political economic orbit, events that have taken place over the intervening years have instigated their now-deliberate secession from the New World Order.

Not only has investment between the countries grown, but they have also sought to change, from the inside, the workings of the current political and economic status quo. In 2013, the BRICS acted to reform IMF voting procedures by pledging to invest $75 billion. However, they have also increased bilateral trade in the currency of each respective nation and they have sought a shared approach in foreign policy, based upon a more constructive and empowering approach for trading partners and their citizens (Ghosh 2013).

The BRICS appeared content to move measuredly toward their goal of greater economic and political integration while continuing to operate within the orbit of the West and its various banking, credit, and exchange institutions. And while there had been talk of an independent bank, there appeared to be no immediate rush to form one. All that, of course, changed rather dramatically.

On July 16, 2014, the BRICS, to offset the extortive tactics of the West's sanctioning regimes, founded a New Development Bank and funded it with $100 billion to be used as a money pool and an additional $50 billion to fund infrastructure projects (Ford 2016). Of course, the hard irony here is that had there been no putsch in Kiev sponsored by the West and no sanctions the New Development Bank may have been a few years off, if, indeed, it ever formed.

The New Development Bank is scheduled to begin making loans in 2016, under decidedly different terms than those provided by the IMF and World Bank. There will be no harsh austerity measures from the new bank and emerging nations will now have a choice of lenders. And so will begin the march away from the Western economic institutions, mandated austerity, and ostensibly the dollar, as alignment with a rising East takes center stage.

Other Eurasian-based organizations currently challenging Western hegemony are the Collective Security Treaty Organization (CSTO) and the soon-to-be Eurasian Economic Union.

NATO sought to checkmate the Russian king by attempting to take one more piece, the final piece, on Zbig's Grand Chessboard: Ukraine. A trap was being set by the West in which it envisioned the Russian state completely surrounded on its western border, cut off from its only warm water port, and completely isolated from the world as a pariah state. Of course, pocketing Ukraine's gold reserves, extracting its natural resources, and putting Ukrainians on a starvation diet via IMF restructuring, was to be yet another critical piece of the Russian chessboard sidelined.

The irony is that the Ukrainian *coup d'é tat*, as orchestrated by the West, served as the trip wire over which the West itself has tripped, and the successive leveling of sanctions have become the pit into which the West is even now still falling.

The West, via Ukraine, has made a geopolitical misstep of proportions so grand that it will shake the very foundation of the socioeconomic and political status quo. Further, the West has provided both Russia and China with a powerful incentive for forging a multipolar geostrategy and has prodded, via its actions, that they make haste in its attainment.

NO GAS FOR THE EU

On December 1, 2014 Russia announced to the world that it had cancelled its South Stream pipeline project, which was scheduled to bring desperately needed natural gas to Europe by 2016. The reason cited for this rather momentous change in direction by President Putin:

> *We believe that the stance of the European Commission was counterproductive. In fact, the European Commission not only provided no help in implementation of [the South Stream pipeline], but, as we see, obstacles were created to its implementation. Well, if Europe doesn't want it implemented, it won't be implemented. We'll be promoting other markets and*

Europe won't receive those volumes, at least not from Russia. We believe that it doesn't meet the economic interests of Europe and it harms our cooperation. But such is the choice of our European friends. (RT 2014)

The other "regions of the world" it turns out, would start with Turkey. President Putin announced to the world, at the selfsame meeting, that the South Stream project would, in fact, be diverted to Turkey instead or "Turk Stream."

The underlying reasons for the cancellation of the South Stream pipeline can be clearly traced to US pressure on the various EU nations and Bulgaria, in particular, to terminate the pipeline and to the EU's own Third Energy Package (TEP), which had been labeled by some as a "rent-extraction" device.

The TEP was adopted by the European Parliament in July 2009 and entered into force on September 3, 2009, two years after the South Stream project had been proposed and signed. The EU sought to retroactively apply conditions via the TEP, that favored the EU to the detriment of Gazprom, a Russian natural gas extractor. As explained by Pepe Escobar (2014) author and journalist for *Asia Times Online*:

> *The EC brilliant "strategy" revolves around the EU's Third Energy Package, which requires that pipelines and the natural gas flowing inside them must be owned by separate companies. The target of this package has always been Gazprom—which owns pipelines in many Central and Eastern European nations. The target within the target has always been South Stream. (Escobar 2014)*

However, the underlying reasoning behind the TEP is explained by Michael Hudson in his article, "Backfired! U.S.

New Cold War Policy Has Backfired–And Created Its Worst Nightmare":

> *The U.S. neoliberal plan has been to insist on non-Russian control of the pipelines that would carry Russian gas and oil to Europe. The idea is to use this pipeline as a tollbooth to siphon off the revenue that Russia had hoped to receive from Europe. (Hudson 2014)*

What were the implications of the TEP in practical person-on-the-street terms? As Hudson states:

> *Imagine that the United States had a law that owners of buildings could not also own the elevators in them. This would mean that the owners of the Empire State Building, for instance, could not own their elevators. Some other investors could buy the elevators, and then tell the building's renters or other occupants that they would have to pay a fee each time they rode up to the 40th floor, the 50th floor, the 60th floor, and so forth.*

> *The result would be that instead of the landlord receiving the rental value of the Empire State Building, the elevator owner could demand the lion's share. Without access, the building would be a walk-up and its rents would fall – unless renters paid the elevator tollbooth. (Hudson 2014)*

In the end, the TEP was, indeed, a scheme by the EU to "carve out a rent-extraction opportunity to siphon off Russian gas revenue" (Hudson 2014). However, in a twist of irony on parallel with a *Twilight Zone* episode, it backfired wickedly.

What was initially hailed, at the time, by Western media as a defeat for Putin and thus Russia, with regard to South Stream's cancellation, has been exposed for its unparalleled cynicism and for the devastating blow that it has leveled at EU energy security.

On January 14, 2015, EU negotiators arrived in Moscow in order to:

> *Pressure Russia to resurrect the canceled South Stream gas pipeline project and build it in accordance with the restrictive rules of the Third Energy Package. (Kettunen 2015)*

The Gazprom response, however, was *nyet* ("no"). Instead Gazprom offered the following solution to its EU clients and would-be rent-extractors:

> *Gazprom will build the pipeline to Turkey and extend it to the Turkish-Greek border. The pipeline will end in a gas distribution hub near the EU border.*

> *If the EU wants to buy gas, it will have to build a pipeline to Turkey at its own expense. It will also need to expand the gas transport capacity between its South European member countries— and do so under the constraints imposed by its own Third Energy Package. (Kettunen 2015)*

But, of course, there's more. The historical problem of the Ukraine siphoning off (stealing and extorting) gas paid for by EU nations would also come to an end after the completion of the new Turk Steam pipeline. Or as summed up by Aleksi Kuttunen in the article, "Gazprom Tells EU No Deal on South Stream Restart, EU Free to Get Russian Gas in Turkey":

> *The final punch to EU arrogance was Gazprom's declaration that after the completion of the gas hub and the Turkish pipeline Gazprom will end all gas transit through Ukraine. Russian gas will only be available through Turkey!*

> *The Ukrainian pipeline network will be used exclusively [to] supply gas to Ukraine. Gazprom based its decision on Ukraine's instability and the high transit risks. (Kettunen 2015)*

It would appear that irony, blowback, a resounding checkmate, and the antics of Keystone Cops, in high office, abound across the Western world. In the end, the EU will have to come hat-in-hand for Russian gas *from Turkey*, with no viable alternatives and a soon-to-be-severed Ukrainian natural gas artery. And Turkey, the endlessly spurned bride to EU "marriage-ship," will have the last laugh and a healthy bank balance.

The Dollar Falls

> *Since the collapse of the USSR, the countries which defied dollar dominance invariably came under heavy pressure and in a number of cases – under devastating attacks. S. Hussein who banned dollar circulation in all spheres of Iraq's economy including oil trade was displaced and executed and his country was left in ruins. M. Gadhafi started switching Libya's oil and gas business to gold-backed Arab currencies and air raids against the country followed almost immediately… Tehran had to put its plan to stay dollar-free on hold to avoid falling victim to aggression.*
>
> —*Leonid Ivashov, Former Joint Chief of Staff of the Russian Armed Forces, General-Colonel*

In the quote above by Mr. Ivashov, Iraq, Libya, and Iran sought to leave the Western economic order, as governed by the US dollar, and subsequently fell into harm's way or, in the case of Iran, has been continually threatened and aggressed economically. The purported reasons for the disastrous fall or harassment of the countries and their leaders have varied from Weapons of Mass Destruction (WMDs) to "killing their own people" to "bringing freedom and democracy." The reasons, in each and every case, have been red herrings, fabrications, and a pack of outright lies. The true reason is that Iran sought another way, a way that US empire did not approve of.

To the present: as the West continually leveled sanctions against Russia for its "aggression" in the Ukraine, a tipping point was reached, to which President Putin declared, "*No mas.*"

Putin's Russia and the other BRICS members have now eclipsed all previous efforts to forgo not only the petrodollar dominance of the West but all of its economic institutions. It is this move that greatly threatens the dollar's reserve status far above Iraq, Libya, or even Iran's attempts.

Furthermore, Russia has itself embarked upon a crusade to de-dollarize the entirety of its trade and replace it with none other than its own currency, the ruble. Less than two decades ago this would have been unthinkable, laughable by Western powers. Today those very same Western powers are circling their financial wagons and aiming their sanctions Winchesters at themselves and each other.

At a meeting held April 24, 2014, and as reported by Prime News:

> *The [Russian] government organized a special meeting dedicated to finding a solution for getting rid of the US dollar in Russian export operations. Top level experts from the energy sector, banks and governmental agencies were summoned and a number of measures were proposed as a response for American sanctions against Russia. (Prime News 2014)*

What are the short to near-term consequences to the G7 nations, whose disintegrating economies (see PIIGS—Portugal Italy Ireland Greece Spain and FUKUS—France United Kingdom United States) are inextricably interwoven into the current imploding economic matrix? The answer, of course, is excruciating, self-inflicted pain, that could easily have been avoided.

It grows increasingly apparent that Western leaders truly make no attempt whatsoever to contemplate the unintended consequences of their actions. This is, unfortunately, the province of ideologues and zealots—*full steam ahead and damn the consequences*. There is ample evidence from Afghanistan, Iraq, Libya, Somalia, and now Syria to provide full bona fides for the above statement.

And it gets ever worse for the Western elite orchestrating the various geostrategic machinations. China, Iran, and India have already agreed to drop the dollar and to trade in their respective currencies. A host of other countries line up to de-dollarize and move out of the Western economic orbit.

On October 14, 2014, Russia and China signed 40 agreements encompassing trade, energy, finance, and technology (Business New Europe 2014). Russian Prime Minister Dmitry Medvedev projected that trade relations between the two countries will double to $200 billion a year. As noted in the *Business New Europe* article "Russia Signs Raft of Deals with China":

> *To financially underpin such a trade surge and move towards stronger use of domestic currencies in trade instead of the dollar, Russia and China agreed to a three-year yuan-rubel swap worth 150bn yuan (roughly $24.5bn), and Beijing state banks agreed to provide credit lines to Russian banks and companies to fund technology imports from China. (Business New Europe 2014)*

And where Russia's largest state-owned bank, Sherbank, relied heavily on high-tech equipment from the US and European companies, China's Huawei Technologies has stepped in to fill the breach (Business New Europe 2014).

But there's still more. On October 24, 2014, Russia, the world's second largest producer of natural gas, launched an independent natural gas exchange to be based in St. Petersburg and it is purported to be the largest market for natural gas trading over the whole of Europe (Schortgen 2014). The new gas exchange will be designated the St. Petersburg International Mercantile Exchange (SPIMEX) and will represent a profound change in that it will be 1) pricing gas independently from oil 2) pricing gas in rubles and not dollars 3) opening up a market for buyers who only seek to purchase gas and not oil 4) creating a more competitive market for natural gas and 5) providing Russia with a mechanism to bypass established market structures and thus punitive sanctions and conspiratorial plots waged to undermine its financial stability (Schortgen 2014). As stated in the article, "Russia's New Gas Exchange Could Lead to Energy Pricing Outside the Dollar":

> *This trade facility will allow for international and domestic gas operations to sell their products in Russia and in a centralized location, and will become part of the growing Eurasian Economic Zone that is emerging in the East as global trade moves away from the dollar and away from US hegemony. (Schortgen 2014)*

In November, Russia and China signed another natural gas deal for a reported $300 billion, taking the combined total of natural gas deals between the countries to a precedent-setting three quarters of a trillion dollars. And, of course, the gas deals will be transacted in rubles and yuan.

However, the most pivotal gambit currently being played by Russia, as led by President Putin, is its amassing of gold. It is a gambit in which the West is even now hopelessly trapped. In chess, the situation in which the West now languishes is called "time trouble (Kalinchenko 2014)" thus it is a matter of time before the game ends quite predictably. Perhaps the battlefield equivalent of this gambit are the "cauldrons" into which the Ukrainian Army was itself checkmated by the Novorrisoyan freedom fighters.

The Western gambit in the Ukraine, on the other hand, has led to unremitting failure. Yet the West attempts another poorly thought-out strategy aimed at destroying the Russian economy, which has taken the form of lowering oil and gas prices, the key drivers of Russia's revenue. However, this new strategy has led the West into yet more "time trouble (cauldron)" from which it will never emerge.

President Putin, as both chess master and Judo champion, is strategically using his opponents strength against him. As stated in the article, "Grandmaster Putin's Golden Trap," Dmitry Kalinichenko (2014) sets the stage:

> *What is the truly tragic predicament of the West and the United States, in which they find themselves? And why all the Western media and leading Western economists are silent about this, as a well guarded military secret? Let's try to understand the essence of current economic events, in the context of the economy, setting aside the factors of morality, ethics and geopolitics. (Kalinichenko 2014)*

Currently, the US Government intentionally suppresses the price of gold via a special department called the Exchange Stabilization Fund (ESF), with the intended aim of stabilizing the dollar. This suppression has, in fact, become law in the US (Kalinchenko 2014):

> *Right now the West spends much of its efforts and resources to suppress the prices of gold and oil. Thereby, on the one hand, to distort the existing economic reality in favor of the US dollar and on the other hand, to destroy the Russian economy, refusing to play the role of obedient vassal of the West. (Kalinchenko 2014)*

As a result, both gold and oil are artificially undervalued, while the dollar flies high against other currencies and the aforementioned commodities.

This brings us to Putin's final gambit. In short, President Putin is quietly selling Russian oil and gas for "physical" gold. And though he still accepts the over-valued dollar in payment, these dollars are then immediately exchanged for under-valued physical gold. This is where the trap becomes "magnetic" and pulls in a West that begins slowly to understand what's happening, but can do literally nothing to change its fate. As Kalinchenko states:

> *Thus, the Western world, built on the hegemony of the petrodollar, is in a catastrophic situation. In which it cannot survive without oil and gas supplies from Russia. And Russia is now ready to sell its oil and gas to the West only in exchange for physical gold! The twist of Putin's game is that the mechanism for the sale of Russian energy to the West only for gold now works regardless of whether the West agrees to pay for Russian oil and gas with its artificially cheap gold, or not. (Kalinchenko 2014)*

So, the US artificially props up the dollar and the Russians use the artificially high dollar to buy the artificially lowered gold and then sells its oil to all other Western players for physical gold. What Russia has, in fact done, is reopened the "gold window," closed by Nixon in 1971 without asking for Washington's permission" (Kalinchenko 2014). Kalinchenko sums that:

> *This truly brilliant economic combination by Putin puts the West led by the United States in a position of a snake, aggressively and diligently devouring its own tail. (Kalinchenko 2014)*

With limited worldwide gold reserves and the West currently hemorrhaging gold eastward to buy oil from Russia, this begs the question: how long will the West be able to buy oil and gas from Russia in exchange for physical gold?

Perhaps this is one of the reasons why Iraq, Libya, Ukraine, and, perhaps, a host of others, have had their gold reserves renditioned to the US, so that the US might attempt to stall the inevitable.

But then there is the most important question: what will happen after the West runs out of physical gold (Kalinchenko 2014)? Checkmate.

The above facts do bring clarity to the fact that a number of Western European countries are asking to repatriate their gold, currently being held in the US.

The combination of the above with regard to imperiling Western hegemony via the dollar as the reserve currency can certainly not be overlooked. Alone, any one of the recent development—BRICS Bank and Investment Bank, historic trading deals executed in currencies other than the dollar, a concerted move away from the SWIFT system, and the current gas bourse—would have been enough to, at least, seriously wound the dollar. Taken together, they represent an ominous and near-term disaster for economies still tied to the dollar.

When the dollar will fall is anyone's guess. That it will fall with an aggressive de-dollarization campaign underway by, arguably, the largest economy in the world, China, and rising Eurasian powers in Russia, India, Iran, and now Turkey, is a certainty. And as Michael Hudson, research professor of economics at University of Missouri—Kansas City, states:

> *Turkey already is moving out of the US-European orbit, by turning to Russia for its energy needs. Iran also has moved into an alliance with Russia. Instead of the Obama administration's neocons dividing and conquering as they had planned, they are isolating America from Europe and Asia. Yet there has been almost no recognition of this in the US press, despite its front-page discussion throughout Europe and Asia. Instead of breaking up the BRICS, the dollar area is coming undone. (Hudson 2014)*

If one believes the point made by Leonid Ivashov, the former joint chief of staff of the Russian Armed Forces, that one of the reasons the West, led by the US, invaded Iraq (banned dollar circulation) and Libya (oil and gas to gold-backed Arab currencies) and has been threatening Iran (Euro-denominated oil bourse) is that each of these countries openly defied dollar dominance. Of course, if these countries were threats with comparatively tiny economies, the current de-dollarization by major countries is assuredly driving the West stark-raving mad.

It may be argued by future historians that this was the greatest and most notable incident of the West shooting itself in the foot over and over again, despite its best aim at its intended victim.

CONCLUSIONS

The Church of the Grand Chessboard

> *"The technotronic era involves the gradual appearance of a more controlled society. Such a society would be dominated by an elite, unrestrained by traditional values. Soon it will be possible to assert almost continuous surveillance over every citizen and maintain up-to-date complete files containing even the most personal information about the citizen. These files will be subject to instantaneous retrieval by the authorities."*
>
> —Zbigniew Brzeziński, from his book Between Two Ages: America's Role in the Technotronic Era (1976)

Perhaps the above quote provides a bit of insight into the heart and soul of the highest of high priests responsible for constructing the Church of the Grand Chessboard.

US foreign policy has, indeed, become a fundamentalist religion as defined by the canons of the Grand Chessboard and the monks of its accompanying sect, the Project for A New American Century. Its priests, priestesses, and monks are zealots in every respect, undeterred by logic, pragmatism, reality, facts, forensic evidence, morality, and even Mutually Assured Destruction (MAD).

The Church of the Grand Chessboard's canons are simple—the universe revolves around the US (more specifically, its financial elite) and the US is "exceptional" standing head and shoulders above all others. Anyone opposing said belief is a heretic, heathen, Hitler, conspiracy theorist, or a candidate for regime change. Further, they of the Grand Chessboard, and their congregants who are incapable of wrong-doing, believe that they are the smartest guys/gals in the world, that their lives are the only lives that matter (though congregants can be expendable in a pinch) and that their god, Mammon, is subordinate to none.

Thus Neocons and Neoliberals are the fanatical high-priests and priestesses of an anachronistic doomsday religion that now holds the fate of the world in its hands. And, unfortunately, the church of the Grand Chessboard has the means to bring about doomsday. Welcome back to the "Dark Ages."

The one thing religious fanatics and zealots fail to realize time and again is that the world is a highly complex, dynamic, and multi-variant system. It is ever-changing. If one were to merely consider the social, political, and economic interactions taking place among nation states from year to year, those changes alone would be nearly impossible to predict. In this same vein, if one were to hold fast to a rigid set of ideological models and attempt to predict the relationship between nation-states some two decades hence, the odds of a successful prediction (even if one were actively engaged in its consummation), would be a non-zero finite sum, approaching zero at light-speed.

Or more simply put, change is inevitable, constant, and part of the natural process of life. Rigid models and ideas are like stagnant, fetid pools of evaporating water. They are not long for the world.

Zbigniew Brzeziński's Grand Chessboard is a stagnant, fetid pool, a scheme frozen in a time and place that no longer exists. Further, it has brought about that which the West has sought to deter with ungodly sums of treasure, countless lives, incessant geopolitical subterfuge, abject hypocrisy, and a universe of lies. And the zealots who now adhere to and execute its precepts are themselves incapable of grasping the horrors that their beliefs, convictions, and ignominious acts call forward.

How do empires fall? How do their fanatical high priests and priestesses exit the stage? Do they exit the stage gracefully, perhaps, as an athlete who knows that his/her time has come? Or do they thrash about causing inconceivable levels of destruction, suffering, and death (bordering on genocide) as they seek to remain imperial?

The US empire, less than three quarters of a century old, with its steroid-fed successor, US hyper-empire, a little more than two decades old, falters on all fronts. Most certainly, the idea of the US having genuine leaders who are principled, courageous, peaceable, pragmatic, and inclusive is the true conspiracy theory of our time, as no such creature now exists.

It appears that the "1 percent" has had quite the hand in fashioning this conspiracy theory—serial assassinations, some quite public, along with a host of other devices that have shorn genuine leaders and potential leaders from any and all positions of leadership.

On the other hand, ungodly amounts of fiat currency that have been dispensed for instigating indentured political servitude, morality-cleanses, and de facto thought control have brought about another creature altogether—the sociopath as political whore, bereft of intellect, integrity, morality, and above all, common sense.

As Peter Dale Scott, former diplomat, Berkeley Professor and author, suggests, there is an "Invisible Empire" that is the true power behind the government, which controls a large measure of the world's resources, its "leaders" and its capital.

President Eisenhower alluded to the culprit, "The Military-Industrial Complex," though he was advised to extract the "congressional" component from his speech. Perhaps, banking oligarchs were also extracted, with the historical record scrubbed clean of this reference altogether.

No doubt, one of the first things that signals the end of an empire is the complete absence of true leaders, the rise to power of the sociopath as "leader" and a congregation of "yes people" who steadily nod their heads, answer the call, and shout down non-believers while happily imbibing the poison-laced imperial Kool-Aid.

Imperial Wars & Planned Chaos—TILT!

The ability of the US to continually engage in de facto wars of imperial conquest, asset stripping/looting, and the purposeful creations of planned chaos is and has been underpinned by the dollar's status as reserve currency. Should that status be disrupted via an alternative currency (ruble, Yuan, or a basket thereof), which is now being aggressively implemented by Russia and China, the gargantuan red chickens of US financial insolvency, estimated at $220 trillion (Lawler 2012), will come home to roost. And non-stop Qualitative Easing (printing money hand over fist) will no longer delay the inevitable — economic collapse.

The attendant consequences will, of course, be the metaphorical shot to the head of the various Western zombie banks, complete Western economic implosion, internal chaos, and a tragic though powerful awakening of the Western masses, long somnambulant via the narcotics of debt-consumerism, entertainment/media programming, hard drugs (legal and illegal), and lies. Perhaps this is one reason US Homeland Security has purchased millions of the illegal Dum-dum bullets (they expand and make big holes in human bodies) and why Posse Commitatus, along with the Bill of Rights, have been suspended or virtually suspended respectively.

If one were to envision an optimistic scenario as a result of Western implosions—the wars, launched by the West, the serial aggression, destabilizations, and resulting chaos—what would it be? It would be a multipolar world with a constructive approach to international relations, a win-win approach to trade, a respect for all life, and different approaches to living on this planet.

Pessimistically, however, should the US not wish to embrace the realization of its status as a zombie financial empire and thus seek to go out with guns blazing...

World War III

> *In desperation, dysfunctional Western capitalism is lashing out recklessly and irrationally, unwilling and unable to preclude the disastrous consequences of its myopic policies. And one possible consequence of current US/NATO policies is thermonuclear war.*
> —Carla Stea, "Pardon Us For Our Country's Existence in the Middle of Your Military Bases," *Global Research* 2014

I recall playing chess with a college friend, whom I had managed to checkmate over the course of several successive games. While moving towards victory in yet another game, my friend, unwilling to take another loss, upset the chessboard. Chess pieces went flying in all directions, as though a bomb had gone off in the middle of the chessboard. It appears that we may all face a similar situation.

As the West stands checkmated on their decades-long Grand Chessboard pilgrimage, with all semblance of intelligence, realpolitik, morality, diplomacy, and sanity in Western Capitals long extinct, will the West upset the chessboard? Will the West do so by titling it towards a nuclear confrontation with Russia and its new best friend for life and strategic partner China?

As Professor Emeritus of Russian Studies Stephen Cohen explains regarding the possibilities of a thermonuclear war between the US and Russia:

> *If the civil war in Ukraine begins again, the military aspect. If the cease fire fails. If Kiev attacks the Donbass again. If Russia feels the need to help the Donbass again militarily, it is being discussed in NATO, the possibility of NATO forces entering Western Ukraine. Now what would that mean? You would have the American led NATO forces in Western Ukraine, whether on the ground or in the air, it doesn't matter. Russian forces in the air or on the ground and that would be a modern version of the Cuban Missile Crisis. (Cohen 2014)*

During the Cuban Missile Crisis the world stood on the knife edge of thermonuclear war, but then there were leaders who understood the consequences and undertook diplomatic initiatives: realpolitik. They clearly understood that speaking to their adversary was critical in order to negotiate a cessation of hostilities. In contrast, today, presidents, prime ministers, and secretaries of state pout, demean, and continually undermine their supposed adversaries with slurs, ad hominem attacks, and marketing slogans straight from Madison Avenue—"He's the devil, he's Hitler, we don't negotiate with the enemy, terrorists, people we don't like."

Professor Cohen laments that an open discussion with opposing points of view is entirely absent from debate in today's US, while the mainstream US media happily toes the line.

> *There is no debate of public opposition in this country about this, unlike the situation 20—5 years ago, when we had real debates and public fights," he said. "I don't know if they [the mainstream media—[RT] know the truth and therefore are not telling the truth, or that they are just caught up in the myths that had been attached to Russia since the end of the Soviet Union. (Cohen 2014)*

Where, indeed, are the voices of reason, sanity, and realpolitik? In light of an AWOL White House and a compliant/subservient media, they are nowhere to be found. And then, of course there is the US Congress and their latest bout of demonstrable insanity, Russian Aggression Prevention Act (RAPA), which states:

> *Use all appropriate elements of United States national power...to protect the independence, sovereignty, and territorial and economic integrity of Ukraine and other sovereign nations in Europe and Eurasia from Russian aggression... [This includes] substantially increasing United States and NATO support for the armed forces of the Republics of Poland, Estonia, Lithuania, and Latvia... [and] substantially increasing the complement of forward-based NATO forces in those states.*

This is not the response of reasonable, sane people to a potential world-ending nuclear conflagration, this is the response of madmen, zealots, sociopaths, high priests and priestesses of a religious cult begging to be destroyed.

> *Having lost our minds and fixated on our brains, we have been taught to be determined, not free. And whether consciously or unconsciously, most have obliged.*
>
> —Edward Curtin, Sociology Professor
> Massachusetts College of Liberal Arts

> *At one rally, the speaker is forced to change his speech halfway through to point out that Oceania is not, and has never been, at war with Eurasia. Rather, the speaker says, Oceania is, and always has been, at war with Eastasia. The people become embarrassed about carrying the anti-Eurasia signs and blame Emmanuel Goldstein's agents for sabotaging them. Nevertheless, they exhibit full-fledged hatred for Eastasia.*
>
> —George Orwell, *1984*

The first quote was taken from a very interesting article called "The Propaganda Trap, Tranquilized by Trivia." In it, Professor Curtin explains how Americans have been programmed twenty-four hours a day and seven days a week to remember and repeat the company line. Its persistence is for us what water is to fish—always there and never questioned or considered.

The second quote taken from Orwell's dystopian saga *1984* finds a present-day parallel as one enemy of the West (Afghanistan, Iraq, Libya, Somalia, Syria, Iran, Russia) is continually switched out for another, right before our very eyes.

So it goes in the Ukraine, as innocent aunts and uncles, grandmothers and grandfathers, wives and husbands, newborns, children, and siblings are labelled as terrorists and killed for the benefit of a defunct strategy and for men and women far too wealthy, powerful, ignorant, and dangerous to be in control of anything, let alone the world.

The West's pursuit of ever more at all costs or with "everything on the table" has led to its moral, cultural, social, and economic bankruptcy and its inevitable decline, now taking place at something near light speed.

Russia pivots east, with its natural resources, flush bank accounts, massive gold reserves, thousands of nuclear missiles, and a rising tech sector, into a bear hug with a dragon, China, also flush with gold, over flowing bank accounts, and its currency flirting with center stage.

The East will continue its now-accelerated rise. The balance of the world will gravitate toward this new magnetic pole and away from the New World Order of the West and its gargantuan hypocrisy, war zealotry, extortive austerity initiatives, and its hyper-gangsterism.

The East with its New Development and Investment Banks, a philosophy that offers constructive engagement, geopolitical pragmatism and win-win investment strategies will be a clear and compelling choice for the world.

The isolation of Russia and China will not materialize from the West/NATO's latest poorly devised gambit, as their attempts to isolate are based upon a seventy-year-old cold war strategy, developed for a world, geostrategic relations, a mindset, and a time that no longer exists.

The world has changed dramatically in the past quarter century. The rise of opposing state media, alternative media, and the internet have made the world smaller, more transparent and the citizens (of at least some countries) more aware of the dynamics at play. It could be argued, though, that karma alone could see an isolated and impotent West.

The various organizations outlined above—BRICS, CTSO, SCO and the countries therein—are not the balls and chains that the former Soviet satellites were. They are all viable independent nations that are rising in their respective geographic sectors.

In the wake of political, economic, geo-strategic, and military dynamics in the year 2014, as a direct result of the US policy on Ukraine, and based upon our prior arguments, the Grand Chessboard strategy, developed and championed by Zbigniew Brzeziński et al. has failed, irrefutably. Irrefutably in that its implementation, over the course of the past two decades, has brought about the precise outcomes that it sought to avoid—Western hegemonic implosion and the formation of multi-poles of power, featuring a rising East and a declining, heavily-indebted and increasingly violent West.

There is a final caveat and that is this: if the West fails to wake from its omnicidal fundamentalist trance, if pragmatism, common sense, morality, and decency go unremembered, then there may be war, accidental or purposeful, and as Albert Einstein so presciently stated:

I know not with what weapons World War III will be fought, but World War IV will be fought with sticks and stones.[1]

—*Albert Einstein*

AFTERWORD

The Russians and Chinese have just signed another mega-billion gas deal reported to be worth $325 billion, which brings the total for the year to three quarters of a trillion dollars. There is no precedent in the history of the world for contracts of this magnitude. The contracts will, no doubt, be conducted in rubles and yuan, which will further displace petrodollar hegemony. This, in turn, will provide a rather impressive turbo charge to the New Silk Road, while, of course, belying Russia's "isolation" and its "economic implosion."

Elections were held in Western Ukraine on October 26, 2014 and in Eastern Ukraine on November 2, 2014.

The elections in Kiev were widely celebrated across the Western capitals as Kiev's "Pro-Western" parties decided, in lockstep, to move Westward.

However, the salient point missing from the "analysis" and praise gushing forth from the West was the intimidation, destruction and outright banning of two of Ukraine's East leaning parties—the Communist Party and the Party of Regions—that had long represented the people of the Donbas. As documented earlier, the various representatives of these parties were intimidated, beaten, publicly tortured, and killed. This is, of course, an inconvenient truth that must be suppressed and ignored by Western governments and mainstream Western media.

Additionally, as stated by Gilbert Doctorow, a research fellow of the American University in Moscow, author, reporter, and one of two members of a fifteen member European Parliamentary Voter Observation Party sent to monitor the elections in Kiev, "that when they decided to visit the city of

Dnepropetrovsk, they witnessed massive cases of violence and intimidation" (RT 2104).

The elections held in the Donbas on November 2, 2014 were widely attended with turnout at 70 percent, nearly two times what it would be in the US (36 percent) in the following days. The voters in Eastern and Southern Ukraine elected a full slate of representatives, with no reports of violence or intimidation.

These elections, however, despite their democratic nature and high voter turnout were both "undemocratic" and "illegal" as voiced by the West and attendant media and once again in lockstep.

Ironically, as a result of the elections, what the Euromaidan activists sought when they waged the protests against President Yanukovych's government—fairness, absence of corruption, a judicial system run by the people—was not what they would get (RT 2014). Instead, they would get more of the same—oligarchs, but now with a sprinkling of neo-Nazis in their Verkhovna Rada parliament.

On the other hand, the Eastern Ukrainians voted to free themselves of oligarchs and not a single neo-Nazi would be seen or heard. Fairness, absence of corruption, and a judicial system run by the people would be exactly what the new leadership proposed for the people of the Donbas.

These are the elections that the West has continuously deemed "illegal," "illegitimate," and "militarily provocative." Yet the irony of the West is clearly stated by Dmitry Linnik, head of the London Bureau of *The Voice of Russia*, who opined on the show Cross Talk:

> *There is one other thing that I'd like to evoke in connection with legitimacy or otherwise. If we could go... rewind back slightly to 1999. We'll recall that the West was out to support the desire of*

> *Kosovo. Well, a majority of the population, obviously, against Belgrade. So what did it [the West] do? It mounted a military campaign against Belgrade to secure the right of the people of Kosovo to a vote for independence. Now if we draw a parallel with the situation in Ukraine, the course would be for military action against Kiev, which is suppressing East Ukraine's right to a vote for independence. (RT 2014)*

As the host, Peter Lavelle commented on the above, "well that would be logical, and Washington doesn't know logical." No, it appears that Washington knows only illogic and cynicism.

Since October, Russia has been forced to cope with a combination of factors that have proven more troublesome than the West's original sanctions: the precipitous drop in oil prices and the parallel devaluation of the ruble.

As a result, Russians are facing a higher inflation rate and a major slowdown in the economy that is expected to culminate in a slump for at least the first half of 2015 (Weafer 2014). However, as usual in the Western mainstream media, hefty amounts of misinformation and hyperbole abound regarding the consequences for Russia. One can almost see the media pundits closing their eyes in childlike fashion and wishing hard for their repeated predictions of Russia's imminent demise—with Putin being yanked out of the Kremlin as he gulps a cyanide capsule—to be true.

The first point of misinformation being bandied about, with Paul Krugman as its most noteworthy disseminator, is the idea that Russia has dangerously high debt liabilities. However, Krugman did not distinguish in his analysis between Russia's government debt and corporate debt. Russia's current government debt is actually only $57 billion. The rest of the $377 billion cited by Western commentators and analysts involves Russian corporations that the state has a stake in but for whose debt the government is not liable (Hellevig 2014).

Furthermore, neither the Russian state nor the Russian corporations involved are at risk of a default (Aris 2014). As we have outlined in this book, Russia has kept a healthy financial balance, holding $400 billion in foreign reserves and gold in addition to rainy day funds and budget surpluses. Russia is actually a creditor nation to the world.

Another point of misinformation involves the implications of the ruble devaluation. While low oil prices and a devalued currency are certainly not a good thing for Russia, the fact that they are happening in tandem protects the Russian budget and trade balance. Hence, the Russian government will have no problem keeping its pension and salary payments in line with inflation for the foreseeable future, ensuring the support of Putin's voting base.

It should also be noted that China and Russia have a currency swap agreement. China has already publicly stated that if the ruble crisis should become perilous and if the Russian government requests it, China will step in and bolster the ruble (Durden 2014).

Putin, for his part, has signaled his opposition to using up financial reserves to support the ruble as well as the use of capital controls, instead allowing the currency to float in order to protect the budget and provide a "soft stimulus for domestic manufacturers," that have seen healthy growth in 2014 (Weafer 2014; Aris 2014).

The Russian government actually has some opportunities in this crisis that can be exploited if it plays its cards right, such as supporting the growth of small-to-medium-sized businesses and domestic manufacturing as Putin discussed in his 2014 Annual Address to the Federal Assembly.

But this would require the ruble to stabilize even if it is at a low value (Aris 2014).

Some wealthy Russians are showing their support by repatriating assets to Russia and borrowing in order to invest in import substitution (Reuters 2014; Aris 2014).

The reaction of the Russian people has ranged from stoic to sanguine. This is partly due to the fact that they have a history of enduring far worse privation and suffering, which they have shown to be quite willing to bear when they see themselves as under attack by outside forces. It is also due to the vast majority of Russians living entirely within the "ruble zone," having no personal financial relationship to other currencies, and Russian legal guarantees of deposit amounts well above what most Russians hold in a bank account—that is, of the small percentage of Russians who even have a bank account as most hoard any extra money (RBTH 2014).

As of December 2014, according to an AP/NORC poll, most Russians still felt their country was moving generally in the right direction and were optimistic about their personal financial future, while Putin still enjoyed an 81 percent approval rating (Bhadrakumar 2014).

And what of World War III? It would appear that the priests and priestesses of the Church of the Grand Chessboard may, indeed, have their apocalyptic coming to god moment.

As of November 5, 2014 the Ukrainian army has once again begun intense shelling across the Donbas, inflicting growing civilian casualties and damage to infrastructure. As detailed by reporter Graham Phillips:

> *Yesterday Kiev ramped the war back up with non-stop shelling across the entire front in Donbass. In Donetsk where the shelling has never stopped, two children were killed and 4 wounded at school #63. in Donetsk. Among others killed in other shelling at*

> *Donetsk was a ten year old girl and her grandmother. They were shredded by an artillery shell direct hit. (RT 2014)*

Readers will not hear this news in the Western mainstream media. Readers will also not be made aware of the fact that, as the war escalates in the Ukraine, the probability of World War III escalates as well. And know this with certainty, as a reader you will not be informed by your President, Prime Minister, Congress or Parliament when the flash point is reached. Instead, readers will be informed by the "facts" on the ground as well as those "facts" exploding above their heads.

However...

If the "crazies," as referred to by George Herbert Walker Bush, the fundamentalist high priests and priestesses can be contained, thwarted, removed, there is every possibility that the military powers that be (the Pentagon, NATO) are extremely concerned about waging a war against an emergent and technologically superior Russia.

"Superior, on what basis?"

In a little-known event in the Black Sea in April 2014, the West, the US in this particular case, was given a ringside seat as to what Western military would face should they attempt to strike Russia.

In the article, "What Frightened the USS Donald Cook So Much in the Black Sea?" we learn that the power and might of one of the US Navy's most sophisticated ships, the USS Donald Cook, a fourth generation guided missile destroyer was literally outmaneuvered in every respect.

But first what are the capabilities of such a ship? As itemized below its key weapons are:

> *Tomahawk cruise missiles with a range of up to 2,500 kilometers, and capable of carrying nuclear explosives. This ship carries 56*

Tomahawk missiles in standard mode, and 96 missiles in attack mode. (Voltaire 2014)

While its combat system is:

...an integrated naval weapons systems which can link together the missile defense systems of all vessels embedded within the same network, so as to ensure the detection, tracking and destruction of hundreds of targets at the same time. In addition, the USS Donald Cook is equipped with 4 large radars, whose power is comparable to that of several stations. For protection, it carries more than fifty anti-aircraft missiles of various types. (Voltaire 2014)

However, on April 12, 2014, a Russian Su-24 tactical bomber, armed only with an electronic warfare device called *Khibiny* (Rossiyskaya Gazeta 2014) mounted under its fuselage, buzzed the USS Donald Cook, which led to the following chain of events:

As the Russian jet approached the US vessel, the electronic device disabled all radars, control circuits, systems, information transmission, etc. on board the US destroyer. In other words, the all-powerful Aegis system, now hooked up—or about to be - with the defense systems installed on NATO's most modern ships was shut down, as turning off the TV set with the remote control. (Voltaire 2014)

Thereafter, the Russian Su-24:

...then simulated a missile attack against the USS Donald Cook, which was left literally deaf and blind. As if carrying out a training exercise, the Russian aircraft—unarmed—repeated the same maneuver 12 times before flying away. (Voltaire 2014)

After the incident:

The 4th generation destroyer immediately set sail towards a port in Romania. No US ship has ever approached Russian territorial waters again. (Voltaire 2014)

The Pentagon would also launch a formal complaint. The Russian research director at the Center on Electronic Warfare, Vladimir Balybine, had the following to say:

The more a radio-electronic system is complex, the easier it is to disable it through the use of electronic warfare. (Voltaire 2014)

Additionally, the military alliance between Russia and China has moved forward at pace. Game-changing weapons systems are now being shared by Moscow with Beijing, and Beijing, more technologically savvy than ever, has embarked on an ambitious program of its own. As touched upon in the article, "The American Century Is Over. The Eurasian Century Has Begun," by Pepe Escobar (Escobar 2014):

The Russia-China symbiosis/strategic partnership visibly expands on energy, finance and, also inevitably, on the military technology front. That includes, crucially, Moscow selling Beijing the S-400 air defense system and, in the future, the S-500.

The S-500 travels at the speed of 15,480 miles an hour, with a range of 2,174 miles—and is capable of shooting down any ICBM Washington can throw at Russia. Translation: Russian airspace sealed to any incoming US nuclear ICBM...The Russian ICBMs deployed at Mach 17, equipped with MIRVs, are simply unbeatable. Beijing, for its part, is already developing its own surface-to-ship missiles that can take out everything the US Navy can muster—from aircraft carriers to submarines and mobile air defense systems. (Escobar 2014)

Perhaps the Russian Bear and the Chinese Dragon have more up their sleeves than anyone at the Pentagon and NATO can contemplate. Perhaps balance, realpolitik, and common sense will once again enter the scene, as the "unknown unknowns" are potentially game changing on a level far above the Church of the Grand Chessboard.

Thank you,

Natylie Baldwin & Kermit E. Heartsong

INDEX

A

A Clean Break · 9, 60, 61
ABM Treaty · 58, 87
Afghanistan · 25, 33, 77, 85, 104, 105, 159, 197, 198, 212, 243, 254, 259, 291, 312, 323, 362
African Union · 103
Al Qaeda · 69
Alain Frachon · 56
Albert Einstein Institute · 153
Alexander Yakimenko · 226
Alexey Pushkov · 81
All-Ukrainian Union · See Svoboda
Anatoly, Chubais · 114, 119, 122
Andriy Parubiy · 182, 188
Armenia · 44, 141
Arseniy Yatsenyuk · 169, 174, 178, 195, 264
Arthur Lepic · 34
asymmetrical war · 147

B

Ban Ki-moon · 70
Banksters · 220
Barack Obama · 35, 58, 63, 64, 68, 69, 72, 73, 74, 136, 168, 218, 238, 242, 245, 248, 273, 284, 292, 346, 347, 348, 349, 351, 352, 357, 358, 359, 360, 365, 370
BBC · 50, 85, 160, 215, 239, 278, 279, 349
Belarus · 44, 141
Benjamin Netanyahu · 58
Black Sea Fleet · 214, 286
Blue Revolution · 152
Boris, Yeltsin · 10, 39, 84, 92, 113, 117, 118, 119, 120, 121, 122, 123, 125, 128, 139, 140, 243, 244, 245
Brezhnev · 25
BRICS · 11, 133, 244, 253, 291, 300, 301, 303, 306, 317, 350, 353
Burisma Holdings · 203

C

Carl Schmitt · 50, 364
Catherine Ashton · 41, 177, 231, 338, 358
cauldron · 199
Cedar Revolution · 152
Central America · 62
Charles De Gaulle · 31
Chechnya · 34, 35, 181
Chernenko · 25
Chicago School · 114, 117, 118, 121
China · 31, 39, 62, 63, 87, 103, 107, 133, 149, 150, 160, 236, 238, 244, 285, 290, 291, 292, 293, 294, 295, 296, 297, 299, 300, 302, 304, 305, 306, 311, 313, 316, 323, 324, 346, 350, 351, 361, 363
Christian Science Monitor · 132, 262, 364
CIA · 32, 33, 34, 53, 54, 59, 89, 139, 149, 193, 228, 231, 247, 248, 347, 352, 355, 361
Clinton, Bill · 84, 85, 183, 217
Cold War · 10, 14, 24, 25, 26, 27, 31, 34, 35, 44, 52, 53, 55, 60, 61, 79, 80, 86, 87, 88, 90, 91, 92, 95, 99, 104, 105, 107, 166, 316, 349, 353, 359, 360
Colin Powell · 49, 57, 85
Colonel Reuven Gal · 151, 153
color revolutions · 10, 147, 148, 149, 150, 152, 153, 157, 206, 356, 357, 360
Communism · 64, 121
Communist Party · 93, 132, 159, 175, 176, 186, 223, 318
Condoleezza Rice · 95, 109
Contract with America · 93
Crimea · 10, 11, 38, 43, 160, 164, 167, 175, 183, 186, 187, 192, 202, 214, 219, 222, 243, 251, 252, 254, 256, 258, 259, 260, 263, 284, 285, 286, 287, 288, 340

D

Daniel Vernet · 56, 352
Darfur · 70
David Rockefeller · 31
Defense Planning Guidance · 56, 364
Deng Xiaoping · 149
Diana Johnstone · 66, 164, 347
Dick Cheney · 51, 57, 63, 100, 140
Dmitry Medvedev · 45
Dmitry Orlov · 18, 244, 246
Dmitry Yarosh · 174

Donald Rumsfeld · 51, 101
Donald Tusk · 164
Donetsk · 197
Douglas Feith · 60
Dr. Anne Cahn · 52
Dr. Bogomolets · 177, 231

E

Eastern Ukraine · 10, 41, 157, 188, 191, 192, 194, 197, 200, 239, 240, 262, 265, 269, 279, 280, 318, 320, 359
Elliot Abrams · 50
EU · 10, 35, 41, 43, 44, 45, 67, 101, 104, 105, 106, 107, 111, 128, 130, 133, 141, 153, 157, 159, 161, 164, 166, 167, 169, 170, 172, 173, 177, 178, 180, 194, 218, 221, 228, 231, 232, 233, 234, 250, 254, 257, 266, 280, 287, 289, 293, 298, 336, 340, 341, 346, 348, 351, 354, 355, 358, 363
Eurasia · 14, 36, 37, 38, 39, 61, 63, 101, 108, 293, 295, 299, 314, 315, 362
Eurasian Economic Union · 44, 302
Euromaidan · 175, 319
European Central Bank · 104
European Neighborhood and Partnership Instrument · 106
European Neighborhood Policy · 105
European Union · 46, 104, 105, 108, 111, 159, 164, 250, 338, 351
exceptionalism · 58, 205, 308

F

Foreign Affairs · 31, 61, 135, 172, 173, 177, 231, 338
Foreign Military Sales Program · 96
Francis Boyle · 67
Franco-Russian · 111, 362
Freedom House · 34, 35, 153
FSB · 92

G

G7 · 116, 118, 304
Gazprom · 128, 136, 290, 350, 356
Gene Sharp · 149, 153
Geoffrey Pyatt · 41, 170, 358
George Kennan · 149
George Orwell - 18, 209, 315

George Schultz · 61
George Soros · 94, 122, 140, 231
Georgia · 10, 15, 45, 46, 106, 109, 152, 159, 160, 161, 162, 239, 284, 346, 348, 351, 352, 362
geostrategy · 14, 294, 302
Gerald Ford · 51
Germany · 14, 30, 46, 53, 75, 78, 79, 85, 87, 88, 90, 104, 105, 128, 173, 197, 209, 236, 257, 287, 350
Global South · 76
Gorbachev · 9, 10, 14, 24, 25, 78, 79, 90, 93, 116, 117, 243, 244, 361, 362
Grand Chessboard · 9, 11, 15, 30, 37, 49, 85, 88, 163, 165, 202, 245, 284, 288, 302, 308, 309, 313, 317, 320, 324, 369

H

Hamas · 59
Harvard Institute for International Development · 114, 119, 124
Harvard Management Company · 122
Heartland Theory · 37
Henry Kissinger · 31, 51, 145
Hezbollah · 59
Hillary Clinton · 36, 47, 63, 72, 164, 261
Hitler, Adolf · 11, 36, 39, 45, 46, 64, 67, 75, 179, 181, 211, 212, 217, 218, 249, 250, 253, 308, 313
House of Trade Unions · 190, 221
House to Trade Unions · 173
Huffington Post · 45, 215, 352
humanitarian interventions · 66

I

IMF · 93, 116, 118, 119, 124, 128, 129, 152, 155, 156, 159, 165, 168, 204, 207, 291, 298, 301, 302, 341
International Center for Non-Violent Conflict · 153
International Court of Justice · 67, 256, 285, 287
International Herald Tribune · 72, 358
International Republican Institute · 153
Iraq · 49, 59, 60, 61, 68, 69, 70, 74, 76, 87, 101, 102, 106, 184, 191, 192, 206, 210, 211, 212, 236, 248, 252, 253, 274, 284, 303, 304, 306, 315, 359, 360
Ivan Katchanovski · 224, 225, 226, 230, 231, 232, 233, 354

J

Jack Matlock · 25, 80, 86, 109
Jacob Heilbrunn · 64
James Baker · 14, 79
Jeffrey Sachs · 94, 118, 119
Jewish holocaust · 64, 66
John Brennan · 193
John Horgan · 65
John McCain · 36, 41, 47, 62, 65, 95, 172, 363

K

Kazakhstan · 44, 79, 141, 299
Kerry · 35, 175, 176, 192, 193, 195, 203, 216, 242, 270, 273, 350, 359
Khmer Rouge · 67
Khodorkovsky's · 140
Kosovo Liberation Army · 67, 218

L

Lawrence Summers · 119, 164
Lawrence Wilkerson · 18, 49, 346, 354
Le Nouvel Observateur · 32
Lech Wałęsa · 91
Leo Strauss · 50, 55
Libya · 9, 71, 72, 73, 74, 75, 76, 103, 106, 152, 191, 192, 206, 218, 248, 252, 253, 284, 303, 304, 306, 315, 347, 349, 355, 358, 360, 364
Lockheed Martin · 95, 98, 100
Lugansk · 196, 197

M

Machiavellian · 32, 237, 251, 252
Madeleine Albright · 31
Magna Carta · 312
Mahdi Darius Nazemroaya · 101
Maidan · 11, 41, 43, 65, 168, 169, 172, 173, 174, 177, 178, 188, 192, 219, 220, 221, 222, 223, 224, 225, 226, 228, 229, 230, 231, 232, 233, 234, 247, 250, 338, 339, 341, 342, 354, 358
Malaysia Airlines flight · 263
Marco Rubio · 36, 47

Marjorie Cohn · 71
Matthew Johnson · 137
Melvin Goodman · 54
Membership Action Plan · 99, 110
MH17 · 11, 219, 252, 256, 260, 261, 262, 263, 264, 265, 266, 267, 270, 271, 272, 273, 274, 275, 276, 278, 279, 280, 281, 282, 354, 355, 364, 365
Michael Ledeen · 50, 53
Middle East · 61, 142, 152
Mikhail Gorbachev · 24, 25, 78, 243, 244
Mikheil Saakashvili · 46, 159
Military Industrial Complex · 310
Mutually Assured Destruction · 55, 308

N

Nathan Gardels · 45
National Endowment for Democracy · 34, 64, 153, 347
National Security Council · 25, 83, 123
NATO · 10, 14, 15, 38, 42, 64, 66, 67, 70, 72, 75, 76, 78, 79, 80, 81, 82, 83, 84, 85, 86, 87, 88, 89, 90, 91, 92, 93, 94, 95, 96, 97, 98, 99, 100, 101, 102, 103, 104, 105, 106, 107, 108, 109, 110, 111, 140, 149, 157, 159, 162, 163, 164, 165, 166, 167, 184, 185, 202, 203, 218, 234, 239, 242, 246, 247, 248, 250, 265, 266, 280, 281, 282, 286, 287, 294, 295, 298, 299, 302, 312, 313, 314, 316, 321, 323, 324, 346, 348, 349, 350, 352, 353, 354, 356, 358, 360, 361, 362, 364
Neocons · 30, 39, 52, 55, 59, 60, 64, 73, 74, 309, 356, 359
Neoconservative · 50, 53, 54, 60
neo-Nazi · 41, 65, 168, 169, 174, 179, 180, 181, 182, 186, 188, 189, 192, 195, 219, 220, 230, 233, 319
New York Times · 27, 56, 78, 160, 239, 281, 347, 352, 355, 359, 361
Nicholas Spykman · 37
Nicolai Petro · 42
Nicolas Sarkozy · 72, 358
Noami Klein · 204
Novorossiyan · 186, 191, 192, 193, 194, 195, 198, 199, 200, 261, 270, 272, 280

O

Office of Special Plans · 60
oligarchs' · 122

Orange Revolution · 10, 110, 152, 157, 158, 159, 163, 231, 360
Organization for Security and Cooperation · 91, 274
Orwell · 18, 209, 315

P

Palestinians · 59
Partnership and Cooperation Agreement · 128
Partnership for Peace program · 92
Party of Regions · 159, 173, 175, 176, 186, 191, 221, 223, 318, 336
Paul Wolfowitz · 50, 52, 57, 95
Paul Wolfowtiz · 56
Pentagon · 26, 49, 55, 89, 91, 96, 97, 108, 152, 159, 212, 282, 321, 323, 324
Peter Beaumont · 61
petrodollar · 15, 298, 303
Pinochet Option · 117
Politico.com · 36, 347
Poroshenko · 164, 181, 196, 197, 198, 200, 320, 342, 363
Posse Commitatus · 312
Project for a New American Century · 61

R

Radoslaw Sikorski · 164
RAND Corporation · 55, 151, 153
Reagan · 9, 25, 26, 52, 53, 54, 55, 56, 61, 86, 157
reciprocal suicide · 56
Responsibility to Protect · 9, 51, 65, 68, 70, 77, 102, 349, 353
Right Sector · 41, 43, 164, 165, 181, 187, 215, 220, 227, 233, 234
Rimland · 37, 364
Robert Kagan · 9, 60, 63, 95, 361
Robert Parry · 58, 73, 163, 188, 260, 273
Ronald Asmus · 95
Rosneft · 136, 284, 291, 292, 356
Russian Federation · 15, 35, 48, 91, 125, 131, 187, 190, 251, 260, 287, 360
Russian TV · 198, 216
Russophobes · 35, 39, 85
Rwandan genocide · 67

S

Saddam Hussein · 59, 86, 274

Saffron Revolution · 152
Salvador Allende · 117
Samantha Power · 73
SCO · See Shanghai Cooperation Organization, See Shanghai Cooperation Organization, See Shanghai Cooperation Organization, See Shanghai Cooperation Organization, See Shanghai Cooperation Organization, See Shanghai Cooperation Organization, See Shanghai Cooperation Organization, See Shanghai Cooperation Organization, See Shanghai Cooperation Organization
Security Council · 71, 103, 182, 227, 271
self-determination · 58, 115, 254, 257
Sergei Lavrov · 109, 233, 254, 272, 365
Seymour Melman · 26
Shanghai Cooperation Organization · 244, 299
Sharon Tennison · 18, 115, 125, 134
Shock Doctrine · 116, 204, 355
shock therapy · 84, 93, 113, 116, 120, 122
Solidarity movement · 93
South Ossetia · 160, 161
sovereignty · 40, 43, 48, 58, 67, 70, 76, 132, 141, 191, 192, 193, 314
Soviet Union · 9, 15, 24, 25, 28, 30, 31, 32, 34, 36, 39, 44, 46, 47, 48, 51, 53, 54, 55, 57, 78, 79, 80, 86, 89, 94, 101, 108, 114, 115, 117, 124, 132, 161, 186, 239, 243, 244, 314, 348
Star Wars · 56
State Department · 31, 42, 60, 61, 64, 91, 96, 153, 169, 210, 211, 212, 213, 215, 219, 228, 240, 242, 243, 247, 251, 261, 269, 282
Stephen Cohen · 18, 88, 111, 166, 213, 216, 313, 353
Stephen Hadley · 95
Superpower Illusions · 109, 357
Susan Rice · 73
Svoboda · 41, 65, 158, 169, 172, 173, 179, 180, 181, 182, 187, 188, 222, 227, 250
Swarm-warfare · 147
Syria · 49, 59, 68, 69, 73, 76, 106, 191, 192, 206, 218, 236, 248, 252, 253, 254, 295, 296, 304, 315, 359

T

Team B · 52, 60
Terry Malloy · 36
Tiananmen Square Massacre · 149
The Economist · 117, 136
The Grand Chessboard · 14, 30, 36, 37, 105, 364
The New Republic · 62, 63, 354

The Observer · 61, 346
The Power of Nightmares · 50, 349
Tony Blair · 82
Trilateral Commission · 31
Tskhinvali · 160, 161
Tulip Revolution · 152

U

US Congress · 46
US foreign policy · 49, 139
Ukrainian Ministry of Health · 173
UN Charter · 103
UN General Assembly · 71, 77
United States · 40, 46, 58, 60, 62, 63, 76, 86, 104, 115, 136, 137, 149, 150, 164, 210, 216, 235, 236, 259, 285, 294, 297, 304, 314, 367
Urmas Paet · 41, 177, 231, 338
US Congress · 34, 314
USAID · 119, 123, 153
USSR · 24, 31, 35, 52, 56, 90, 91, 244, 259, 302

V

Verkhovna Rada · 174, 175, 176, 177, 180, 319
Victoria Nuland · 9, 41, 60, 63, 169, 170, 178, 334
Vietnam War · 75, 98
Yanukovych · 41, 111, 141, 157, 158, 164, 165, 167, 168, 169, 170, 171, 172, 173, 174, 176, 189, 193, 220, 221, 224, 225, 226, 228, 229, 230, 232, 250, 251, 255, 256, 319, 334, 336, 339, 342, 343, 355
Viktor Yushchenko · 110, 157, 231
Vilnius Group · 100
Vitali Klitschko · 169, 175
Vladimir, Putin · 10, 11, 15, 36, 39, 44, 45, 46, 47, 48, 63, 64, 74, 82, 83, 84, 85, 87, 107, 108, 109, 110, 121, 125, 127, 128, 130, 135, 137, 138, 139, 140, 141, 142, 143, 144, 164, 166, 192, 197, 198, 212, 214, 242, 244, 249, 250, 251, 252, 253, 254, 261, 269, 272, 280, 281, 284, 286, 287, 289, 291, 292, 296, 303, 346, 347, 349, 350, 351, 352, 353, 354, 358, 360, 361, 362, 363, 364, 365

W

Washington · 22, 35, 36, 49, 61, 62, 64, 73, 81, 88, 90, 94, 99, 105, 110, 117, 119, 121, 150, 153, 154, 158, 163, 164, 166, 183, 214, 216, 242, 245, 246, 286, 288, 293, 320, 335, 347, 349, 352, 355, 362, 364
Wikileaks · 150, 348
William Kristol · 50, 61
Wilson Center · 39, 347
Wolfowitz Doctrine · 9, 56, 57, 364
World Bank · 116, 118, 119, 124, 152, 159, 207, 291, 298, 301, 352
WWII · 26, 30, 50, 62, 66, 90, 104, 115, 137, 139

Y

Yulia Tymoshenko · 110, 158, 167, 215, 286
Yuri, Andropov · 25

Z

Brzeziński · 9, 14, 30, 31, 32, 33, 34, 35, 36, 37, 38, 39, 41, 43, 44, 45, 46, 47, 48, 49, 85, 88, 89, 93, 95, 98, 100, 105, 308, 309, 317, 347, 348, 351, 352, 364, 365

APPENDIX I

Phone Transcript Nuland and Pyatt

Full transcript of the February 6, 2014 telephone talk between US Assistant Secretary of State Victoria Nuland and US Ambassador to Ukraine Geoffrey R. Pyatt (Oriental Review 2014):

Victoria Nuland (V.N.): What do you think?

Geoffrey R. Pyatt (G.P.): I think we are in play. The Klitchko piece is obviously the most complicated electron here, especially the announcement of him as Deputy Prime Minister. You have seen my notes on trouble in the marriage right now, so we are trying to get a read really fast where he is on the staff. But I think your argument to him which you'll need to make, I think that's the next phone call that you want to set up is exactly the one you made to Yats [Yatsenuk's nickname]. I'm glad you put him on the spot. <…> He fits in this scenario. And I am very glad he said what he said.

V.N.: Good. I don't think Klitsch [Klitschko's nickname] should be in the government. I don't think it's necessary, I don't think it's a good idea.

G.P.: Yeah, I mean, I guess… In terms of him not going into the government… I'd just let him stay out and do his political homework. I'm just thinking, in terms of sort of the process moving ahead, we want to keep the moderate democrats together. The problem is gonna be with Tyahnibok and his guys. And, you know, I am sure that is part of what Yanukovych is calculating on all this.

V.N.: I think Yats is the guy. He has economic experience and governing experience. He is the guy. You know, what he needs is Klitsch and Tyahnibok on the outside. He needs to be talking to them four times a week. You know, I just think if Klitchko gets in, he's going to be at that level working for Yatsenuk, it's just not gonna work…

G.P.: Yeah, yeah, I think that's right. Ok, good. Would you like us to set up a call with him as the next step?

V.N.: My understanding from that call that you tell me was that the big three were going into their own meeting and that Yats was gonna offer in this context, you know, a «three plus one» conversation or a «three plus two» conversation with you. Is that not how you understood it?

G.P.: No. I think that was what he proposed but I think that knowing the dynamic that's been with them where Klitchko has been the top dog, he'll show up for whatever meetings they've got and he's probably talking to his guys at this point. So, I think you reaching out directly to him, helps with the personality management among the three. And it also gives you a chance to move fast on all this stuff and put us behind it, before they all sit down and he explains why he doesn't like it.

V.N.: Ok. Good. I am happy. Why don't you reach out to him and see if he wants to talk before or after.

G.P.: Ok, I will do it. Thanks.

V.N.: I can't remember if I told you this or if I only told Washington this: when I talked to Jeff Feltman this morning he had a new name for the UN guy – Robert Serry. I wrote you about it this morning.

G.P.: Yeah, I saw that.

V.N.: Ok. He's gotten now both Serry and Ban Ki-moon to agree that Serry will come on Monday or Tuesday. That would be great I think to help glue this thing and to have the UN help glue it and, if you like, fuck the EU.

G.P.: No, exactly. And I think we've got to do something to make it stick together because you can be pretty sure that if it does start to gain altitude that the Russians will be working behind the scenes to try to torpedo it. And again the fact that this is out there right now, I am still trying to figure out in my mind why Yanukovych <…> that. In the meantime there is a Party of Regions faction meeting going on right now and I am sure there is a lively argument going on in that group at this point. But anyway, we could land jelly side up on this one if we move fast. So let me work on Klitschko and if you can just keep… I think we just want to try to get somebody with an international personality to come out here and help to midwife this thing. The other issue is some kind of outreach to Yanukovych but we probably regroup on that tomorrow as we see how things start to fall into place.

V.N.: So on that piece, Jeff, when I wrote the note Sullivan's come back to me V.F.R., saying you need Biden and I said probably tomorrow for an atta boy and to get the details to stick. So, Biden's willing.

G.P.: Ok. Great, thanks.

APPENDIX II

Phone Transcript Paet and Ashton

The following conversation between Estonian Foreign Minister Urmas Paet and Catherine Ashton, high representative of the Union for Foreign Affairs and Security Policy for the European Union, was apparently leaked by Ukrainian Security Forces. The conversation has Paet and Ashton dicussing the Maidan sniper shooting. Paet believes based upon the information that he has received while visiting that the new Ukrainian government is the responsible party.

CONVERSATION W/INTIAL CONNECTIONS OMITTED:

Catherine Ashton: Hello.

Urmas Paet: Hello.

Ashton: Hello, how are you?

Paet: I am fine
.
Ashton: Good.

Paet: And you?

Ashton: Good. I am good. I just wanted to catch up with you on what you thought when you were there.

Paet: Ok, yes. I returned last night already, so that I was one day.

Ashton: Yeah. Impressions?

Paet: Impressions are sad.

Ashton: Um hum.

Paet: I met with representatives of Regions Party [originally Yanukovych's party, but it had dissociated from him by this point in time], also new coalition representatives, and also civil society [Ukrainian non-governmental organizations or NGOs]. There is this lady called Olga [Dr. Olga Bogomolets, who was tending to wounded protesters] who is head of the doctors. Yes, yes. You know her?

Ashton: I do.

Paet: Yes, so that, well, my impression is indeed sad that there is, well, no trust towards also these politicians who will return now to the coalition. Well, people from Maidan and from civil society, they say that they know everybody who will be in new government – all these guys have a dirty past.

Ashton: Yeah.

Paet: So that, well, they made some proposals to the same Olga and some others from civil society to join new government. But this Olga, for example, she says directly that she is ready to go to the government only in the case if she can take with her, her team of foreign experts to start real health care reforms.

Ashton: Yeah.

Paet: So that, well, basically, it is that the trust level is absolutely low. On the other hand, all the security problems, this integrity problems, Crimea, all this stuff. Regions Party was absolutely upset. They say that, well, they accept, they accept this that now there will be new government. And there will be external elections. But there is enormous pressure against members of parliament – that there are uninvited visitors during the night ... to party members. Well, journalists ... some journalists who were with me, they saw during the day that one member of parliament was just beaten in front of the parliament building by these guys with the guns on the streets.

Ashton: Yeah.

Paet: So that all this mess is still there. And, of course, this Olga and others from civil society, they were absolutely sure that people will not leave the streets before they see that the real reforms will start. So that it's not enough that there is just change of government. So that that is the main impression. So that, from EU's and also well Estonia's point of view, of course, we should ready to put this financial package together. Also together with others. This very clear message is needed that it's not enough that there is change of government, but they say real reforms – you know, real action to increase the level of trust. Otherwise, it will end badly. Because the Regions Party also said that, well, we will see that if the people from the eastern part of Ukraine will really wake up, and will start to demand their rights. Some people also with me, they were also in Donetsk. There people said that, well, we can't wait. How long still the occupation of Ukraine lasts in Donetsk. That it is real Russian city, and we would like now to see that, well, Russia will take over. So that well ... short impressions.

Ashton: No, very, very interesting. I just had a big meeting here with Olli Rehn [EU Commissioner for Economic and Monetary Affairs] and the other commissioners about what we can do. I mean, we're working on financial packages – short, medium, long-term. Everything from how we get money in quickly. How we support the IMF. And how we get a kind of ... investment packages and business leaders and so on. On the political side, we've worked [?out?] what resources we have got, and I offered to civil society, and to Yatsenyuk [Aresniy Yatsenyuk became the interim prime minister when what is now the "new coaltion" became the interim Ukrainian government] and Klitchko [Vitali Klitchko, one of the leaders of the new coalition, a former boxer, and now mayor of Kiev], and everybody I met yesterday: "We can offer you people who know how to do political and economic reform. The countries that are closest to Ukraine have been going through dramatic changes and have done big political and economic reforms. So we have got loads of experience to give you, which we're happy to give." I said to the people in Maidan, "Yes, you want real reforms, but you've got to get through the short-term first. So you need to find ways in which you can establish a process that will have anticorruption at its heart, that will have people working alongside until the elections, and that you could be confident in the process.

Then I said to Olga, "You may not be Health Minister now, but you need to think about becoming Health Minister in the future, because people like you are going to be needed to be able to get and make sure that [?reform?] happens. I also said to them, "If you simply barricade the buildings now, and the government doesn't function, we cannot get money in, because we need a partner to partner with.

Paet: Absolutely.

Ashton: And I said to the opposition leaders, shortly to become government, "You need to reach out to Maidan. You need to be, you know, engaging with them. You also need to get ordinary police officers back on the streets under a new sense of their roles, so that people feel safe. I said to the Party of the Regions people, "You have to go and lay flowers for the people [who] died. You have to show that you understand what you have … what has happened here. Because what you were experiencing is anger of people who have seen the way that Yanukovych lived and the corruption. And they assume you are all the same." And, also the people who have lost people and who feel that, you know, he ordered that to happen. There is quite a lot of shock I think in the city. A lot of sadness and shock, and that is going to come out in some very strange ways if they are not careful. I think all of us, we just have to work on this. We did a big meeting here today to try and get this in place. But, yeah, very interesting, your observations.

Paet: It is. And, well, actually, the only politician [whom] the people from civil society mentioned positively was Poroshenko [Petro Poroshenko, known as "the chocolate king" was elected president of Ukraine in the May 25 election].

Ashton: Yeah, yeah.

Paet: So that he has some sort of, how to say, trust among all this Maidan people and civil society. And, in fact, what was quite disturbing, the same Olga told that, well, all the evidence shows that people who were killed by snipers, from both sides, among policemen and then people from the streets, that they were the same snipers, killing people from both sides.

Aston: Well, that's ... yeah.

Paet: So that, then she also showed me some photos. She said that as [a] medical doctor she can, you know, say that it is the same handwriting, the same type of bullets, and it's really disturbing that now the new coalition, that they don't want to investigate what exactly happened. So that there is now stronger and stronger understanding that behind [the] snipers, they were ... it was not Yanukovych, but it was somebody from the new coalition.

Ashton: I think we do want to investigate. I mean, I didn't pick that up. It's interesting. Gosh.

Paet: Yeah. So that it was [?indeed?] disturbing that, if it starts now to live its own life very powerfully, that it already discreditates [sic] from [the] very beginning also this new coalition.

Ashton: I mean this is what they have got to be careful of as well, that they need to demand great change, but they have got to let the Rada [Ukrainian Parliament] function. If the Rada doesn't function, then they have complete chaos. So that, it's all, you know, being an activist and a doctor is very, very important. But it means that you're not a politician. And somehow they've got to come to a kind of accommodation for the next few weeks, which is how the country is actually going to run. And then we get the elections and things can change. And that's, I think, going to be quite pop... I am planning to go back early next week, probably on Monday.

Paet: It's really important that now, well, people from Europe and also [the] West show up there so that it's absolutely...

Ashton: Well, [?Verislav?] is going with the Visegrad Group [an alliance of the Czech Republic, Hungary, Poland, and Slovakia] Friday. Friday, Saturday. William Haig (unintelligible) on Sunday. I will be back again Monday.

Paet: Yes, I heard also that Canadian Minister is going on Friday. And yesterday also William Burns [the American Deputy Secretary of State] was there, so we met ...

Ashton: Yes, I saw Bill.

Paet: We met also with Burns there in Kiev yesterday. Ashton: Yeah, good. Yeah, I didn't know that John Baird was going. I will get hold of him. Okay, my friend. It was great to talk to you.

Paet: Well, thanks for these comments, and wish you well. Nice Australia.

Ashton: Yeah. What?

Paet: Nice Australia. Enjoy!

Ashton: I am not going to go. I got to delay it because I'm going to do more Ukraine instead.

Paet: OK, good, good.

Ashton: All right, my friend …

Paet: OK. Thank you. Thank you. And all the best to you. Bye.

Ashton: Bye.

BIBLIOGRAPHY

Adomanis, Mark. "3 Things Obama Got Wrong About Russia." Forbes. August 4, 2014.

Ahmed, Nafeez. "Ukraine crisis is about Great Power Oil, Gas Pipeline Rivalry." The Guardian. March 6th, 2014

Armstrong, Patrick. "The EU Report: Little and Late." Russia Other Points of View. October 8, 2009.

Asmus, Ronald. Opening NATO's Door. Columbia University Press. NY, NY. 2002.

Baldwin, Natylie. Telephone Interview with Col. Lawrence Wilkerson. August 7, 2014.

Barabanov, Mikhail. "Three Military Analyses of the 4 Day War Between Russia and Georgia." Vineyard of the Saker. September 16th, 2008

Barria, Carlos. "China, Russia reported to build huge seaport in North Asia." Reuters. September 11, 2014

Becker, Richard. "Who's who in Ukraine's New [Semi-fascist] Government." Liberation. March 6th, 2014

Beaumont, Peter. "A Neocon By Any Other Name." The Observer. April 26, 2008.

Bespalova, Natalia. "Ukraine: Straddling Between the EU and the Customs Union." Russia Beyond the Headlines. March 12, 2013.

Bhadrakumar, MK. "Putin Points to the Russia of the Future." Asia Times Online. May 16, 2006.

Bidder, Benjamin. "New Report on Russia-Georgia War: EU Investigators Debunk Saakashvili's Lies." Spiegel Online. October 1st, 2009

Blair, Eric. "25 Recent Events in Ukraine the US Wants You To Forget." Global Research. July 27, 2014

Blum, William. "Trojan Horse: National Endowment for Democracy." Third World Traveler.com. 2000.

Blum, William. Killing Hope: US Military and CIA Interventions Since World War II. Common Courage Press. Monroe, ME. 2000.

Borger, Julian. "Ukraine Crisis: Geneva Talks Produce Agreement on Defusing Conflict." The Guardian. April 17th, 2014

Boyle, Francis. Destroying Libya and World Order: The Three Decade US Campaign to Terminate the Qaddafi Revolution. Clarity Press, Inc. Atlanta, GA. 2013.

Bricmont, Jean. (Translated by Diana Johnstone). Humanitarian Imperialism: Using Human Rights to Sell War. Monthly Review Press. NY, NY. 2006.

Brinkley, Douglas. "Out of the Loop." New York Times. December 29, 2002.

Broad, William J. and David Sanger. "US Ramping Up Major Renewal in Nuclear Arms." New York Times. September 22, 2014.

Brown, Jeff. "Operation Rescue Russia." OpEd News. August 25, 2014.

Brzeziński, Zbigniew. "What Is To Be Done? Putin's Aggression in Ukraine Needs a Response." Washington Post. March 3, 2014.

Brzeziński, Zbigniew. "What Obama Should Tell Americans About Ukraine." Politico.com. May 2, 2014.

Brzeziński, Zbigniew. The Grand Chessboad: American Primacy and Its Geostrategic Imperatives. Basic Books. NY, NY. 1997.

Brzeziński, Zbigniew. "Confronting Russian Chauvinism." Transcript of Speech at Wilson Center on June 16, 2014. The American Interest.

Brzeziński, Zbigniew. Testimony Before Senate Foreign Relations Committee. July 7, 2014.

Brzeziński, Zbigniew "Introductory Statement on NATO Enlargement." Federation of American Scientists. October 9, 1997.

Bureau of Labor Statistics – US Department of Labor. "Regional and State Unemployment: 2013 Annual Averages." February 28, 2014.

Burns, William. "Nyet Means Nyet: Russia's NATO Enlargement Red Lines." Wikileaks. February, 2008.

Business New Europe. "Russia to Crack Down on Tax Evasion." October 17, 2014.

Byzantium. "Will the EU Crack Up the Way the Soviet Union Did?" Russia Insider. November 7th, 2014

Caralucci, Tony. "Spinning the Odessa Massacre." Land Destroyer. May 4th, 2014

Chicago Tribune. "Clinton and Dole and the Polish Vote." May 20, 1996.

Christison, Bill and Kathleen. "A Rose by Another Name: The Bush Administration's Dual Loyalties." Counterpunch. December 13, 2002.

Chomsky, Noam and Edward S. Herman. Manufacturing Consent: The Political Economy of the Mass Media. Pantheon Books. New York, NY. 1988.

Chomsky, Noam. "Ossetia-Russia-Georgia." Chomsky.info. September 9, 2008

Chossudovsky, Michel., "America's Neo-Nazi Government in Kiev. Towards a Scenario of Military Escalation?" Global Research. 4 May, 2014

Chossudovsky, Prof. Michel. "Obama is a Liar. Fake NATO Evidence. OSCE Confirms that No Russian Troops, No

Tanks, Have Crossed the Russia-Ukraine Border." Global Research. September 04, 2014

CIA Intelligence Memorandum. "The Impending Soviet Oil Crisis." March, 1977.

Clark, Neil. "A Funny Sort of Democracy." New Statesman. November 17, 2003.

Clark, Neil. "Putin Demonized For Thwarting Neocon Plan For Global Domination." Information Clearing House. November 15, 2014

Clinton, Hillary. "We Came, We Saw, He Died." https://www.youtube.com/watch?v=Fgcd1ghag5Y

Cloughley, Brian. "Washington And Media Russia Bashing Is Riddled With Lies, Hysteria And Humbug." Counterpunch. July 26, 2014

Cohen, Jeff. "Internet Samizdat Releases Suppressed Voices and History." Fairness and Accuracy in Reporting. December 1, 2001.

Cohen, Stephen. Soviet Fates and Lost Alternatives: From Stalinism to the New Cold War. Columbia University Press. NY, NY. 2011.

Cohen, Stephen F. "Distorting Russia: How the American Media Misrepresent Putin, Sochi and Ukraine." The Nation. February 11th, 2013

Cohen, Stephen F. "Patriotic Heresy vs. the New Cold War." The Nation. August 27, 2014

Cohen, Stephen F. "The Silence of American Hawks About Kiev's Atrocities." The Nation. June 30th, 2014

Cohn, Marjorie. "The Responsibility to Protect – The Cases of Libya and Ivory Coast." Truthout. May 16, 2011.

Cooper, Julian. The Soviet Defense Industry: Conversion and Economic Reform. The Royal Institute of International Affairs Council on Foreign Relations Press. 1991.

Cunningham, Finian. "Washington and NATO's New Surrealpolitik." Strategic Culture Foundation. April 9th, 2014

Curtis, Adam (director). "The Power of Nightmares (Parts 1 – 3)." BBC. Originally aired October and November, 2004

Democracy Now Headlines for August 11, 2014. "Obama: US Intervening to Protect American Personnel."

Democracy Now Headlines for August 14, 2014. "US: Siege of Mount Sinjar Broken, Rescue Mission Unlikely."

Dinucci, Manlio. "NATO's Global Offensive." Voltaire.net. July 30, 2014

Ditz, Jason. "US Invents Reports of Russia Attacking Ukraine Bases: No Reports Out of Ukraine on Any Such Incidents." AntiWar.com. July 24, 2014

Draitser, Eric. "Waging War against Russia, One Pipeline at a Time." Reuters. June 27, 2014

Drake, Bruce. "In Germany, US, Poll Finds Little Support for Military Aid to Ukraine." Pew Research. April 14, 2014.

Dunham, Will. "Kerry Condemns Russia's 'Incredible Act of Aggression' in Ukraine." Reuters. Mar 2, 2014

Durden, Tyler. "Company In Which Joe Biden's Son Is Director Prepares To Drill Shale Gas In East Ukraine." Zero Hedge. July 25th, 2014

Durden, Tyler. "Russia's Response To European Capital Sanctions In One Word." Zero Hedge. September 8th, 2014

Durden, Tyler, "The Nail In The Petrodollar Coffin: Gazprom Begins Accepting Payment For Oil In Ruble, Yuan," Information Clearing House, August 29th, 2014

Durden, Tyler. "Was The Price Of Ukraine's "Liberation" The Handover Of Its Gold To The Fed?" Zero Hedge. March 10th, 2014

Durden, Tyler. "What Petrodollar: Russia, China To Create SWIFT Alternative." Zero Hedge. 10 September, 2014

Engdahl, William. "The Emerging Russian Giant Plays its Cards Strategically. " Engdahl Oil Geopolitics.net. October 20, 2006.

Engdahl, William. "Putin and BRICS Form Seed Crystal of a New International Monetary Pole." Boiling Frogs. July 25, 2014.

Engdahl, William. "Obama's Stupid Sanctions Give Putin New Oil Bonanza." New Eastern Outlook (NEO) October 13th, 2014

Engdahl, William, "The Rape of Ukraine: Phase Two Begins: The Events in Ukraine Since November 2013 are So Astonishing as Almost to Defy Belief." 21st Century Wire. February 28th, 2014

Engdahl, William F. "Ukraine: Secretive Neo-Nazi Military Organization Involved in Euromaidan Sniper Shootings." Global Research. March 3, 2014

Ernesto, Chris. "The Eurasian Chessboard: Brzeziński Mapped Out the Battle for Ukraine in 1997." Antiwar.com. March 15, 2014.

Escobar, Pepe. "Russia 1, Western Wannabe Regime Changers 0: The World Watches as Neo-Nazis Take Over Ukraine, with E.U. Funding." Alter Net. March 17th, 2014

Euronews. "The Economics of the EU-Russia Relationship." March 18, 2014.

European Union. "Independent International Fact Finding Mission on the Conflict in Georgia." Official Journal of the European Union. September, 2009.

Eurostat. "December 2013: Euro Area Unemployment Rate at 12%." News Release, Euro Indicators, January 31, 2014.

Federation of American Scientists. "Central and Eastern European Security Concerns."

Ford, Peter. "Brazil, Russia, India, China, and South Africa Have Founded a $100 Billion 'New Development Bank' That Will Lend to Members and Other Developing Countries, a Potential Alternative to the Washington-based World Bank." AFP. July 16, 2014

Frachon, Alain and Daniel Vernet. "The Strategist and the Philosopher." Counterpunch. May 29, 2003.

Fry, Douglas. The Human Potential for Peace: An Anthropological Challenge to Assumptions About War and Peace. Oxford University Press. NY, NY. 2006.

Gardels, Nathan. "Brzeziński: Russia's Invasion of Georgia is Reminiscent of Stalin's Attack on Finland." Huffington Post. September 10, 2008.

Gati, Charles. Zbig: The Strategy and Statecraft of Zbigniew Brzeziński. John Hopkins University Press. Baltimore, MD. 2013.

Gerth, Jeff and Tim Weiner. "Arms Makers See Bonanza in Selling NATO Expansion." New York Times. June 29, 1997.

Giraldi, Philip. "Does the CIA Believe Obama?" The American Conservative. September 6, 2014

Glazyev, Sergey and Mikhail Khazin, et al. "Putin Advisors Mikhail Khazin and Sergey Glazyev Discuss Western Sanctions and Russian Economic Policy on Russia Today." Vineyard of the Saker. 2014.

Global Issues. "World Military Spending: Global Distribution of Military Expenditure in 2012." (Pie chart).

Golinger, Eva. "Colored Revolutions: A New Form of Regime Change, Made in USA." Global Research. March 05, 2014

Golstein, Prof. Vladimir. "Why Everything You've Read About Ukraine Is Wrong." Forbes. May 19th, 2014

Goodman, Amy. Interview with Seymour Hersh on Democracy Now. April 7, 2014.

Graham, Thomas. "A Russia Problem, Not a Putin Problem." Carnegie Forum. August 20, 2014.

Greppi, Edoardo Prof. "The Responsibility to Protect: An Introduction." University of Torino. 2009.

Grossman, David Lt. Col. On Killing: The Psychological Cost of Learning to Kill in War and Society. Back Bay Books. NY, NY. 1996.

Hackard, Mark. "National Nihilism." Oriental Review. June 19th, 2014

Hallinan, Conn. "BRICS and the SCO: Let A Thousand Poles Bloom." International Policy Digest. October 10, 2014

Hamm, Bernd. "The End Of Democracy As We Knew It." Information Clearing House. March, 2014

Hartmann, Thom. "The New Cold War." Interview with Stephen Cohen on The Big Picture. November 14, 2014.

Hartung, William. "The Hidden Costs of NATO Expansion." Arms Trade Resource Center. March, 1998.

Hersh, Seymour. "The Red Line and the Rat Line." London Review of Books. April, 2014.

Horgan, John. The End of War. McSweeny's Books. San Francisco, CA. 2012.

Howell, Elizabeth. "US Too Dependent on Russian Rocket Engines, Experts Tell Lawmakers." Space.com. July 17, 2014.

Hudson, Michael. "New Cold War's Ukraine Gambit." Michael-Hudson.com. May 13, 2014.

Hudson, Michael. "The New Cold War Policy Has Backfired." Strategic Culture Foundation. December 11th, 2014.

Hudson, Michael. "West Looks to Carve Up Ukraine & Privatize Industries Held By Kleptocrats."Video Interview With Michael Hudson, Real News Network. April 9, 2014

Hussain, Haris. "Malaysia Accuses US and EU backed Ukraine Regime of MH17 Shoot-down." New Straits Times Online. August 7th, 2014

Jackson, Bruce. Testimony on NATO Enlargement Before Senate Foreign Relations Committee. April 1, 2003.

Jacobson, Brad. "Why War Isn't Inevitable: A Science Writer Studies the Secret to Peaceful Societies." Alternet. March 18, 2012.

Johnson, Matthew. Russian Populist: The Political Thought of Vladimir Putin. The Barnes Review. 2012.

Johnson, Matthew. "Dealing with the 'Authoritarian' Label: Putin and the Fraud of American Exceptionalism - Analysis." Eurasian Review. May 13, 2014.

Johnson, Matthew. "Globalization and Decline of the West: Eurasianism, the State, and Rebirth of Ethnic Socialism." Eurasian Review. May 2, 2014.

Johnstone, Diana. "R2P and Genocide Prevention: The Good Intentions That Pave the Road to War." Counterpunch. February 1, 2013.

Kagan, Robert. "Superpowers Don't Get to Retire." The New Republic. May 26, 2014.

Kagan, Robert, "US Needs a Discussion on 'When, Not Whether, to use Force." Washington Post. July 15, 2014

Kall, Rob. Interview with Col. Lawrence Wilkerson. OpEd News. May 28, 2014.

Katchanovski, Ivan. "The Snipers Massacre on the Maidan in Ukraine." Chair of Ukrainian Studies Seminar at the University of Ottawa, Ottawa. October 1, 2014

Keck, Zachary. "India Backs Russia's 'Legitimate Interests' in Ukraine." The Diplomat. March 08, 2014

Kissner, Jason. "Malaysian Airlines MH370 and MH17. A Criminologist Questions: What are the Probabilities? Is it a Mere Coincidence? Vladimir Putin is to Blame, According to the Mainstream Media." Global Research. July 20, 2014

Keck, Zachary. "Russian Military Spending Soars." The Diplomat. April 8, 2014.

Kennan, George F. "A Fateful Error." New York Times. February 5, 1997.

Khalidi, NA. "Afghanistan: Demographic Consequences of War, 1978-1987." Central Asian Survey, Volume 10, No. 3, pp. 101-126. 1991.

Klein, Naomi. The Shock Doctrine: The Rise of Disaster Capitalism. Picador. NY, NY. 2007.

Koenig, Peter, "Civilization of the Neocons," Information Clearing House, January 23, 2015

Koenig, Peter, "Russian Invasion" – How long is Screaming 'Wolf!' Having an Impact on the Western Populations? – Until Full Spectrum Dominance has Been Attained?" Vineyard of the Saker. August 30th, 2014

Kornbluh, Peter and Kate Doyle. "CIA and Assassinations: The Guatemala 1954 Documents." National Security Archive.

Korybko, Andrew. "Washington's Nightmare Comes True: The Russian-Chinese Strategic Partnership Goes Global." Global Research. August 23, 2014.

Kuzio, Taras. "Ukraine at Crossroads After Rejecting EU Pact President Yanukovych is Struggling to Balance Ukrainian, Russian and European Priorities." Al Jazeera. November 29, 2013

Kovacevic, Dejan. "The Winter Olympics in Sochi Are a Success…But Don't Tell Russia." Triblive.com. February 23, 2014.

Krasnow, George W. "Suzanne Massie's Advice to President Obama: Revive Reagan's Policy Toward Russia." Russia Other Points of View. December 5, 2008.

Kuperman, Alan. "Lessons from Libya: How Not to Intervene." Belfer Center for Science and International Affairs. September, 2013.

Kuttenen, Aleksi, "Gazprom Tells EU No Deal on South Stream Restart, EU Free to Get Russian Gas in Turkey," Russia Insider. January 15, 2015

Landler, Mark. "Obama Hosts Foreign Policy Experts, Laying Groundwork for Speech on ISIS." New York Times. September 8, 2014

Lantier, Alex. " Malaysia Accuses US and EU Backed Ukraine Regime of MH17 Shoot-down." World Socialist Website. August 9th, 2014

Laughland, John. "The Chechens' American Friends." The Guardian. September 8, 2004.

Lawler, Joseph. "Economist Laurence Kotlikoff: US $222 Trillion in Debt." Real Clear Policy. December 1, 2012

Lendman, Stephen, "Color Revolutions, Old and New." Stephen Lendman Blog. June 29, 2009

Lendman, Stephen. "Kiev Waging War on Its Own People." PRN. May 17th, 2014

Lendman, Stephen. "Meet Obama's New Ukrainian Friends." Veterans Today. March 13th, 2014

Lepic, Arthur. "The Outrageous Strategy to Destroy Russia." Voltaire.net. October 22, 2004.

Lekic, Slobodan. "Despite Cuts, NATO Still Accounts for Most of World's Military Spending." Stars and Stripes. February 25, 2014.

Lloyd, Richard. "Possible Implications of Faulty US Technical Intelligence in the Damascus Nerve Agent Attack of August 21, 2013." MIT Science, Technology and Global Security Working Group.

Lobe, Jim. "Neocons Shaken, But Not Deterred." Inter Press Service. January 24, 2008.

Lossan, Alexei. "Rosneft and Gazprom Overtake Google and Apple in Corporate Transparency." Russia Beyond the Headlines. November 12, 2014.

Sławomir Łukasiewicz. "Jan Nowak-Jeziorański: A Sketch for a Portrait." New Eastern Europe. October 2, 2014.

Luhn, Alec. "Protestors Guard Biggest Weapons Cache in Eastern Europe." The Guardian. April 24, 2014

Madsen, Wayne. "Ukraine: NATO's Eastern Prize." Voltaire Network. December, 16th, 2013

Madsen, Wayne. "Ukrainian Phone Wrecks The Secret Agenda of Ashton and Nuland Revealed." Voltaire Network. March, 2014

Malinkin, Mary Elizabeth. "Reagan's Evolving Views of Russians and Their Relevance Today." Article Covering Lecture by Suzanne Massie at Kennan Institute on December 1, 2008.

Martenson, Chris. "The West's Reckless Rush Towards War With Russia." Zero Hedge. July 31st, 2014

Matlock, Jack. Superpower Illusions: How Myths and False Ideologies Led America Astray and How to Return to Reality. Yale University Press. New Haven, CT. 2010.

Maupin, Caleb T. "America's Foreign Policy Script: False Flags, "Humanitarian Crises" and Russia's "Phantom Tanks."Global Research. September 06, 2014

McCauley, Lauren. "Obama: US Airstrikes Will Be Long Term Project." Commondreams. August 9, 2014.

McGovern, Ray. "Rebuilding the Obama-Putin Trust." Consortium News. January 3, 2015.

McGovern, Ray. "The Risk of a Ukraine Bloodbath." Information Clearing House. July 3rd, 2014

McGovern, Ray. "Ukraine: One 'Regime Change' Too Many?" Antiwar.com. 2 March, 2014

Mellow, Craig. "What the US Could Learn from Russia." Minyanville. October 10, 2013.

Melman, Seymour. After Capitalism: From Managerialism to Workplace Democracy. Alfred A. Knopf Publishers. 2001.

Melman, Seyhour. "The Economic Conversion Comparative: Eleven Propositions." August, 1990. Available at Global Makeover.com

Meyssan, Thierry. "Perfecting The Method of "color revolutions: Western Leaders Slip Back into Childhood." Information Clearing House. August 7th, 2012

Meyssan, Thierry. "The Day Before the Revolution, a Ukrainian Deputy Revealed the Conspiracy." Voltiare Network. February 19, 2015.

Meyssan, Thierry. "Ukraine: Poland Trained Putchists Two Months in Advance." Information Clearing House. April 21st, 2014

Mezyaev, Alexander. "Is the Crimean Referendum Legal?" Dissident Voice. March 14th, 2014

National Priorities Project. "Fighting For a US Federal Budget That Works For All."

Naylor, S. "When Anti-Maidan was Destroyed I Fled from Kiev..." Slavyangrad. September 1, 2014

Nazemroaya, Mahdi Darius. The Globalization of NATO. Clarity Press, Inc. Atlanta, GA. 2012.

Nazemroaya, Mahdi D. "Euromaidan Coup: Why the West Supported the Toppling of the Ukrainian Government." Boiling Frogs, February 26, 2014

Nazemroaya, Mahdi D. "Welcome to Nulandistan: A Multimedia Look at What the US and EU Have Unleashed on Ukraine." Global Research, 12 May, 2014

Nuland, Victoria and Geoffrey Pyatt. Transcript of Telephone Conversation. February, 2014.

Obama, Barack, Nicolas Sarkozy and David Cameron. "Libya's Pathway to Peace." International Herald Tribune. April 14, 2011.

O'Neill, James, "A View from Australia: Why the Secrecy on the MH17 Investigation?" Counterpunch. January 17, 2014.

Orlov, Dmitry. "America's Foreign Policy Fiascos." ClubOrlov. June 16th, 2014

Orlov, Dmitry. "How Can You Tell Whether Russia Has Invaded Ukraine?" ClubOrlov.com. Saturday, August 30, 2014

Orlov, Dmitry. "The Crimean Crisis and Western Bias." Club Orlov. March 11th, 2014

Orlov, Dmitry. "The Madness of President Putin." ClubOrlov. September 09, 2014

Paet, Urmas and Catherine Ashton. Transcript of Telephone Conversation. March, 2014.

Parry, Robert. "Burning Ukraine's Protesters Alive. Neo-Nazi "Shock Troops" Supported by US." Consortium News, May 11, 2014

Parry, Robert. "The Human Price of Neocon Havoc." Consortium News. July 17, 2014.

Parry, Robert. "What's the Matter with John Kerry?" Consortium News. April 14, 2014.

Parry, Robert. "The Dangerous Neocon-R2P Alliance." Consortium News. April 18, 2014.

Parry, Robert. "Loving a Putsch – Cheering a "Democratic Neo-Nazi Coup" in Ukraine." Consortium News, February 27, 2014

Parry, Robert. "Malaysia Airlines Whodunnit Still a Mystery." Consortium News, September 9, 2014

Parry, Robert. "Neocons Double Down on Iraq and Syria." Consortium News. June 13, 2014.

Parry, Robert. "NYT Is Lost in Its Ukraine Propaganda." Consortium News. January 24th, 2015

Parry, Robert, "Sidestepping Ukraine's 'N-Word' for Nazi." Consortium News. September 6, 2014

Parry, Robert. "The Mystery of a Ukrainian Army 'Defector'." Consortium News, July 22nd, 2014

Parry, Robert. "The New York Times Dishes More Ukraine Propaganda." Consortium News. July 07, 2014

Parry, Robert. "Ukraine's Neo-Nazi Imperative: The Mainstream Media's One-Sided Propaganda." Global Research, April 20, 2014

Parry, Robert. "The Victory of 'Perception Management'" Consortium News. December 28, 2014.

Parsons, Michelle A. Dying Unneeded: The Cultural Context of the Russian Mortality Crisis. Vanderbilt University Press. Nashville, TN. 2014.

Petras, Prof. James. "Obama Destabilizes Europe's Economy: Sanctions Deepen the Recession." Global Research. August 23, 2014

Petras, James. "The Kiev Putsch: Rebel Workers Take Power in the East." Information Clearing House. May 7th, 2014

Petro, Nicolai. "Eastern Ukraine: The Never Ending Crisis." The National Interest. September 3, 2014.

Petro, Nicolai. "How We Won the Cold War But Lost the Peace." The National Interest. September 14, 2014.

Pfaff, William. "America Started This Ukraine Crisis." WilliamPfaff.com. August, 7th, 2014

Pieraccini, Federico. "Here's How the Resistance Beat the Ukrainian Army Without Much Help From Russia." Russia Insider. September 4, 2014

"Poland NATO Report." Center for International Relations – Euro Atlantic Association. Warsaw, Poland. 1994.

Polish American Congress. "Review of the Role of the Polish American Congress in Bringing Poland into NATO (Timeline)."

Polk, William R. "What's Behind the Conflict Between Russia and Ukriane?" History News Network. December 21, 2014

Pollack, Norman. "Resumption of Cold War in Earnest: NATO, Spearhead of Western Fascism." Counterpunch. September 08, 2014

Pushkov, Alexey. "Broken Promises." The National Interest. April 16, 2007.

Putin, Vladimir. Annual Address to the Federal Assembly of the Russian Federation. April 25, 2005.

Putin, Vladimir. Statement to International Press Regarding UN Resolution on Libya. RT. August, 2011.

Putin, Vladimir. Prepared Remarks at 43rd Annual Munich Security Conference. February 11, 2007.

Putin, Vladimir. Annual Address to the Federal Assembly of the Russian Federation. December, 2013.

Putin, Vladimir. "We Need a New Economy." RT. January 30, 2014.

Putin, Vladimir. Prepared Remarks at the Davos World Economic Forum. January 29, 2009.

Queally, John. "Obama Bombs Iraq in Order to Save It." Commondreams. August 8, 2014.

Raimondo, Justin. "The Orange Revolution, Peeled: The Color Revolutions Revisited." Antiwar.com. February 8, 2010

Reynolds, Douglas B. "Peak Oil and the Fall of the Soviet Union: Lessons on the 20th Anniversary of the Collapse." The Oil Drum. May 27, 2011.

Reynolds, Lionel. "The Ukraine Crisis and the Big Game: The Geneva Agreement Changes Nothing." Global Research. April 18, 2014

RIA Novosti. "Gorbachev Blasts NATO Eastward Expansion." April 2, 2009.

RIA Novosti. "Russia's Economy Under Vladimir Putin." January 3, 2008.

Rightweb – Robert Kagan. http://www.rightweb.irc-online.org/profile/kagan_robert

Rightweb – US Committee on NATO. http://rightweb.irc-online.org/profile/US_Committee_on_NATO

Risen, James. "Secrets of History: The CIA in Iran." New York Times. April 16, 2000.

Rohde, David and Arshad Mohammed. "Special Report: How US Made its Putin Problem Worse." Reuters. April 19, 2014.

Roxburgh, Angus. Strongman: Vladimir Putin and the Struggle for Russia. Palgrave MacMillan. NY, NY. 2013.

Rozoff, Rick. "NATO Expansion, Missile Deployments and Russia's New Military Doctrine." Voltaire.net. February 15, 2010.

Rozoff, Rick. "NATO's Incremental Absorption of Ukraine." Voltaire.net. April 26, 2014.

RT. "Russia Gains 11 Points in Global Competitiveness Report." September 3, 2014.

RT. "China, Russia Reported to Build Huge Sea Port in North Asia." September 11, 2014.

RT. "Russia's Import Ban Means Big Business for Latin America." August 7, 2014.

Russia Today. "White House confirms CIA Director Visited Ukraine Over Weekend." Russia Today. April 15, 2014

Ryan, John. "The Media's Disinformation Campaign on Ukraine: "There are No Neo-Nazis in the Interim Government." Global Research. April 3rd, 2014

Sakwa, Richard. "The Soviet Collapse: Contradictions and Neo-Modernisation." Journal of Eurasian Studies. July 31, 2012.

Sarich, Christina. "The Russians Prove Organic Small Scale Farming CAN Feed the World." Natural Society. May 29, 2013.

Sarotte, Mary Elise. "Not One Inch Eastward: Bush, Baker, Kohl, Genscher, Gorbachev, and the Origin of Russian Resentment Toward NATO Enlargement in February of 1990." Diplomatic History Journal. January 6, 2010.

Schweizer, Peter. Victory: The Reagan Administration's Secret Strategy That Hastened the Collapse of the Soviet Union. The Atlantic Monthly Press. New York, NY. 1994.

Shakarian, Pietro. "Will Georgia Be the Next Ukraine? Political Tensions, Exacerbated by Western Regional Expansion, are Raising the Risk of Violence." The Nation. September 25, 2014

Shamir, Israel. "The Ukraine in Turmoil." Vineyard of the Saker. May 18th, 2014

Simha, Rakesh K. "How Sanctions are Hastening the World Without the West." Russia & India Report. September 13, 2014

Sinclair, Jim. "Russia Could Crush the Petrodollar." George Washington Blog. March 21st, 2013

Slavyangrad. "Franco-Russian Dialogue on Ukraine." September 1, 2014.

Snyder, Michael. "Why Is The Mainstream Media Ignoring The Rabid Anti-Semitism In The New Ukraine Government?" The Truth. March 4th, 2014

Stea, Carla. "The US Says the Ukrainian People Must Decide Their Fate, NATO Wants Something Else." Global Research. December 29, 2013.

Stryker, Deena. "What Putin's Eurasia Project Could Mean for Europe." OpEd News. August 22, 2014.

Suchan, Vladimir. "Putin's Dilemma and Rubicon When Making Favorable References to the Devil Bent on Invading Russia," Vladimir Suchan.com. June 8th, 2014

Szamuely, Tibor. The Russian Tradition. Fontana Press. London. 1974. Chapters 1 – 5.

Tarifa, Fatos. To Albania With Love. University Press of America. Lanham, MD. 2007. pp. 85-88.

TASS Russian News Agency. "East Ukraine Militias Seize Large Amount of Ukrainian Armor – Kiev's Hacked Data." August 28, 2014.

Tavrovsky, Yury. "Russia and China: Together Like Teeth and Lips." Carnegie Moscow Center. September 8, 2014

Taylor, Adam. "John McCain Went to Ukraine and Stood on a Stage With a Man Accused of Being an Anti-Semitic Neo-Nazi." Business Insider. December 16, 2013.

Tennison, Sharon. The Power of Impossible Ideas: Ordinary Citizens' Extraordinary Efforts to Avert International Crises. Odenwald Press. 2012.

Tennison, Sharon. "Who is Vladimir Putin? Why Does the US Government Hate Him?" Global Research. May 8, 2014.

Tennison, Sharon. "Reality Check from Russia." Email Report. September 19, 2014.

The Saker. "Is the US Getting Ready to Dump Poroshenko? It Looks Like Poroshenko's Days are Numbered. His Most Likely Replacement? The Extreme Right." Russia Insider. October 14, 2014

Thomas, Jeff. "How Empires End." Information Clearing House. September 09, 2014

Todhunter, Colin. "Ukraine: Russia's Response to a US-EU Sponsored Coup d'Etat. Violation of International Law?" Global Research. March 03, 2014

Ulher, Walter C. "Who's Responsible for Shooting Down Malaysian Airlines Flight, MH17?" July 19th, 2014 http://www.walter-c-uhler.com.

Ukolova, Alina. "Organic Farms: A Growth Area in Russia." UK Telegraph. April 30, 2013.

Valiente, Alexandra. "The Grand Chessboard: Ukraine Enthralled by Brzeziński's Paradigm." Libya 360. December 16, 2013

Valiente, Alexandra. "Odessa Massacre Planned and Executed by the Fascist Interim Rulers of Ukraine." Antifascist. May 15th, 2014

Von Sponeck, Hans. "The United Nations and NATO: Which Security and For Whom?" Current Concerns. April 14, 2009.

Wahlberg, Eric. "Vladimir Putin and Russia's White Revolution." Global Research. February 9, 2012.

Watson, Paul J. "Whistleblower: US Satellite Images Show Ukrainian Troops Shooting Down MH17: Source Tells Award Winning Reporter Washington Lying About Responsibility for Tragedy." Global Research. July 22, 2014

Wedel, Janine. "Harvard Boys Do Russia." The Nation. 1997.

Weir, Fred. "Is the US Bent on Bringing Down Russia? Some in the Kremlin Say Yes." Christian Science Monitor. July 23, 2014.

Wikipedia – Zbigniew Brzeziński.

Wikipedia – List of Wars Between Democracies.

Wikipedia – Carl Schmitt.

Wikipedia – Rimland.

Wikipedia – The Geographical Pivot of History.

Williamson, Anne. Testimony Before House of Representatives. September 21, 1999.

Williamson, Clint. "Statement of Chief Prosecutor of the SITF." Special Investigative Task Force. July 29, 2014.

Wolfowitz, Paul. "Defense Planning Guidance for 1994 – 1999 (aka Wolfowitz Doctrine)." 1992. National Security Archives.

World's Top Exports. "Russia's Top 10 Exports." 2013.

Yakovlev, Andrei. "State-Business Relations and Improvement of Corporate Governance in Russia." Bank of Finland. 2008.

Zakaria, Fareed. Interview with Zbigniew Brzeziński on CNN. July 20, 2014.

Zinn, Howard. Terrorism and War. Seven Stories Press. NY, NY. 2002.

Zivulovic, Srdjan. "Russian Foreign Minister Sergei Lavrov Russia Says West Taking No Action to Settle Ukraine Conflict." Reuters, July 28th, 2014

Zeese, Kevin, "US Empire Reaches Breaking Point. "Greatest Threat to Humanity—Time To End It." Global Research. July 20, 2014

Zuckert Michael and Catherine. "Leo Strauss and The Problem of Political Philosophy, University of Chicago Press, 2014.

Zuesse, Eric. "Falsehoods in the NYT's Editorial, 'Mr. Putin Tests the West in Ukraine." OpEdNews.com. September 5, 2014

Zuesse, Eric. "Evidence Is Now Conclusive: Two Ukrainian Government Fighter-Jets Shot Down Malaysian Airlines MH17. It was Not a 'Buk' Surface to Air Missile." Global Research. August 4th, 2014

Zuesse, Eric. "Obama Is Defeated in Ukraine. Status-Quo Truce-Lines Agreed." Global Research. September 21, 2014

Zwarich, Raymond. "What Price These Lies?" Dissident Voice. September 8th, 2014

If there is no President Bush, then there is no President Obama. If there is no President Obama, then there is no resurrection of the once very nearly dead Republican Party. There's a dance step going on here folks, one need only "see" it, to get the moves down.

—Kermit E. Heartsong, *Author, Publisher*

Next Revelation

BIOGRAPHIES

Natylie Baldwin lives in the San Francisco Bay Area. Her fiction and nonfiction have appeared in various publications including *Sun Monthly, Dissident Voice, Energy Bulletin, Newtopia Magazine, The Common Line, New York Journal of Books, OpEd News,* and *The Lakeshore*. She is a graduate of Cal State East Bay and enjoys walking, hiking, the beach, movies, and classic television dramas. She is currently working on two novels.

Kermit E. Heartsong a San Francisco native and author, has written two non-fiction books—*The United States of Mammon* (2013) and *Illusions, Dystopia & Monsters* (2014), with *The God in Us Knows* to debut in 2017. Heartsong, an empirical scientist, has been a keen observer of the macroscopic developments of social, economic, and political systems for the past twenty-five years. He has been featured in *Entrepreneur, Entrepreneur Young Millionaire, Success, Essence,* and in author Carol Adrienne's *The Story of Your Life*.

It is no measure of health to be well adjusted to a profoundly sick society.

—*Jiddu Krishnamurti*

UKRAINE

ZBIG'S GRAND CHESSBOARD

&

HOW THE WEST WAS
CHECKMATED

CPSIA information can be obtained
at www.ICGtesting.com
Printed in the USA
BVOW04s0846311016
466280BV00001B/2/P